THE HISTORY OF AL-ṬABARĪ

AN ANNOTATED TRANSLATION

VOLUME XXXVI

The Revolt of the Zanj

A.D. 869–879/A.H. 255–265

The History of al-Ṭabarī

Editorial Board

Ihsan Abbas, University of Jordan, Amman

C. E. Bosworth, The University of Manchester

Franz Rosenthal, Yale University

Everett K. Rowson, The University of Pennsylvania

Ehsan Yar-Shater, Columbia University (*General Editor*)

Estelle Whelan, *Editorial Coordinator*

Center for Iranian Studies

Columbia University

SUNY

SERIES IN NEAR EASTERN STUDIES

Said Amir Arjomand, Editor

The preparation of this volume was made possible in part by a grant from the National Endowment for the Humanities, an independent federal agency.

Bibliotheca Persica
Edited by Ehsan Yar-Shater

The History of al-Ṭabarī

(Ta'rīkh al-rusul wa'l-mulūk)

VOLUME XXXVI

The Revolt of the Zanj

translated and annotated
by

David Waines

Lancaster University

State University of New York Press

Published by
State University of New York Press, Albany

Printed in the United States of America

For information, address the State University of New York Press,
90 State Street, Suite 700, Albany, NY 12207

Library of Congress Cataloging in Publication Data

Ṭabarī, 838?–923.

[Ta 'rīkh al-rusul wa-al-mulūk. English. Selections]

The revolt of the Zanj : A.D. 869–879 / A.H. 255–265 / translated and annotated by David Waines.

p. cm.—(Bibliotheca Persica) (The history al-Ṭabarī = Ta'rīkh al-rusul wa'l-mulūk ; v. 36) (SUNY series in Near Eastern studies)

Translation of extracts from: Ta'rīkh al-rusul wa-al-mulūk.

Includes bibliography: (p.) and index.

ISBN 0-7914-0763-2 (acid-free). — ISBN 0-7914-0764-0 (pb : acid free)

1. Iraq—History—Zanj Rebellion, 868–883. 2. Islamic Empire—History—750–1258. I. Waines, David. II. Title. III. Series.
838?–923. Ta'rīkh al-rusul wa-al-mulūk. English; v. 36.
DS38.2.T313 1985 vol. 36
[DS76.4]
956.7'02—dc20

90-1032[illegible]
CIP

Preface

The History of Prophets and Kings *(Ta'rīkh al-rusul wa'l-mulūk)* by Abū Ja'far Muḥammad b. Jarīr al-Ṭabarī (839–923), here rendered as *The History of al-Ṭabarī,* is by common consent the most important universal history produced in the world of Islam. It has been translated here in its entirety for the first time for the benefit of non-Arabists, with historical and philological notes for those interested in the particulars of the text.

Al-Ṭabarī's monumental work explores the history of the ancient nations, with special emphasis on biblical peoples and prophets, the legendary and factual history of ancient Iran, and, in great detail, the rise of Islam, the life of the Prophet Muḥammad, and the history of the Islamic world down to the year 915. The first volume of this translation contains a biography of al-Ṭabarī and a discussion of the method, scope, and value of his work. It also provides information on some of the technical considerations that have guided the work of the translators.

The *History* has been divided here into 39 volumes, each of which covers about two hundred pages of the original Arabic text in the Leiden edition. An attempt has been made to draw the dividing lines between the individual volumes in such a way that each is to some degree independent and can be read as such. The page numbers of the Leiden edition appear on the margins of the translated volumes.

Al-Ṭabarī very often quotes his sources verbatim and traces the chain of transmission (*isnād*) to an original source. The chains of transmitters are, for the sake of brevity, rendered by only a dash (—)

between the individual links in the chain. Thus, "According to Ibn Ḥumayd—Salamah—Ibn Isḥāq" means that al-Ṭabarī received the report from Ibn Ḥumayd, who said that he was told by Salamah, who said that he was told by Ibn Isḥāq, and so on. The numerous subtle and important differences in the original Arabic wording have been disregarded.

The table of contents at the beginning of each volume gives a brief survey of the topics dealt with in that particular volume. It also includes the headings and subheadings as they appear in al-Ṭabarī's text, as well as those occasionally introduced by the translator.

Well-known place names, such as, for instance, Mecca, Baghdad, Jerusalem, Damascus, and the Yemen, are given in their English spellings. Less common place names, which are the vast majority, are transliterated. Biblical figures appear in the accepted English spelling. Iranian names are usually transcribed according to their Arabic forms, and the presumed Iranian forms are often discussed in the footnotes.

Technical terms have been translated wherever possible, but some, such as dirham and imām, have been retained in Arabic forms. Others that cannot be translated with sufficient precision have been retained and italicized, as well as footnoted.

The annotation aims chiefly at clarifying difficult passages, identifying individuals and place names, and discussing textual difficulties. Much leeway has been left to the translators to include in the footnotes whatever they consider necessary and helpful.

The bibliographies list all the sources mentioned in the annotation.

The index in each volume contains all the names of persons and places referred to in the text, as well as those mentioned in the notes as far as they refer to the medieval period. It does not include the names of modern scholars. A general index, it is hoped, will appear after all the volumes have been published.

For further details concerning the series and acknowledgments, see Preface to Volume I.

Ehsan Yar-Shater

To Martin Hinds,
in memory of
a long
and
valued
friendship

Contents

Preface / v

Abbreviations / xiii

Translator's Foreword / xv

Map I. The Lower Part of Southern Iraq in the Third/Ninth Century / xix

The Caliphate of Ibn al-Wāthiq: Al-Muhtadī bi-Allāh

The Events of the Year 255 (cont'd) (868/869) / 1

An Account of the Causes and Consequences of [the] Disturbances [in Baghdad] / 3
An Account of [the] Deaths of [Aḥmad b. Isrā'īl and Abū Nūḥ] / 10
An Account of [the] Events [of Ramaḍān 255] / 13
An Account of Mūsā's Departure / 25
The First ʿAlawite Rebellion in al-Baṣrah / 29
An Account of [ʿAlī b. Muḥammad b. ʿAbd al-Raḥīm's] Expedition and What Determined Him to Revolt There / 30
An Account of the Zanj Leader's Advance upon al-Baṣrah with His Army / 59

The Events of the Year 256 (869/870) / 68

An Account of Ṣāliḥ's Discovery in Hiding and His Death / 72
An Account of [al-Muhtadī's] Removal and Death / 91
Other Accounts of al-Muhtadī's Death / 95
News of [the] Encounter [between Juʿlān and the Zanj] / 108
An Account of the Zanj Occupation of al-Ubullah / 110
The Account of [the Zanj Leader's] Summons for [the] Surrender [of the Inhabitants of ʿAbbādān] / 111
An Account of [the Occupation of al-Ahwāz] / 111

The Caliphate of al-Muʿtamid ʿalā-Allāh

The Events of the Year 256 (cont'd) (869/870) / 115

The Events of the Year 257 (870/871) / 119

An Account of the Battle [between Saʿīd al-Ḥājib and the Zanj] / 121
An Account of the Battle [between Manṣūr b. Jaʿfar and the Zanj] / 122
The Death of Shāhīn b. Bisṭām and the Flight of Ibrāhīm b. Sīmā / 123
The Events that Led up to [the] Entry of al-Baṣrah [by the Zanj] and What Transpired Thereafter / 125
An Account of al-Muwallad's Expedition / 134

The Events of the Year 258 (871/872) / 136

An Account of [Manṣūr b. Jaʿfar's] Death / 137
An Account of [Mufliḥ's] Death / 139
An Account of [Yaḥyā b. Muḥammad's] Capture and Death / 142
An Account of [Abū Aḥmad's] Withdrawal to Wāsiṭ / 146

The Events of the Year 259 (872/873) / 150

An Account of [Kanjūr's] Death / 150
An Account of [the] Battle [at Sūq al-Ahwāz] and How the Army Commander of the Central Authorities Was Killed / 152

An Account of How [Mūsā b. Bughā's Commanders] Fared against the Zanj / 153
An Account of [Ya'qūb b. al-Layth's Entry into Naysābūr] / 156

The Events of the Year 260 (873/874) / 158

An Account of [the] Battle [in Ṭabaristān] / 158
An Account of [al-Azdī's] Death / 161

The Events of the Year 261 (874/875) / 163

An Account of [the] Battle [of Rāmhurmuz] / 164

The Events of the Year 262 (875/876) / 168

An Account of [the Zanj Attack on the Salt Flats] / 174
An Account of the Battle and Capture of al-Ṣu'lūk / 181

The Events of the Year 263 (876/877) / 185

An Account of [the] Battle [at 'Askar Mukram] / 186
An Account of [Ya'qūb] al-Ṣaffār's Activities This Year / 187

The Events of the Year 264 (877/878) / 189

An Account of [the] Capture [of 'Abdallāh b. Rashīd] / 190
An Account of [the] Battle [at Wāsiṭ] / 190
An Account of How the Abominable One Prepared His Zanj to Occupy Wāsiṭ (and Other Events of the Year 264) / 193

The Events of the Year 265 (878/879) / 200

An Account of [the] Battle [of Junbulā'] / 200
An Account of Takīn's Arrival in al-Ahwāz / 205

Bibliography of Cited Works / 209

Index / 213

Abbreviations

EI[1]: *Encyclopaedia of Islam*, first edition. 4 volumes and supplement. Leiden: 1913–42.
EI[2]: *Encyclopaedia of Islam*, new edition. Leiden and London, 1960–.

Translator's Foreword

The present volume of Ṭabarī's voluminous history covers the years 255–65/869–79. It deals with some of the most dramatic events, if not of the entire *History*, certainly of the lifetime of the historian himself. Ṭabarī was already a mature scholar of about thirty when al-Muhtadī became caliph in 255/868 and the leader of the Zanj commenced his uprising in the very heartland of the ʿAbbāsid domains, southern Iraq. These events marked a most severe test for the caliphate and were part of a prolonged internal crisis, not only political in nature, but economic and social as well, a crisis from which the ʿAbbāsids never fully recovered.[1]

The seat of the caliphate was still at Sāmarrā, where the Caliph al-Muʿtaṣim had transferred affairs of state from Baghdad in 221/836. The move was occasioned by the desire to settle his new Turkish elite military forces and thus avoid tensions between them and the older established political and commercial sections of Baghdad's population. However, the concentration of Turks in Sāmarrā helped foster rivalries among them, as well as struggles between them and their masters, the caliphs. The assassination of al-Mutawakkil (247/861) ushered in a period of anarchy that came to an end only with the death of al-Muhtadī (255/868), when the Turkish leaders felt more secure of their position within the state apparatus. The new caliph, al-Muʿtamid (with the invaluable support of his brother Abū Aḥmad al-Muwaffaq), remained on the caliphal throne in Sāmarrā for more than twenty years and died a natural death, in con-

1. See D. Waines, "The Crisis of the ʿAbbāsid Third Century."

trast to the violent deaths of the five previous caliphs in the space of a decade.

But, although a period of relative tranquillity began in the capital, danger signals were flashing in territories adjacent to the imperial heartlands. The situation in Sāmarrā, which had paralyzed central government, had allowed provincial dissent to emerge into the open. Ṭabarī deals here with one such expression of dissent in the career of Yaʿqūb b. al-Layth, a coppersmith (al-Ṣaffār) who, having become master of the province of Sīstān, next moved to challenge the Ṭāhirids of Khurāsān, long-standing supporters of the ʿAbbāsids both in the east and in Baghdad. The central government attempted to win Yaʿqūb's support by granting him the governorship of several eastern regions, but a greater danger then arose when he marched westward toward al-Ahwāz and advanced upon Baghdad itself. Ultimately this particular danger was averted but not before it had seemed possible that Yaʿqūb might join forces with ʿAlī b. Muḥammad and his army of the Zanj in the southern marshlands (*baṭāʾiḥ*) of Iraq.

The Zanj revolt occupies the bulk of the narrative in the present volume, from its tentative beginnings in 255/869 through the traumatic capture of al-Baṣrah in 257/871 to the sacking of Wāsiṭ in 264/878. The period covered here, in fact, marks what Alexandre Popovic has correctly called the first distinct phase of the revolt.[2] The movement was crushed only when the Zanj capital, Mukhtārah, fell to al-Muwaffaq's forces in 269/882 and the Zanj leader died the following year. In all, the revolt had occupied the central government's attention for fifteen years.

Ṭabarī's account of these events is of primary importance, "tant par la qualité que par la quantité de ses informations," as Popovic acknowledges.[3] Ṭabarī's skills as a historian are apparent from the manner in which he has constructed his account around reports from those who participated in or witnessed the events recorded. He also displays the storyteller's touch in his inclusion of certain selected anecdotes that bring the narrative to life. My favorite is the picture of a fleeing Zanj soldier who attempts to halt the advance of his pursuer first by tossing his armor at him and finally by trying to stop him with a metal field-oven that he had been carrying. More-

2. A. Popovic, *La révolte des esclaves en Iraq au III/IX siècle*, 83.
3. Popovic, 13.

over, Ṭabarī seems to have been living in Baghdad through at least some of the period of the revolt, as is attested in his brief account of the serial murderer of women who was captured and executed, and whose corpse was publicly displayed in the city, and more particularly in his mention of having been present at the departure of al-Muwaffaq's large and well-equipped army to engage the Zanj in the south. Ṭabarī, for the most part, avoids making judgments on the persons and events he is dealing with, yet he cannot restrain himself entirely from expression of feeling on such momentous events. For example, until the infamous incident of the "Day of the Barges" outside al-Baṣrah, he refers to ʿAlī b. Muḥammad as the Zanj leader; thereafter, however, ʿAlī is designated "the enemy of God," "the cursed one," and, most frequently, simply *al-khabīth* "the abominable one."

A brief comment on the annotation is apposite here. The primary importance of Ṭabarī's account, as already noted, lies in the mass of detail unique to him. Some personal names and place names, especially in the account of developments within the Zanj camp, occur only here and often only once, which makes complete identification virtually impossible. As far as possible, I have cited the works of Le Strange for the identification of place names, as readers of this translation may wish to pursue certain points in a language accessible to them. Tribal names have generally, been left unannotated. References to earlier passages in the *History* are confined to providing a fuller context for events at the beginning of this translation, linking them with earlier or alternative accounts of the same incidents or with immediate antecedent events. The labor of this translation would have been much greater but for the exhaustive study of the revolt by Popovic; my indebtedness to him will be evident from the footnotes.

It remains for me to thank those who have kindly responded to pleas for assistance on points of obscurity and difficulty in the text. To Professor C. E. Bosworth, Basim Musallam, Nasser Tuwaim, and Goudah al-Batanuni I offer gratitude. A more special thanks is owed to the edior, Ehsan Yar-Shater, for reviewing the text and to Everett Rowson for his painstaking scrutiny of the translation, his corrections, and numerous helpful suggestions. And finally, a word of appreciation to Estelle Whelan for her unfailing good humor at moments of mutual vexation.

David Waines

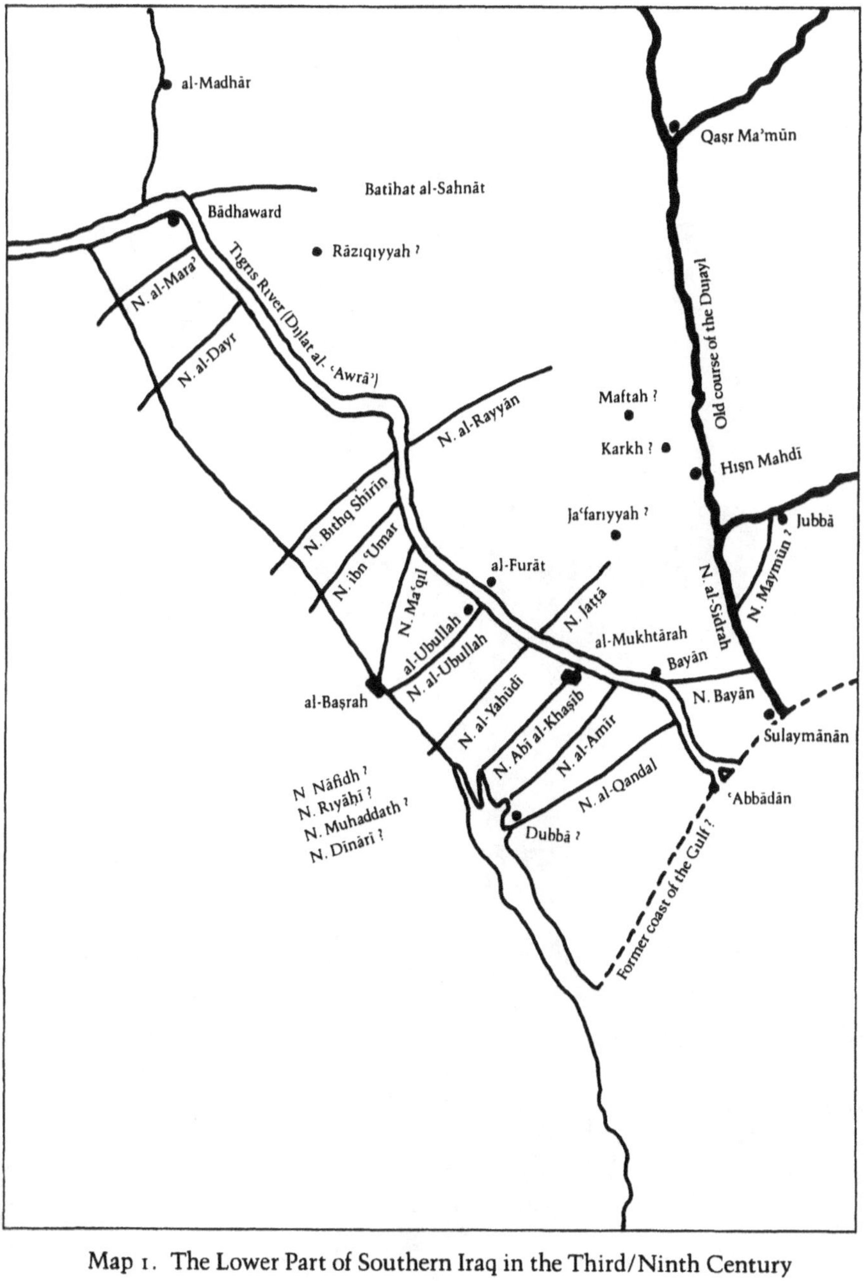

Map 1. The Lower Part of Southern Iraq in the Third/Ninth Century

The Caliphate of Ibn al-Wāthiq: Al-Muhtadī bi-Allāh

The Events of the Year 255 (cont'd) [1712]

(December 20, 868–December 8, 869)

On Wednesday, the last day of Rajab[1] of this year 255 (July 14, 869), Muḥammad the son of al-Wāthiq was rendered the oath of allegiance as caliph. He was called al-Muhtadī bi-Allāh.[2] His agnomen was Abū ʿAbdallāh. His mother, a Byzantine, was called Qurb.

It was reported on the authority of an eyewitness that Muḥammad b. al-Wāthiq refused to accept the oath of allegiance from anyone until al-Muʿtazz came before him and submitted his abdication, confirming his inability to administer matters entrusted to him and, moreover, expressing his desire to relinquish these matters into the care of Ibn al-Wāthiq.[3]

Extending his hand, al-Muʿtazz acknowledged his allegiance to Muḥammad b. al-Wāthiq, and only then was the new caliph given the honorific title of al-Muhtadī. Thereupon al-Muʿtazz withdrew,

1. The last day of the month was, in fact, Thursday.

2. See *EI*,[1] s.v. "al-Muhtadī"; Masʿūdī, *Murūj al-dhahab wa-maʿādin al-jawhar*, VIII, 1–41.

3. Al-Muʿtazz had become caliph in al-Muḥarram 252 (January 866), achieving the rank through the forced abdication of his predecessor, al-Mustaʿīn. See *EI*,[1] s.v. "al-Muʿtazz."

and the inner circle of clients (*mawālī*)[4] rendered their own oaths of allegiance.

The text of the statement concerning al-Muʿtazz's abdication is as follows:

> In the name of God, the Compassionate, the Merciful. The following is what the witnesses, named in this document below, were called upon to testify. They witnessed that Abū ʿAbdallāh, the son of the Commander of the Faithful al-Mutawakkil ʿalā-Allāh (while calling upon them to attest that he was of sound mind and that he lawfully performed this act of his own free will and without compulsion) acknowledged that he had reflected carefully upon matters concerning his title to the caliphate and the administration of the Muslims' affairs. He had reached the conclusion that he no longer felt suited to the task, as he was unable to fulfill his [1713] duties. He was unequal to the responsibilities he had to shoulder. Thus he voluntarily withdrew from office, declaring himself free of the burden, removing it by means of abdication. He released from their oaths those of his entourage who had sworn allegiance to him. Likewise anyone else who had sworn before him an oath of allegiance, or covenants and compacts, or oaths of divorce, of the emancipation of slaves, the voluntary payment of alms (*ṣadaqah*) or of pilgrimage, indeed every manner of oath, he redeemed these from them.
>
> After it had become clear to al-Muʿtazz that the best course both for himself and for all Muslims was to give up the caliphal office and to abdicate, he set free all those with obligations to him.
>
> He called to witness for him, regarding everything that was cited and described in this document, all the witnesses named below and all those present after the document had been carefully read aloud to him and he had acknowledged freely and without compulsion his full awareness of its contents.

4. The word *mawlā*, pl. *mawālī*, in the ʿAbbāsid period refers mainly to military personnel employed by the caliphs and who were mainly, if not exclusively, of central Asian origin. See P. Crone, *Slaves on Horses*.

This occurred on Monday, the 27th day of Rajab in the year 255 (July 11, 869).[5]

In his own hand al-Muʿtazz signed his consent to its contents with the words, "I Abū ʿAbdallāh acknowledge all that is contained in this document." It was dated Monday, the 27th day of Rajab, 255 (July 11, 869), and witnessed by the following persons: al-Ḥasan b. Muḥammad, Muḥammad b. Yahyā, Aḥmad b. Janāb, Yaḥyā b. Zakariyāʾ b. Abī Yaʿqūb al-Iṣbahānī, ʿAbdallāh b. Muḥammad al-ʿĀmirī, Aḥmad b. al-Faḍl b. Yaḥyā, Ḥammād b. Isḥāq, ʿAbdallāh b. Muḥammad, and Ibrāhīm b. Muḥammad.[6] [1714]

In Baghdad at the end of Rajab of this year there were disturbances and riots among the populace against Sulaymān b. ʿAbdallāh b. Ṭāhir.[7]

An Account of the Causes and Consequences of [the] Disturbances [in Baghdad]

One Thursday, toward the end of Rajab,[8] Sulaymān, who was in Baghdad, received a despatch from Muḥammad b. al-Wāthiq in-

---

5. The document, which is less a formal declaration of abdication than a report on the event itself, seems to end here. See Ṭabarī, III, 1709–12 for details of the deposition. Al-Muʿtazz's death was announced in public shortly afterward, on the 2nd of Shaʿbān (July 16, 869).

6. Only the first name in this list has been identified. Al-Ḥasan b. Muḥammad b. Abī al-Shawārib had been appointed chief judge in 252/866 (see Ṭabarī, III, 1684; his arrest is noted in Dhū al-Qaʿdah 255 [October 11–November 9, 869], 1787; see also D. Sourdel, *Le vizirat ʿabbāside*, I, 307), and his presence would have been deemed necessary to give the abdication/deposition at least the appearance of legitimacy. He did not, however, draw up the actual abdication document, which was undertaken by another of the company mentioned, Yaḥyā b. Zakariyāʾ al-Iṣbahānī. Ibn Abī al-Shawārib confirmed orally that the sister, son, and mother of al-Muʿtazz would be provided with safe-conduct. See Ṭabarī, III, 1710–11.

7. A scion of the famous Ṭāhirid family from Khurāsān, which had long supported the caliphs from the days of al-Maʾmūn (d. 218/833). As well as supplying governors of the eastern provinces, which led to the founding of an autonomous dynasty with its capital at Naysābūr, the family was deeply involved in the affairs of Baghdad. Sulaymān had been governor of Ṭabaristān in 250/864–865 and, earlier in the present year, on the 6th of Rabīʿah II (March 25, 869), he had been appointed chief of security in Baghdad and the districts of the *sawād* (see Ṭabarī, III, 1706). See *EI*,[1] s.v. "Ṭāhirids"; also C. E. Bosworth, "The Ṭāhirids and Ṣaffārids."

8. The expression *salkh*, meaning "in the last stage of," is used when the precise date of an event is not known but only its approximate occurrence in a phase or stage of the lunar month. See M. Ocaña Jiménez, *Nuevas tablas de conversión de datas islámicas a cristianas y viceverersa*, 45.

forming him of the people's oath of allegiance to him as caliph. At the time Abū Aḥmad, a son of al-Mutawakkil, was also in Baghdad.[9] His brother al-Muʿtazz had banished Abū Aḥmad to al-Baṣrah when he quarreled with his brother[10] al-Muʾayyad. Later, when factionalism erupted in al-Baṣrah, al-Muʿtazz had him brought back to Baghdad, where he continued to reside.[11] Sulaymān b. ʿAbdallāh b. Ṭāhir, who was at the time in charge of the office of security in Baghdad, sent for Abū Aḥmad and had him brought to his palace. The troops stationed in Baghdad and the mob (*al-ghawghāʾ*)[12] heard of the matter concerning the abdication of al-Muʿtazz and Ibn al-Wāthiq's accession to the caliphate. They gathered in front of Sulaymān's palace, creating a great uproar, but broke up somewhat later when they were informed that there was no confirmation of the report of what had happened. On the following day, Friday, there were again disturbances, and once again people were told the same thing as on the previous day. Prayers were performed in the two main mosques of the city and invocations offered in the name of al-Muʿtazz. Then, on the Saturday morning, troops attacked Sulaymān's palace, calling out in
[1715] the name of Abū Aḥmad (b. al-Mutawakkil) and demanding that he be rendered the oath of allegiance. Confronting Sulaymān in his palace, they asked him to produce Abū Aḥmad b. al-Mutawakkil. He brought him before them, and he promised to meet their wishes if there was delay in their fulfillment. The crowd departed, having been reassured of his guarantee.

Yārjūkh[13] arrived and camped at al-Baradān.[14] He was transporting thirty thousand dinars for the pay of the troops (*al-jund*) of Madīnat al-Salām.[15] He then advanced to al-Shammāsiyyah[16] and the

9. He was later known by the honorific title al-Muwaffaq.

10. *Akhi min ummihi*. Ṭabarī notes that Abū Aḥmad and al-Muʾayyad were brothers by the same mother.

11. Abū Aḥmad had been banished first to Wāsiṭ, thence to al-Baṣrah in 253/867. See Ṭabarī, III, 1693.

12. See n. 17, below.

13. Ṭabarī first mentions this Turkish officer during the course of events of this year in an engagement with the rebel Musāwir, who defeated him, forcing his flight to Sāmarrā. See Ṭabarī, III, 1706.

14. A town lying on the east bank of the Tigris just to the north of Baghdad. The road from it passed through the Baradān Gate on Baghdad's eastern side. See Le Strange, *Baghdad during the Abbasid Caliphate*, 174.

15. At this time Madīnat al-Salām was synonymous with Baghdad, and the expression has been retained here wherever it occurs.

16. One of the northern quarters of eastern Baghdad, Shammāsiyyah has the mean-

following morning entered Baghdad. When word of this got around, the troops (*al-nās*) created an uproar as they rushed out to meet him. Yārjūkh was informed of their approach, and he returned to al-Baradān to remain there. Despatches were exchanged between him and the central authorities until he finally sent money to the troops (*ahl*)[17] of Baghdad, with which they were content. Al-Muhtadī was rendered the oath of allegiance by the inner circle [of clients][18] in Baghdad on Thursday, the 7th of Shaʿbān (July 21, 869). Prayers were offered for him on Friday, the 8th of Shaʿbān, following an outbreak of violence (*fitnah*)[19] in Baghdad, during which some people were killed, others were drowned in the Tigris, while yet others suffered various injuries. This violence occurred because Sulaymān had his palace guarded with a group of armed Ṭabariyyah,[20] against whom the troops of Baghdad waged a pitched battle in Tigris Street and at the Bridge.[21] Thereafter order and peace were restored.

In the month of Ramaḍān of this year (August 13–September 9,

---

ing "deaconry," as the place had originally been occupied by several monasteries. See Le Strange, *Baghdad*, 202.

17. Ṭabarī at the beginning of the paragraph employs the common word for a military force, troops, or soldiers, *al-jund*, and then resorts to the more euphemistic terms *al-nas* and *ahl*, which literally mean "people" in general. However, a few lines earlier (see n. 12, above) Ṭabarī uses another term in association with *al-jund*, namely *al-ghawghā'*, which normally has no military connotation. Thus, despite Ṭabarī's rather loose style, he nevertheless conveys the picture of disorder caused by both military and civilian elements in the city. This is underlined by his use of the word *al-ʿāmmah* "the populace" in introducing the account of these events. See Ṭabarī, III, 1714.

18. The word *al-khāṣṣah* alone is taken here to mean those close to the court and the Caliph's person, as in the phrase *khāṣṣat al-mawālī*, used by Ṭabarī, III, 1712.

19. Ṭabarī's use of the word *fitnah* here suggests the rising tempo of violence in Baghdad, which had moved from demonstrations of anger to open violence leading to deaths. Sulaymān's deployment of a "foreign" contingent of soldiers around his palace was seen as highly provocative by troops based in Baghdad.

20. A contingent of soldiers from the province of Ṭabaristān. These troops may have been brought by Sulaymān b. ʿAbdallāh on his journey from Khurāsān to Sāmarrā. See Ṭabarī, III, 1706.

21. *Al-jisr*. There were three pontoon bridges (pl. *al-jusūr*) across the Tigris, joining western and eastern Baghdad. See Le Strange, *Baghdad*, 177–86, for a description of them. J. Lassner, *The Shaping of ʿAbbāsid Rule*, 299 n. 109 (and 294 n. 63) says that *al-jisr* signifies the Main Bridge joining the quarter of the Khuld on the western side with the Bāb al-Ṭāq on the east. Of the various scholarly views concerning the precise location of these bridges, Lassner follows Le Strange. See Lassner, *The Topography of Baghdad in the Early Middle Ages*, 173–76, 280 n. 1, 281 n. 6. Another problem about which there can be no certainty is when, whether in Ṭabarī's time or later, the term *al-jisr* became applied specifically to the Main Bridge.

869) Qabīḥah[22] went to the Turks and revealed to them the location of some of her possessions, including a hoard of treasures and jewels. That reportedly occurred because she had planned to assassinate Ṣāliḥ (b. Waṣīf)[23] and plotted to do so with a number of secretaries
[1716] whom Ṣāliḥ had already maltreated.[24] When Ṣāliḥ [again] submitted them to torture and Qabīḥah learned that they had withheld no information from Ṣāliḥ, owing to the punishment he meted out to them, she became convinced her own life was in danger. She undertook to save herself and thus removed the contents of her treasure stores from inside the Jawsaq palace,[25] which included money, jewels, and other precious goods; she deposited them for safekeeping along with other goods of the same kind she had previously deposited.

Qabīḥah was unsure of being able to act swiftly in the event of such circumstances as eventually overwhelmed her and her son, so she devised a strategem for her escape. A tunnel was excavated leading from one of her private chambers inside the palace to a place that would not be detected. When she learned of the circumstances [surrounding her son's abdication] she hastened to the tunnel without a second thought and escaped from the palace confines. When those who had rebelled against her son had succeeded [in imposing the situation] they wanted, they then set out in search of Qabīḥah, confident of her capture. But they found the palace empty. She had vanished without a trace, leaving them no clue where to search. Finally, however, they stumbled across the tunnel. Realizing this must have

---

22. The mother of al-Muʿtazz.

23. Ṣāliḥ was a prominent military leader, whose father had been murdered two years earlier by his Turkish rivals. He was now attempting to restore the power of his own faction and bore grievances against both the deposed Caliph, al-Muʿtazz, and some of his government officials. Qabīḥah clearly felt Ṣāliḥ would not honor his pledge of securing her safety. See Sourdel, *Vizirat*, I, 297–98.

24. Prominent among those who were subjected to Ṣāliḥ's interrogation methods were Abū Jaʿfar Aḥmad b. Isrāʾīl al-Anbārī, al-Muʿtazz's vizier, who, together with Abū Nūḥ ʿĪsā b. Ibrāhīm and Ḥasan b. Makhlad, were the major pillars of the Caliph's administration. In addition, Ḥasan was also secretary to Qabīḥah. As such they became the target of Ṣāliḥ b. Waṣīf's ambitions in his bid for power. See Ṭabarī, III, 1706–9; Sourdel, *Vizirat*, I, 295–98, for details of relevant parallel sources.

25. This palace, built by the Caliph al-Muʿtaṣim, was located on the eastern side of the Tigris at Sāmarrā. See Le Strange, *The Lands of the Eastern Caliphate*, 55. It should not be confused with the palace al-Jawsaq al-Muḥdath situated in Baghdad. See Le Strange, *Baghdad*, 257. The architectural details of the palace are discussed in K. A. C. Creswell, *A Short Account of Early Muslim Architecture*, 259–60.

been her escape route, they followed it as far as the secret exit and became certain of her successful escape. They surmised that she would have sought a safe and secure refuge, and what better way than to seek shelter with Ḥabīb, the wife of Mūsā b. Bughā,[26] whom he had married from among the concubines of al-Mutawakkil? They set out for this quarter of the city, but being loath to expose themselves to any of her supporters, they organized a surveillance team to watch her. A threat was publicly announced against anyone with information of her whereabouts who then did not inform them of it. Thus matters stood until, in the month of Ramaḍān, she suddenly appeared and went to Ṣāliḥ b. Waṣīf. A female apothecary in whom she had trust acted as her intermediary with Ṣāliḥ. Qabīḥah had wealth in Baghdad, and so she sent written instructions for some of it to be brought to Sāmarrā. [1717]

On Tuesday, the 11th of Ramaḍān in this year (August 23, 869), it was reported, a sum of five hundred thousand dinars arrived in Sāmarrā. The money had been raised for Qabīḥah from the treasure she had in Baghdad and despatched according to her instructions. The central authorities profited greatly from this source, while in Baghdad itself the non-Arab troops (*al-jund*) and the Shākiriyyah[27] who received regular stipends were assigned considerable sums from it as well. The sale of these hoards continued to raise money in Baghdad and Sāmarrā for several months until, at last, they were depleted. Qabīḥah remained in Sāmarrā until people departed for Mecca on that year's pilgrimage. She was sent in the company of Rajāʾ al-Rabābī and Waḥash, a *mawlā* of al-Muhtadī. It was reported that someone heard her along the way imploring God in a loud voice

---

26. Mūsā was the son of the army commander the elder Bughā. See *EI*,[2] s.v. "Bughā al-Kabīr."

27. A name variously applied to a group or groups of soldiers who became rivals of troops commanded by the Turkish commanders in Sāmarrā. See Masʿūdī, *Murūj*, VII, 276; also R. Levy, *The Social Structure of Islam*, 418, states the word is derived from the Persian *chākir* "servant or apprentice" and that, as a contingent, they were distinct from the *jund*, or regular soldiers. A more precise distinction may be found in the organization of military administration during the earlier reign of al-Mutawakkil (d. 248/861), when there existed a branch of the department of the army called the *Diwān al-jund wa-al-Shākiriyyah*; *jund* referred to non-Arab troops while Shākiriyyah meant mercenaries. See Sourdel, *Vizirat*, II, 596; *EI*,[2] s.v. "Djund." Thus, in instances where Ṭabarī uses these two terms in conjunction, the word *jund* will be rendered as "non-Arab troops"; otherwise it will be rendered variously as "soldiers," "troops," "army," and the like.

[1718] against Ṣāliḥ b. Waṣīf, saying: "Oh God, humiliate Ṣāliḥ b. Waṣīf just as he has dishonored me, murdered my son, seized my property, squandered my goods, banished me from my home, and behaved obscenely toward me." When the pilgrims set out on their return journey, Qabīḥah was detained in prison in Mecca.

It was reported that, when the Turks became agitated and roused against al-Muʿtazz, they demanded fifty thousand dinars from him, promising in return to kill Ṣāliḥ b. Waṣīf and then become pacific. Al-Muʿtazz sent word to his mother of the Turks' grievances against him and of his fear for his life. She replied, "I have no liquid resources. We have received some promissory notes,[28] and, if the Turks can wait until they are redeemed, we could then pay them."[29]

When al-Muʿtazz had been killed, Ṣāliḥ made contact with a jeweler, who recounted the following story: "I went to Ṣāliḥ. Aḥmad b. Khāqān[30] was present with him at the time. Aḥmad said to me, 'Woe upon you! This is it. Do you see what a fix I'm in?' Ṣāliḥ had been alarmed by the Turks, who had demanded money of him that he did not have. He said to me, pointing out one of the company present, 'I have been informed that Qabīḥah has treasure hidden in a place to which this man can guide you. Go, and take Aḥmad b. Khāqān with you. Should you uncover anything, make a record of it, hand it over to him, and come with him to me.'

When I had performed my prayers[31] in the congregational mosque, this man took us to a tidy dwelling, which we entered and searched
[1719] from top to bottom without finding anything. The man began to abuse Aḥmad b. Khāqān, who in turn menaced, threatened, and abused him and accused him of making an error. The man fetched an ax and commenced piercing the walls with it, searching for a place where the money might be hidden. He continued exploring in this fashion until the ax struck a spot in the wall that, by the sound it made, indicated that something was concealed there. By demolishing the wall, a door was revealed behind it. We opened it and entered. It led to a tunnel, and we found ourselves in a chamber built

28. *Safātij*.

29. See Ṭabarī, III, 1709, for slightly different details of these events.

30. This is Aḥmad b. Khāqān al-Wāthiqī, a freedman of the Caliph al-Wāthiq, who appears briefly later; p. 73, below.

31. *Ila al-ṣufūf*, the reading favored by the editor of the Leiden text. Although each of the recensions has a different reading, none of them is satisfactory.

beneath the dwelling we had entered above, identical in structure and floor plan. There, stored in baskets placed upon shelves, we located the money, amounting to something in the order of a million dinars. Aḥmad and his companion removed three hundred thousand dinars. Then we discovered three baskets; one contained a *makkūk*[32] of emeralds, but of a kind that I could imagine neither al-Mutawakkil nor indeed anyone else possessing. Another smaller basket contained half a *makkūk* of large beads which, by God, I had never dreamed al-Mutawakkil or anyone else could possess. The third yet smaller basket contained a *kaylajah* of rubies, the likes of which I had never before seen or even imagined existing anywhere in the world. Estimating the market value of it all, it came to two million dinars. We removed the entire treasure and took it to Ṣāliḥ. When he heard of its value, he could scarcely believe it and remained unconvinced until he was shown the actual goods. He then re- [1720] marked, 'May God do such-and-such to her! Al-Muʿtazz's mother condemned her son to death for want of the miserable sum of fifty thousand dinars, when she actually had in only one of her treasuries such wealth as this!'"

The mother[33] of Muʿtazz b. al-Wāthiq (al-Muhtadī) died before the oath of allegiance had been rendered to him. She had been one of al-Mustaʿīn's wives, and when he was slain al-Muʿtazz transferred her to the palace of al-Ruṣāfah,[34] where he kept his harem. After al-Muhtadī became caliph he one day said to a company of his *mawlās*, "I now [unlike al-Muʿtazz] have no mother who requires the sum of ten million dinars every year as expenses for her maids and servants and hangers-on; as for myself and my children, I want only sufficient food and nothing extra, except for my brothers, as they have fallen upon hard times."

Aḥmad b. Isrāʾīl and Abū Nūḥ were killed on the 27th of Ramaḍān of this year (September 8, 869).

---

32. Measures like this and *kaylajah*, below, were subject to regional variation. A *makkūk* in Baghdad and al-Kūfah weighed 5.625 kg., while in al-Baṣrah and Wāsiṭ it weighed 6 kg. In Iraq a *kaylajah* was one-third of a *makkūk*. See W. Hinz, *Islamische Masse und Gewichte*, 40, 44.

33. This was Qurb, the Byzantine woman mentioned above, p. 1.

34. Located in the northeastern quarter of Baghdad, the palace was orginally built by the Caliph al-Mahdī and probably restored or enlarged by Hārūn al-Rashīd. See Le Strange, *Baghdad*, 189; Lassner, *Topography*, index, q.v.

An Account of [the] Deaths [of Aḥmad b. Isrā'īl and Abū Nūḥ]

We have already mentioned the cause that led them to their deaths.[35] As for the nature of their deaths, it is reported that, when Ṣāliḥ b. Waṣīf had seized all their property and that of al-Ḥasan b. Makhlad as well, he did so by torturing them with beatings and chains and placing braziers of red-hot coals next to them, while depriving them of any respite the whole time they were in his custody. They were
[1721] accused of grave crimes of treason, of intending to degrade the central authorities, and of attempting to prolong civil disorder by plotting dissent among Muslims. Al-Muhtadī did nothing to interfere with Ṣāliḥ in these matters, though he disapproved of and did not accept his violent behavior toward them. Then, in the month of Ramaḍān (August 13 – September 11, 869), Ṣāliḥ ordered al-Ḥasan b. Sulaymān al-Dūshābī[36] to supervise the extraction of any remaining property that they had concealed from him.

Al-Ḥasan b. Sulaymān related that, when Aḥmad b. Isrā'īl had been brought to him, he abused him, saying "You wretch, do you think that God will give you respite and that the Commander of the Faithful will not sanction your death, though you are the cause of discord, an accomplice in murder and treason, and a corrupter of purpose and character? For the very least of these crimes you deserve to be made an example of, just as those before you have deserved such treatment. Death in this life and torment and ignominy in the life hereafter are your lot if you do not receive God's pardon and mercy, and your Imām's pardon and forgiveness. Protect yourself from incurring the punishment you deserve by being truthful concerning your wealth; if you do so and your truthfulness is confirmed, you can save yourself."

Aḥmad replied that he had nothing left, nor had anyone until then left him property or estates.

Al-Ḥasan said, "I then called for whips to be brought out and ordered that Aḥmad be stood outside in the sun. I assailed him with
[1722] ferocity, though triumph could have slipped through my hands if he had shown a little courage and fortitude. Finally, however, he con-

---

35. See Ṭabarī, III, 1706–9.
36. No further information on this man has been found.

ceded to an amount of nineteen thousand dinars, and I accepted his bond on it."

Al-Ḥasan continued, "Thereafter I had Abū Nūḥ ʿĪsā b. Ibrāhīm brought to me and told him the same as I had to Aḥmad, or words to the same effect, elaborating somewhat upon them. "Withal, you remain a Christian, violating Muslim women while proclaiming yourself free from Islam and its followers. What better indicates this than the fact that you remain a Christian in private among your family and children? God has permitted such persons to be lawfully killed. But Abū Nūḥ gave no reply to any of this, weak and miserable man that he was."[37]

Al-Ḥasan continued: "As for al-Ḥasan b. Makhlad, I had him brought to me next, but when I addressed him I was speaking to someone already weak and humiliated. I chided him for appearing this way. I said, 'Someone who has grooms to accompany him on his *shihrī* steed, who judges matters as you do, and desires what you do, should never appear humbled or impotent.' I kept up the pressure on him in this manner until he signed his bond for a jewel the value of which was some thirty thousand dinars. After this I departed, and they were then all returned to their places." Al-Ḥasan b. Sulaymān al-Dūshābī's examination of these men was the last involving them. According to the information that has reached me, no similar examination was held during the remaining days of al-Muhtadī.

On Thursday, the 27th of Ramaḍān (September 8, 869), Aḥmad b. Isrāʾīl and Abū Nūḥ ʿĪsā b. Ibrāhīm were brought to the Public Gate. [1723]
Ṣāliḥ b. Waṣīf, who presided in the public audience hall, ordered Ḥammād b. Muḥammad b. Ḥammād b. Danqash[38] to beat them. Aḥmad b. Isrāʾīl was prepared, and Ibn Danqash cried out "Scourge him!" Each flogger lashed him twice, then stepped aside for the next one until Aḥmad had received five hundred strokes. They next prepared Abū Nūḥ and administered five hundred severe lashes on him as well. The two wretches were then placed face down upon the backs of donkeys of water sellers, their heads toward the rear of the animals, so that their lacerated backs were plain for all to see. When

---

37. At this time there were in the administration several scribes of Nestorian origin, some of whom had been recently converted. To this general group belonged Aḥmad b. Ismāʿīl, al-Ḥasan b. Makhlad, and Abū Nūḥ ʿĪsā b. Ibrāhīm. See Sourdel, *Vizirat*, I, 304.

38. No further information on this person has been found.

the procession reached Khashabat Bābak,[39] Aḥmad died and Abū Nūḥ died when the procession came to an end. Aḥmad was buried between the walls [of the city] and, according to another account, Abū Nūḥ died the same day in the prison of al-Sarakhsī, who was the deputy of Ṭalmajūr,[40] in charge of the special police. For his part, al-Ḥasan b. Makhlad remained in prison.

Someone who had been present at these proceedings reportedly said, "I heard Ḥammād b. Muḥammad b. Ḥammād b. Danqash berate the floggers saying, 'Exert yourselves, you sons of harlots, may you never be addressed in respectful terms![41] Punish them! Change the whips and replace the teams of torturers with others!' Aḥmad b. Isrā'īl and ʿĪsā (b. Ibrāhīm) cried out for mercy."

When news of this reached al-Muhtadī, he said, "Is there no choice of punishment other than either the whip or death? Is there nothing better? Is imprisonment not enough? We are God's, and to Him we shall return."[42] He repeated this last phrase over and over again.

Al-Ḥasan b. Makhlad is reported to have said that their whole af-
[1724] fair involving Ṣāliḥ would have come to naught had ʿAbdallāh b. Muḥammad b. Yazdād[43] not been present and in such a ruthless mood. He urged upon Ṣāliḥ to "beat and torture them; indeed it would be best to go beyond that and kill them. If they escape, you will never be sure their injustices will not visit you in the end, let alone what those seeking to avenge them might do." He then mentioned what vile things that he had heard concerning them, which delighted Ṣāliḥ.

Ibn Makhlad continued: "Dā'ūd b. al-ʿAbbās al-Ṭūsī[44] used to

39. For Bābak, the leader of the Kurramite sect, and the place in Sāmarrā that carries his name, see *EI*,[2] s.v. "Bābak." For the quarter of Khashabat Bābak, see Yaʿqūbī, *Kitāb al-Buldān*, 259. The quarter in these years was the site of public executions. See Ṭabarī, III, 1658.

40. The name is uncertain, other variants being given as Ṭalmaḥūn and Ṭalḥūr.

41. That is, they would not be addressed by their patronymics. See *EI*,[2] s.v. "Kunya," on the honorific nature of this form of address.

42. A phrase that occurs in the Qur'ān several times.

43. Abū Ṣāliḥ ʿAbdallāh b. Muḥammad b. Yazdād al-Marwazī was the son of the Caliph al-Ma'mūn's last secretary; ʿAbdallāh himself was briefly vizier under al-Mustaʿīn and was last encountered being summoned by al-Muʿtazz to be appointed vizier during the events here recounted. See Ṭabarī, III, 1707; Sourdel, *Vizirat*, I, 292.

44. His name is otherwise given as Dā'ūd b. Muḥammad b. Abī al-ʿAbbās al-Ṭūsī. See Ṭabarī, index, s.v. "Dā'ūd b. al-ʿAbbās." No other information about him is available, but see n. 45, below.

bring us to Ṣāliḥ, saying, 'May God give you strength, what are these people that they should have caused you such anger?' We thought he might influence Ṣāliḥ to treat us leniently until he said, 'But by God, I know that if they were set free they would perpetrate immense evil and corruption throughout the domain of Islam.' Before he departed Dā'ūd provided a legal opinion (*fatwā*)[45] justifying our execution and advised Ṣāliḥ to have us put to death. This legal opinion and the other things he said about us increased Ṣāliḥ's anger and his willingness to do us harm."

Someone who had some firsthand knowledge of these developments was once asked how al-Ḥasan b. Makhlad was spared the fate of his two companions. The reply was twofold. First, al-Ḥasan had at once truthfully revealed to Ṣāliḥ the information he required, also providing proof that what he said was true. Ṣāliḥ had promised to pardon al-Ḥasan if he told the truth and swore an oath to that effect. The second reason was that the Commander of the Faithful had mentioned his case to Ṣāliḥ, telling him of the esteem he had for his family and hinting that he desired to have al-Ḥasan rehabilitated. He thereby restrained him from doing anything too reprehensible to [1725] him. The informant also thought that, if Ṣāliḥ had held al-Ḥasan longer in custody, he would have released him in any case and treated him well. But in the matter of government secretaries, Ṣāliḥ was not content to sequester their wealth and that of their children. He went so far as to threaten their relatives and other near relations with sequestration of their wealth and extended his influence even over their hangers-on.

On the 13th of Ramaḍān of this year 255 (August 25, 869) the prison in Baghdad was breached. The Shākiriyyah and reserve soldiers (*al-nā'ibah*) in the city attacked Muḥammad b. Aws al-Balkhī.

An Account of [the] Events [of Ramaḍān 255]

The cause of these developments was the arrival in Baghdad of Muḥammad b. Aws,[46] who was accompanying Sulaymān b. ʿAbdallāh

45. This phrase would suggest that Dā'ūd b. al-ʿAbbās al-Ṭūsī was a *muftī*, a canon lawyer, competent to render such an opinion. See *EI*,[2] s.v. "Fatwā."

46. In his account of events of the year 250/864–65 Ṭabarī notes that Muḥammad b. Aws had virtually wrested Ṭabaristān from the control of its governor, Sulaymān b. ʿAbdallāh, by placing his own offspring in key positions of power. Their brutality

b. Ṭāhir.[47] Muḥammad was in charge of the army coming with Sulaymān from Khurāsān, in addition to the riffraff[48] whom Sulaymān had assembled while in al-Rayy but whose names were not recorded in the *dīwān* of the central authorities in Iraq.[49] Sulaymān had been given no instructions concerning them. The prevailing practice for such recruits, however, was to pay those who accompanied him from Khurāsān a rate of pay in Iraq equivalent to that paid to their like in Khurāsān, to be drawn from the revenues of the [Iraqī] estates[50] of
[1726] heirs of the Ṭāhirid family.[51] Instructions were then sent to Khurāsān concerning the matter, to arrange that the heirs there were compensated from the public treasury [in Khurāsān] for what was paid out from their property in Iraq. When Sulaymān b. ʿAbdallāh arrived in Iraq, however, he discovered that the treasury of the heirs' property was depleted. Once this information was confirmed, ʿUbaydallāh b. ʿAbdallāh b. Ṭāhir[52] had undertaken to transfer to his brother, Sulaymān [responsibility for] the task[53] to which he had been assigned. ʿUbaydallāh secured the amount accumulated in the coffers of the heirs of his father and grandfather while demanding payment

---

and arrogance had created much ill feeling against them among the population of the province. See Ṭabarī, III, 1524–25.

47. Sulaymān b. ʿAbdallāh had been appointed by al-Muʿtazz as chief of security in Baghdad and the Sawād on the 6th of Rajab II (March 24, 869). After receiving robes of honor from the Caliph, he departed for Baghdad. See Ṭabarī, III, 1706. His arrival there was the cause for the disturbances recounted on pp. 3–5, above.

48. *Ṣaʿālīk*, pl. of *ṣuʿlūk*. The word means a poor or needy person and, by extension, a thief and robber. In the present context they may be understood as a group of untrained conscripts; in any event, they appear to have been quartered together as a group, as will appear in the subsequent narrative. See n. 81, below, and p. 164, where one Abū Dāʾūd al-Ṣaʿlūk was engaged in warlike activities.

49. On the organization of the army in ʿAbbāsid times, see *EI*,[2] s.v. "Djaysh"; Bosworth, "Recruitment, Muster and Review in medieval Islamic Armies."

50. *Ḍīyāʿ warathah dhī al-yamīnayn*. The Ṭāhirids were acting as bankers for the army.

51. The text reads *dhū al-yamīnayn*. The epithet, meaning ambidextrous, was given to the founder of the Ṭāhirid dynasty, Ṭāhir b. al-Ḥusayn, owing to his ability to use a sword in battle with either hand. See Bosworth, "Ṭāhirids," 90–5; H. Kennedy, *The Prophet and the Age of the Caliphs*, 150–52; *EI*,[1] s.v. "Ṭāhir b. al-Ḥusayn."

52. Muḥammad b. ʿAbdallāh, the brother of ʿUbaydallāh, had deputized him in his will to assume his duties in the event of his death. When Muḥammad died in Dhū al-Qaʿdah 253 (November 867) al-Muʿtazz gave ʿUbaydallāh robes of honor and a document signifying that he was the governor of Baghdad; Ṭabarī, III, 1691–92. In the next year, 254/868, ʿUbaydallāh was in Baghdad, tracking down the sons of the Turkish commander Bughā the Younger, murdered at the instigation of the Caliph, III, 1696.

53. That is, the governorship of Baghdad.

of taxes in advance on immature crops. Payments[54] from tax collectors were brought forward to a time when they were not yet due. Nevertheless, he managed to gather the entire amount required.

Thereafter ʿUbaydallāh set out and established camp in al-Juwayth,[55] which was situated on the eastern side of the Tigris. Later he crossed over to the western side. Thus Sulaymān found himself in dire straits as the Shākiriyyah and the non-Arab soldiers[56] agitated for payment of their allotments. Sulaymān corresponded with Abū ʿAbdallāh al-Muʿtazz on the matter, estimating the amount of revenue required for these payments. He added an estimate as well for those who had accompanied him from Khurāsān. He instructed his secretary, Muḥammad b. ʿĪsā b. ʿAbd al-Raḥmān al-Kātib al-Khurāsānī, to deal with the matter. After some negotiations Sulaymān received a reply that funds under the control of the tax agents of the Sawād would be assigned to him,[57] on condition of his assuming responsibility for their repayment. The funds would be for the pay of [troops] in Madīnat al-Salām and the garrisons of the Sawād; they were not to meet needs of [Sulaymān's] reserves or the troops accompanying them. Sulaymān was not able to get access to any of the funds. Ibn Aws, the riffraff, and his troops arrived, but the revenue was insufficient for his needs and the needs of those reserves who had anticipated receiving it. They thus found out about this sit- [1727]
uation and its harmful consequences to them.

The riffraff and others who had arrived in Baghdad with Sulaymān began to disturb the peace of the local neighborhoods, openly displaying foul behavior and attacking women, slaves (*al-ʿabīd*),[58] and servants (*al-ghilmān*).[59] They were able to assault these classes be-

---

54. *Amwāl nujūm. Najm* signifies the time when a payment falls due, hence also an installment.

55. The reading is uncertain, the name in manuscripts B and C being unpointed.

56. Ṭabarī again employs the term *al-jund* here. See n. 27, above. It is, however, unclear whether he is referring to troops already stationed in Baghdad or to soldiers who accompanied Sulaymān.

57. *Subbiba lahu. Tasbīb* was a form of direct payment made to soldiers either as a salary or as an assignment on a specific source of taxation. See Ṭabarī, *Glossarium*; CCLXXXIV see also Bosworth, "Recruitment," 75; Bosworth, "Abū ʿAbdallāh al-Khwārazmī on the Technical Terms of the Secretary's Art," 139–40.

58. On this term, pl. of *ʿabd*, see, *EI*,[2] s.v. "ʿAbd."

59. On the complex of meanings of this term, pl. of *ghulām*, see *EI*,[2] s.v. "Ghulām." In the urban contexts of Sāmarrā and Baghdad the term may be rendered as "attendant, guard, servant, and page." See also *EI*,[2] s.v. "Djaysh," especially at 507, for the

cause of their standing with the central authorities, and such behavior aroused against them the anger and fury of the people.

Now it happened that Sulaymān b. ʿAbdallāh had developed a deep resentment against al-Ḥusayn b. Ismāʿīl b. Ibrāhīm b. Muṣʿab b. Ruzayq[60] because of the position granted him by ʿUbaydallāh b. ʿAbdallāh, as well as the support and maintenance ʿUbaydallāh provided him. Sulaymān also resented al-Ḥusayn's separation from himself and his supporters. After al-Ḥusayn b. Ismāʿīl had returned to Baghdad at the end of his appointment in charge of the non-Arab troops and the Shākiriyyah on behalf of ʿUbaydallāh, Sulaymān imprisoned al-Ḥusayn's secretary in al-Maṭbaq[61] and his chamberlain in the prison by the Syrian Gate.[62] He also placed troops to guard the residence of al-Ḥusayn b. Ismāʿīl under the command of Ibrāhīm b. Isḥāq b. Ibrāhīm. Sulaymān had put this Ibrāhīm in charge of the double bridge[63] of Baghdad and the administrative districts (sg. *ṭassūj*) of Qaṭrabbul, Maskin, and al-Anbār.[64] These were the very same duties that al-Ḥusayn b. Ismāʿīl, on ʿUbaydallāh's behalf, had been responsible for previously.

Events transpired as they did in the wake of al-Muhtadī's accession to the caliphate with the revolt of the troops and the Shākiriyyah in Madīnat al-Salām and the outbreak of general unrest. During this period, Muḥammad b. Aws severely maltreated an inhabitant from Marv who was a partisan of the Shīʿah. In Sulay-

---

term "young soldier," which might at times also apply in these same contexts. For a contrasting usage, see n. 139, below.

60. One of the military commanders who had been in the service of Muḥammad b. ʿAbdallāh b. Ṭāhir in Baghdad; he then served as one of ʿUbaydallāh's commanders. See Ṭabarī, III, 1664–68.

61. Built by the Caliph al-Manṣūr, this prison is located by Le Strange in the southern part of the Round City at the intersection of roads leading to the al-Baṣrah and al-Kūfah Gates. Le Strange, *Baghdad*, 27.

62. This prison, also built by al-Manṣūr, was located by the Syrian Gate of the Round City. Le Strange, *Baghdad*, 130.

63. *Jisrayn*. From the use of this expression and from an earlier context (see Ṭabarī, III, 1663–64), it is possible to suggest that there existed a double pontoon bridge in Baghdad, even before the one known to have been erected in the mid-eleventh century. See Lassner, *Topography*, 173–76, 281 n. 6; and note 72, below.

64. These districts formed part of a larger suburban area to the north and west of Baghdad, extending as far as the Euphrates river. See Le Strange, *Lands*, 51; Le Strange, *Baghdad*, 50–51; Lassner, *Topography*, index, q.vv. On the *ṭassūj*, see Bosworth, "Abū ʿAbdallāh," 140; F. Løkkegaard, *Islamic Taxation, in the Classic Period*, 164–65.

mān's palace, Muḥammad administered to him three hundred brutal lashes and then imprisoned him at the Syrian Gate. It happened that the man was among al-Ḥusayn b. Ismāʿīl's inner circle. So [1728] when this [unrest] occurred, there was need of al-Ḥusayn b. Ismāʿīl, because of his fortitude and courage. The troops placed in charge of guarding his palace were removed, and he came out. His own troops, after having been distributed among the contingents of other army commanders, a large number of them being attached to the commander Muḥammad b. Abī Awn,[65] returned to him without orders.

It was reported that, when those who had been thus assigned to Ibn Abī Awn arrived at [al-Ḥusayn's] palace, he dispensed among them from his own resources ten dirhams for each foot soldier and a dinar for each horseman. After they thus returned to al-Ḥusayn, Ibn Abī Awn lodged a complaint regarding that, but no appointment [returning the soldiers to him] or order regarding that was forthcoming.

The position remained the same, and the non-Arab soldiers and the Shākiriyyah clamored for the payment due to them upon the accession of the new caliph[66] and for the remainder of their advance allotments. Arrangements for the distribution of their pay and their receipt [of it] had now passed again into the hands of al-Ḥusayn, along the same lines as in the days of ʿUbaydallāh b. ʿAbdallāh b. Ṭāhir. Al-Ḥusayn was continuously haranguing them about Muḥammad b. Abī Awn's behavior and that of those who had come with Sulaymān, how these were trying to get their hands on the troops' money and keep it from them, until their hearts were filled [with resentment].

On Friday the 13th of Ramaḍān (August 25, 869) a contingent of non-Arab troops and the Shākiriyyah assembled together with a crowd of the local populace. Under the cover of night they proceeded to the prison at the Syrian Gate, broke down its doors, and released most of the inmates, leaving behind only those criminals who were [1729] either too weak or sick or were loaded with fetters. Among those who managed to escape that night were a number belonging to the

65. He had formerly been one of Muḥammad b. ʿAbdallāh b. Ṭāhir's commanders, and had been appointed by al-Muʿtazz in 252/866 to govern al-Baṣrah, Yamāmah, and al-Baḥrayn. See Ṭabarī, III, 1658.

66. *Māl al-bayʿah*. See *EI*,[2] s.v. "Māl al-bayʿa."

family of Musāwir b. ʿAbd al-Ḥamīd the Khārijite.[67] The man from Marv who had been maltreated by Muḥammad b. Aws was also set free. So too was a group of those to whom the central authorities had sent some fifty million[68] before being captured.[69]

When people went out on Friday morning, they found the prison gates opened. [The inmates] who could walk away did so; for those who were unable to walk riding animals were hired. They milled about without let or hindrance. This was one of the most significant events that caused both the privileged and the common people to lose any fear they had of Sulaymān b. ʿAbdallāh. Finally, the doors of the prison at the Syrian Gate were sealed with bricks and clay. No indication was known of any action whatsoever taken that night on the part of Ibrāhīm b. Isḥāq[70] or any of his associates. It was rumored among the people that the person suspected of planning the assault on the prison was someone acting on behalf of, and in order to release, the man from Marv whom Ibn Aws had badly beaten.

Scarcely five days had elapsed after these events when Ibn Aws quarreled with al-Ḥusayn b. Ismāʿīl over the matter of paying the reserve forces. Ibn Aws wanted the money for his own troops, but al-Ḥusayn would have none of it. Foul words were exchanged between them, and Muḥammad (Ibn Aws) departed livid with anger. The next
[1730] morning he set out for Sulaymān's palace; al-Ḥusayn b. Ismāʿīl and al-Shāh b. Mīkāl, a *mawlā* of Ṭāhir,[71] did likewise. Among the

67. Musāwir was one of the *dihqāns* of al-Bawāzīj, a town in the eastern part of the Jazīrah area, on the bank of the Lesser Zāb river (see Le Strange, *Lands*, 91). Ṭabarī calls him a Khārijite (*muḥakkim*, meaning "one who asserts there is no judgment, *ḥukm*, but God's," a known Khārijite principle) where he notes the commencement of his rebellion in Rajab 253 (July 7–August 5, 876), III, 1688–94. Here, as in all later references, Ṭabarī refers to him as al-Shārī, literally, "seller," a Khārijite term meaning "one who sells his soul for the cause of God," echoing Qur'ān 2:203.

68. *Khamsīn alf alf*. The text does not mention to what the figure refers; indeed, the copyist may have inadvertently repeated the *alf* (thousand) and the figure intended may have been fifty thousand.

69. The translation of this last sentence is tentative; the entire passage is quite obscure.

70. This incident appears to have been the sequel to an earlier clash in Baghdad between the mob and the clients of Isḥāq b. Ibrāhīm, who sided with Ṭāhir b. Muḥammad b. ʿAbdallāh against Muḥammad's brother ʿUbaydallāh in what was a petty interfamily squabble. See Ṭabarī, III, 1691–92.

71. Al-Shāh b. Mīkāl had been one of Muḥammad b. ʿAbdallāh b. Ṭāhir's loyal commanders in Baghdad. He had a brother Muḥammad who was a commander in the service of another member of the Ṭāhirid family and who was killed in 250/864–65.

crowd gathered in front of Sulaymān's residence some of Ibn Aws's troops were engaged in loud, heated discussion with the reserves. Then the troops of Ibn Aws and the newcomers [from Khurāsān] hastened across to the island,[72] followed by Ibn Aws himself and his sons. Men summoned one another to arms. Al-Ḥusayn b. Ismāʿīl, al-Shāh b. Mīkāl, and al-Muẓaffar b. Saysal[73] departed with their own troops, and the men called to the mob, "Join us, those who want to plunder!" It is said that during the day some hundred thousand of the populace crossed over the double bridge (*al-jisrayn*) of boats.[74] The non-Arab troops and the Shakiriyyah arrived at the island armed, followed by the vanguard of the populace. Suddenly a man from Sarakhs attacked the eldest son of Muḥammad b. Aws and stabbed him, knocking him from the *shihrī* horse he was riding. He received sword wounds while his supporters fled without raising a finger. Lying there injured, he was stripped clean and then dumped into a boat and carried across the river to the palace of Sulaymān b. ʿAbdallāh b. Ṭāhir, where he was left.

Someone who was present with Sulaymān at the time reported that, when Sulaymān saw the wounded man, his eyes filled with tears. A bed was prepared for him, and he was attended by physicians. Ibn Aws left immediately for his residence in a palace belonging to the family of Aḥmad b. Ṣāliḥ b. Shīrzād.[75] This was situated in the quarter of al-Dūr,[76] adjacent to the palace of Jaʿfar b. Yaḥyā b. [1731]

See Ṭabarī, III, 1532. Al-Shāh b. Mīkāl appears again, charged with putting down an ʿAlid revolt in al-Kūfah, on p. 115, below.

72. The topography in this passage is obscure. There is a reference by Ṭabarī, III, 1616, to "an island opposite the palace of Muḥammad b. ʿAbdallāh (b. Ṭāhir)," where a crowd of Banū Hāshim gathered demanding their stipends in 251/865–66. The island in the present passage could be the same, if Sulaymān occupied Muḥammad's palace after his brother's death or else had his own palace adjacent to it. The double bridge (*al-jisrayn*) mentioned in the passage, therefore, could be the one noted by Le Strange, *Baghdad*, 179, which was known as the Zandaward Bridge. If this identification is correct, then the bridge that, according to Le Strange, had been "temporarily" established by al-Amīn, was still in existence many years later. See also Lassner, *Topography*, 281, n. 6.

73. A former commander of Muḥammad b. ʿAbdallāh b. Ṭāhir. See Ṭabarī, III, 1590, 1623.

74. See n. 72, above.

75. Aḥmad b. Ṣāliḥ b. Shīrzād had been secretary to the Turkish commander Waṣīf. See Ṭabarī, III, 1542.

76. The quarter lay along the road leading out of east Baghdad near the Shammāsiyyah Gate where a number of palaces (*al-dūr*) of the Barmak family were located. See Le Strange, *Baghdad*, 200.

Khālid b. Barmak.[77] The troops[78] of Baghdad searched everywhere for them, along with the military commanders, until at last they were found. Fighting broke out between the two sides in al-Dūr, which lasted from about two in the afternoon until seven in the evening. Each side fired arrows at the other, tossed spears, and attacked with their swords. Ibn Aws was supported by his neighbors from the Qaṭūṭā market[79] and boatmen from among the skiffs of al-Dūr. Fighting intensified until the Baghdādī troops sent for some naphtha throwers[80] from Sulaymān's palace; but, when his chamberlain informed him of this, he forbade their use. Ibn Aws himself fought tenaciously until he was overcome by wounds from arrows and spear thrusts, at which point he and his troops were defeated. He had managed to evacuate his family from the palace, but the troops followed them until they were expelled beyond the Shammāsiyyah Gate. Ibn Aws's residence was then ransacked of all its contents. It was reported that the value of its goods amounted to two million dirhams, or at least one million fifty thousand dirhams. The plunder included a hundred pantaloons lined with sable, beside those lined with camel or goat hair, which resembled the others. Furnishings of Ṭabaristān silk, together with brocade material and rich vestments to the value of a million dirhams, were also taken. The crowd then left,
[1732] as the regular soldiers began to throng the palace of Sulaymān, bringing with them their booty and creating a great clamor. No one restrained or checked their passage.

Meanwhile, Ibn Aws remained that night in the Shammāsiyyah quarter with those of his troops who had stuck by him. The Baghdādī troops next took to attacking the dwellings where the riffraff[81] [from al-Rayy] were quartered. They plundered their dwellings and dealt harshly with any of the inhabitants who happened to linger be-

77. On the Barmakids, the famous family of viziers who dominated the political scene during the first decade of the rule of the Caliph Hārūn al-Rashīd (170–80/786–96), see *EI*,[2] s.v. "Barāmika"; and Sourdel, *Vizirat*, I, 127–81. When the family suddenly fell from favor, Ja'far, who had been Hārūn's closest companion, was murdered. See *EI*,[2] s.v. "Dja'far b. Yaḥyā."

78. *Ahl Baghdād.* Here and several times in the following lines the expression is used; it literally means "people" or "populace," and Ṭabarī could be using it deliberately in a somewhat pejorative sense.

79. See Lassner, *Topography*, 105.

80. *Al-naffāṭīn.* See Levy, *Social Structure*, 439.

81. *Ṣa'ālīk.* See n. 48, above.

hind. Having been suddenly forced to flee, not one of them appeared openly in Baghdad the following day.

It was reported that during the same evening Sulaymān sent clothing, furnishings, and food to Ibn Aws. There is, however, disagreement as to whether he accepted them or sent them back.

The next morning al-Ḥusayn b. Ismāʿīl and al-Muẓaffar b. Saysal went to the palace of al-Shāh b. Mīkāl, where they were joined by some of the leading Shākiriyyah, the reserves (*al-nāʾibah*), and others. They remained there, avoiding contact with Sulaymān b. ʿAbdallāh b. Ṭāhir. Indeed, his palace was practically deserted; only a handful of persons were present. Sulaymān sent word to them with Muḥammad b. Naṣr b. Ḥamzah b. Mālik al-Khuzāʿī,[82] who was unaware of what agreement they had come to. This Muḥammad was to let them know that their behavior toward Muḥammad b. Aws was shameful and to instruct them in what was due him because of his honor and reputation. If they would apprise Muḥammad of what it was about Ibn Aws that they rejected, then progress could be made to rectify the situation in a manner satisfactory to them all.

At this the Shākiriyyah who were present in the palace of al-Shāh [1733] b. Mīkāl raised a great hue and cry. They said, "We refuse to accept any clientship[83] with Ibn Aws or with any of his men or with the riffraff who have been assigned to him." Moreover, if anyone were to attempt to force them to do so against their will, they would conclude their own agreement, forsaking Ibn Aws and repudiating anyone who demanded their compliance to him. Al-Shāh b. Mīkāl, al-Ḥusayn b. Ismāʿīl, and al-Muẓaffar b. Saysal reluctantly supported them. The messenger returned to Sulaymān with this information. Sulaymān sent him back on another matter and assured them that he was confident of their word and guarantee, without requiring oaths or formal pledges. Thereafter he retired in a dignified fashion.

Nevertheless, Sulaymān continued to regard Muḥammad b. Aws, the riffraff, and others of his crowd of hangers-on as an unwelcome nuisance. He was well aware of their covetousness and corrupt behavior and the fact that Muḥammad b. Aws prized himself so highly, in addition to his passion for meddling in anything that might insti-

---

82. He had been in the employ of Muḥammad b. ʿAbdallāh b. Ṭāhir. Ṭabarī, III, 1668.

83. *Mujāwirah*. See E. W. Lane, *An Arabic-English Lexicon*, s.v. "j-w-r."

gate dissension and division. Sulaymān's musing upon these concerns led him to exaggerate greatly their import, to the point where he confessed that in his prayers he had been driven to plead for respite from Muḥammad b. Aws. Finally, he turned to Muḥammad b. ʿAlī b. Ṭāhir[84] and ordered him to go to Muḥammad b. Aws and present him with the decision that he must return to Khurāsān. He was
[1734] to inform him as well that there was no way for him to return to Madīnat al-Salām or to handle the affairs that he had been entrusted with on Sulaymān's behalf.

When the news reached Muḥammad b. Aws, he left al-Shammāsiyyah for Raqqat al-Baradān,[85] situated on the Tigris. For some days he remained there while he reassembled those of his troops who had become dispersed. From Raqqat al-Baradān he moved to al-Nahrawān,[86] where he established his camp and settled. He had written to Bāyakbāk[87] and Ṣāliḥ b. Waṣīf, submitting his grievances to them at the way he had been treated. But he found no satisfaction from them.

Muḥammad b. ʿĪsā b. ʿAbd al-Raḥmān (al-Kātib al-Khurāsānī) had stayed behind in Sāmarrā to carry out Sulaymān's orders. Muḥammad loathed Ibn Aws and completely avoided him, while Ibn Aws, for his part, was greatly disturbed by the hostile presence of the secretary Muḥammad b. ʿĪsā. So, when Ibn Aws and his troops were deprived of material support, they began to prey upon villagers and travelers, the attacks and plundering becoming more frequent until Ibn Aws settled in al-Nahrawān.

It was reported from someone whom Ibn Aws's troops had gone off to plunder and who had reminded them of the afterlife and tried to instill in them a fear of God that they had replied to him, "If plunder and murder are acceptable in Madīnat al-Salām, the shrine of Islam, and the renowned seat of the caliph, why should anyone disapprove of such things in the countryside and deserts?" After leaving the

---

84. Another of the Ṭāhirid clan, he was last mentioned by Ṭabarī, III, 1533, as unsuccessfully engaged in suppressing a Shīʿite revolt in al-Rayy in 250/864–65.

85. A town located to the north of Baghdad. *Raqqah* is the term for the swampy terrain beside a river that is subject to periodic inundation. See Le Strange, *Lands*, 59, 101.

86. This town was the first stage eastward out of Baghdad along the great Khurāsān Road.

87. Bāyakbāk had been one of the military chiefs and special bodyguard of the Turkish commander Bughā, from whom he later (in 254/868) became estranged. Ṭabarī, III, 1694–95.

marks of his rapacious behavior on the district, Ibn Aws departed from al-Nahrawān. He relieved the populace of money and food, which he had transported by boat from al-Nahrawān to Iskāf Banī Junayd[88] to sell there. [1735]

Muḥammad b. al-Muẓaffar b. Saysal was in al-Madā'in[89] at the time he heard of Ibn Aws's arrival in al-Nahrawān. Fearing for his own safety because of his father's presence and role in the battle [against Ibn Aws], Muḥammad made for his residence in al-Nuʿmāniyyah in the district of the Zābs.[90]

Muḥammad b. Naṣr b. Manṣūr b. Bassām, whose estate was in ʿAbartā,[91] reported that his agent had fled the place after having given Ibn Aws, under duress and from fear of death, nearly fifteen hundred dinars. Ibn Aws remained in the district, coming and going, behaving in turns with closed fist and open hand, alternating severity with lenience. His campaign of intimidation lasted until he received a communication from Bāyakbāk granting him, on his behalf, control of the Khurāsān Road. The lapse of time between Ibn Aws's departure from Madīnat al-Salām and the arrival of this letter of appointment was two months and fifteen days.

One of the sons of ʿĀṣim b. Yūnus al-ʿIjlī reported that his father had been made steward of the estates belonging to al-Nūshurī[92] in the district of the Khurāsān Road. He wrote to al-Nūshurī, mentioning what he had been able to learn of the strength of Ibn Aws's forces and the apparent state of their matériel. He advised that this information should be passed on to Bāyakbāk, describing as well the absence along the Khurāsān Road of any of the central authority's forces to control it and protect the people. Moreover, the army [of Ibn Aws] was already encamped in the district with infantry, equipment, and supplies.

---

88. Also known simply as Iskāf, this location was east of Baghdad on the Nahrawān canal. See Le Strange, *Lands*, 59–60.

89. Located on the Tigris to the south of Baghdad, al-Madā'in had been known as Ctesiphon under the Sāsānian emperors. See Le Strange, *Lands*, 25, 32–35.

90. Situated on the western bank of the Tigris, al-Nuʿmāniyyah was about halfway between Baghdad and Wāsiṭ and thus farther to the south, away from the threat of Ibn Aws in al-Nahrawān. See Le Strange, *Lands*, 37.

91. See Le Strange, *Lands*, 59. The name means "crossing place" marked by a bridge of boats.

92. He was one of Ṣāliḥ b. Waṣīf's commanders (see p. 71, below) and was also married to his sister (see p. 90, below).

[1736] Al-Nūshurī mentioned these matters to Bāyakbāk, advising him to appoint Ibn Aws over the Khurāsān Road, thus reducing the burden upon the central government. Bāyakbāk accepted this advice and ordered Ibn Aws to be contacted by letter regarding it. He was entrusted with the Khurāsān Road in Dhū al-Qaʿdah of the year 255 (October 11–November 9, 869).

Mūsā, the deputy of the Khārijite Musāwir b. ʿAbd al-Ḥamīd, was stationed in al-Daskarah[93] and its environs with around three hundred men. Musāwir had placed him in charge of the area from Bāb Ḥulwān up to al-Sūs[94] on the Khurāsān Road and Baṭn Jūkhā,[95] together with the nearby administrative districts of the Sawād.

During the course of this year al-Muhtadī banished the male and female singers[96] from Sāmarrā. He exiled them to Baghdad after an order to this effect had been submitted from Qabīḥah. This was before misfortune had befallen her son. Al-Muhtadī had also ordered that the lions that were kept in the caliphal palace be killed, that the dogs be cast out, and that all frivolous entertainments cease. He reintroduced the court of appeals (*maẓālim*),[97] and he himself sat and heard the cases of the commoners. During his reign all the domains of Islam were beset by faction and fighting.

Mūsā b. Bughā,[98] his *mawlās*, and troops of the central authorities set out from al-Rayy, while Mufliḥ[99] departed from Ṭabaristān after his arrival there. This Mufliḥ vanquished al-Ḥasan b. Zayd[100] and drove him from Ṭabaristān into the land of al-Daylam.

---

93. Also Daskarat al-Mālik; it was the next station after al-Nahrawān on the Khurāsān Road, northeast of Baghdad. See Le Strange, *Lands*, 62.

94. A stage on the road between Wāsiṭ and Ahwāz in the province of Khūzistān. See Le Strange, *Lands*, 82.

95. Located in the district of Wāsiṭ. See Le Strange, *Lands*, 42.

96. For a contemporary description of this profession, to which the Caliph objected, see Jāḥiẓ, *The Epistle on Singing Girls*.

97. A form of justice of last resort, derived from the absolute authority of the sovereign and from his fundamental competence to deal with all litigation and to right all wrongs. See Sourdel, *Vizirat*, II, 640–49, for details of its functioning in this period. More generally, see Emile Tyan "Judicial Organization," 109–17.

98. The son of the famous Turkish army commander Bughā al-Sharābī. Mūsā was also the brother-in-law of Ṣāliḥ b. Waṣīf. See Ṭabarī, III, 1694.

99. Mufliḥ was one of Mūsā b. Bughā's commanders. See Ṭabarī, III, 1687.

100. In the account of events at the beginning of this year, 255/868–69, Ṭabarī narrates Mufliḥ's defeat of the Shīʿah rebel al-Ḥasan b. Zayd in Ṭabaristān, thus driving him into an alliance with the Daylamites. Mufliḥ also destroyed al-Ḥasan's residences in Āmul and then set out against him in Daylam. See Ṭabarī, III, 1688.

An Account of Mūsā's Departure

It is reported that, when Qabīḥah, the mother of al-Muʿtazz, became aware of the Turks' unrest and was incensed by their behavior, she [1737] communicated with Mūsā b. Bughā, asking him to come and support her. She had hoped that he would arrive before events took the course they did, involving herself and her son, al-Muʿtazz. Mūsā resolved to set out to help her. Qabīḥah's letter had arrived while Mufliḥ was in Ṭabaristān, and Mūsā wrote to him ordering him to join him in al-Rayy.

One of our acquaintances from Ṭabaristān informed me that Mufliḥ had received Mūsā's letter when he had already set out for the region of al-Daylam to hunt down al-Ḥasan b. Zayd al-Ṭālibī. When Mufliḥ received the letter, he returned to his point of departure, much to the distress of a group of notables from Ṭabaristān. They were fleeing from al-Ḥasan b. Zayd before Mufliḥ came to their aid. They thus expected Mufliḥ's arrival would settle the problem of al-Ḥasan b. Zayd and enable them to return to their towns and homes. Mufliḥ had indeed promised to pursue al-Ḥasan b. Zayd wherever he was, until he either defeated him or was himself vanquished. According to the account I heard, Mufliḥ had boasted to them that, if he tossed his cap down anywhere in al-Daylam, none of Ibn Zayd's followers would have the courage to come near it. But when the notables of Ṭabaristān saw him returning from his expedition without any of al-Ḥasan's [captured] army, indeed not even a single Daylamite, they demanded to know the reason for his failure to fulfill his promise to pursue Ibn Zayd. According to what I was told, they went on speaking to him, while he seemed confused and perplexed and failed to answer their queries. When they persisted, Mufliḥ said, "I [1738] have received a despatch from the commander, Mūsā, insisting that his instructions be carried out and for me to join him at once. Although I am concerned to settle matters uppermost in your minds, there is no way of disobeying the commander."

Mūsā had not completed his preparations to leave al-Rayy for Sāmarrā when he received a despatch concerning the death of al-Muʿtazz and the establishment of al-Muhtadī as caliph. Because he could not now attain what he had hoped for from al-Muʿtazz, Mūsā's resolve to leave for Sāmarrā was dampened. When he received the news that al-Muhtadī had been rendered the oath of allegiance, his own troops at first prevented him from submitting his. Eventually they conceded, and their [own] oath of allegiance arrived in Sāmarrā on the 13th of Ramaḍān of this year (August 25, 869).

Later, the *mawlās* in Mūsā's army learned of Ṣāliḥ b. Waṣīf's extraction of money from the secretaries and supporters of al-Muʿtazz and al-Mutawakkil. They begrudged the enjoyment of this money by the troops stationed in Sāmarrā, and they urged Mūsā to depart with them for the city. Mufliḥ then joined Mūsā at al-Rayy, having left Ṭabaristān to al-Ḥasan b. Zayd.

Al-Qāshānī reported that his cousin wrote to him from al-Rayy, mentioning that he had met Mufliḥ there and had enquired of him his reasons for departing from al-Daylam. Mufliḥ said that the *mawlās* had refused to stay and that, when they left, he was unable to manage without them.

On Sunday, at the time of the new moon in Ramaḍān 255 (August 13 – September 11, 869), Mūsā demanded the collection of the tax (*kharāj*)[101] for the year 256 (December 9, 869 – November 29, 870). According to reports, he raised that day five hundred thousand dirhams.

[1739] The inhabitants of al-Rayy assembled and said to him: "May God honor the commander! You claim that the *mawlās* wish to return to Sāmarrā because they have the prospect of greater pay there, while you and your troops here are better off than the troops there. If you desire to [continue] manning this frontier post[102] and expect your reward to come from its people, and impose on us as taxes on our private property whatever you think we can bear from which to pay your followers, then you should do so." But Mūsā did not comply with their requests. However, they persisted; "May God guide the commander. If he has decided to leave us, what is the sense of extracting the taxes (*kharāj*) for an agricultural year in which we have not even begun cultivation? Moreover the bulk of the crop of this current year upon which the commander has levied taxes is situated in open areas (*ṣaḥārā*), to which we would not have access after he had departed from us." But Mūsā paid no attention to any of their arguments or requests.

---

101. See *EI*,[2] s.v. "Kharādj," for details on the perception of this tax and the method of collecting it; cf. Levy, *Social Structure*, 309–16.

102. This is, at al-Rayy.

Now, when al-Muhtadī received word of Mūsā's [imminent] departure, he sent several letters to him which made no impression. When he heard that Mūsā was actually on his way from al-Rayy, without al-Muhtadī's despatches having had any effect, the caliph sent two men of the Banū Hāshim[103] bearing a message for Mūsā and for those *mawlās* attached to his army. They were to state frankly to the arrivals the true situation in the capital, the lack of resources there, and the general apprehension that what they left behind would be lost and that Ṭālibīs[104] would take control of it and their influence spread to the territory of al-Jabal.[105] One of these Hāshimites was called ʿAbd al-Ṣamad b. Mūsā, and the second was Abū ʿĪsā Yaḥyā b. Isḥāq b. Mūsā b. ʿĪsā b. ʿAlī b. ʿAbdallāh b. ʿAbbās. The two men, with a number of *mawlas*, set out to fulfill their commission, as Mūsā and those accompanying him approached. Meanwhile Ṣāliḥ b. Waṣīf made much of Mūsā's departure with al-Muhtadī, attempting to ascribe to him dissent and rebellion. Indeed, he imputed far worse than this to him and declared before God his own innocence of anything Mūsā did. [1740]

A despatch from the master of the post (*ṣāḥib al-barīd*)[106] in Hamadhān concerning Mūsā's departure from there reportedly reached al-Muhtadī. Al-Muhtadī raised his hands to the sky and, after expressing his thanks to God and extolling Him, he exclaimed, "O God! Before You I am free of any guilt for the actions of Mūsā b. Bughā and his neglect of the defense of the frontier and his leaving it open to the enemy. I am absolved of any bonds between us. O God! Remove the artifice of [this] deceiver of Muslims. O God! Make the armies of Muslims victorious wherever they may be. O God! Wherever Muslims are afflicted, I shall freely venture forth with a firm resolve and give them support and defend them. O God! Reward my

103. The Banū Hāshim were kinsmen of the Prophet Muḥammad by common descent from Hāshim, his great-grandfather. During the ʿAbbāsid period they enjoyed certain privileges, such as pensions paid by the state, exemption from payment of the alms tax, and having a special magistrate appointed by the caliph to attend their affairs. See *EI*,[2] s.v. "Hāshimids."

104. That is, the Shīʿite rebels led by al-Ḥasan b. Zayd.

105. Literally, "the mountains," referring to the mountainous region stretching from the Mesopotamian plain on the west to the large desert region of Persia on the east. See Le Strange, *Lands*, 185.

106. The master of the post also fulfilled the function of intelligence officer, gathering, and sending information to his superiors. See *EI*,[2] s.v. "Barīd."

intention since I am deprived of effective supporters." He then broke into tears, weeping.

Someone who was present at al-Muhtadī's assemblies reported what he had said on this particular occasion. Sulaymān b. Wahb[107] was also present and he asked, "Is the Commander of the Faithful
[1741] ordering me to write to Mūsā what I have heard?" Al-Muhtadī replied that this was so, saying, "If you could engrave my words in stone, then [I would tell you to] do so!"

The two Hāshimite messengers met with Mūsā on the road [to Sāmarrā], but without achieving anything. The *mawlas* began to clamor and nearly set upon the envoys. Mūsā replied to the caliph's comminiqué, presenting as his excuse that his troops would fail to pay any attention to what he said to them before reaching the Commander of the Faithful's court. Were he to try to go against them, he would not feel safe from them, and he adduced in his defense what the envoys themselves had witnessed. The messengers arrived with the reply, Mūsā having sent with them a delegation from his army. They reached Sāmarrā on the 4th of al-Muḥarram, 256 (December 12, 869).

In this same year Kanjūr[108] left ʿAlī b. al-Ḥusayn b. Quraysh.[109] In the days of al-Muʿtazz he had been banished to Fārs, where ʿAlī b. al-Ḥusayn was placed in charge of him and imprisoned him. After ʿAlī had decided to wage war against Yaʿqūb b. al-Layth,[110] he released Kanjūr from prison and gave him command of cavalry and infantry. When ʿAlī b. al-Ḥusayn's supporters were defeated, Kanjūr escaped

---

107. Sulaymān, one of a number of "Nestorian scribes" in the administration, was descended from a Christian family in Wāsiṭ. Formerly secretary to the military commander Mūsā b. Bughā, he was briefly vizier under al-Muhtadī and again for brief intervals during 263–65/877–79 under al-Muʿtamid. See Sourdel, *Vizirat* I, 300–303, 310–13; *EI*,[1] s.v. "Sulaymān b. Wahb."

108. Kanjūr was the chamberlain (*ḥājib*) of al-Muʿtazz's brother Ibrāhīm al-Muʾayyad at the time the Caliph imprisoned the two of them in the Jawsaq palace in 252/866. Later Kanjūr was sent in chains to Baghdad and was finally imprisoned in al-Yamāmah. See Ṭabarī, III, 1668–69.

109. The battle in which ʿAlī b. al-Ḥusayn, another contemporary Shīʿite rebel, was defeated occurred near Shīrāz, and he was taken prisoner by Yaʿqūb b. al-Layth. See Ṭabarī, III, 1702–3.

110. Born in Sīstān, Yaʿqūb b. al-Layth was a coppersmith (*al-ṣaffār*) by trade, but his military ambitions took him from membership in a band of marauders to control of Sīstān province in 247/861. His influence spread into eastern Afghanistān before he turned against the caliphal authorities in Iraq and the Ṭāhirids in Khurasan. See Bosworth, "Ṭāhirids," 109–17; cf. Ibn al-Athīr, *al-Kāmil fī al-taʾrīkh*, VII, 191–94.

to the district of al-Ahwāz, where he made a considerable impact on Rāmhurmuz. He then joined Ibn Abī Dulaf[111] in Hamadhān, but he treated Waṣīf's[112] dependents badly, as well as his estates and agents in the district. Next he joined the army of Mūsā (b. Bughā). When Mūsā approached Sāmarrā with the troops who had joined him, word of this reached Ṣāliḥ. On the authority of al-Muhtadī he sent instructions that Kanjūr be brought to the caliph's palace bound in chains, but the *mawlās* refused to do this. [1742]

Communiqués on this matter continued to go back and forth until Mūsā's army reached and encamped in al-Qāṭūl.[113] It soon became apparent that Ṣāliḥ was nursing a deep dislike of Mūsā and that Mūsā had set out for Sāmarrā determined to avoid Ṣāliḥ and those who sympathized with him. Mūsā stayed in al-Qāṭūl for two days, during which time Bāyakbāk joined his forces. Al-Muhtadī sent his brother on his mother's side, Ibrāhīm, to tell Mūsā that the *mawlās* in Sāmarrā had unanimously refused to allow Kanjūr to enter the city. The Caliph ordered Mūsā to place him in chains and take him to Madīnat al-Salām, but things did not turn out as Ṣāliḥ had anticipated. Mūsā's reply was that, when they entered Sāmarrā, they would obey whatever the Commander of the Faithful ordered regarding Kanjūr or anyone else.

The First ʿAlawite Rebellion in al-Baṣrah[114]

In the middle of Shawwāl of the year 255 (September 10–October 8, 869) a man who claimed to be ʿAlī b. Muḥammad b. Aḥmad b. ʿAlī b. ʿĪsā b. Zayd b. ʿAlī b. al-Ḥusayn b. ʿAlī b. Abī Ṭālib[115] appeared in Furāt al-Baṣrah.[116] He assembled his forces from among the Zanj,[117]

111. See Ṭabarī, III, 1605.
112. The Turkish commander, killed in 253/867; he was the father of Ṣāliḥ. See Ṭabarī, III, 1687.
113. In the vicinity of Sāmarrā. See Yāqūt, *Muʿjam al-buldān*, III, 174; Yaʿqūbī, *Kitāb al-buldān*, 256.
114. See Popovic, *Révolte*, 83–93; Ibn al-Athīr, *Kāmil*, VII, 205–14.
115. See Popovic, *Révolte*, 71–81; *EI*,[2] s.v. "ʿAlī b. Muḥammad al-Zandjī." See also Masʿūdī, *Murūj*, VIII, 31–33.
116. See Yāqūt, *Muʿjam*, III, 861–62; *EI*,[2] s.v. "al-Furāt."
117. The word is not Arabic, and, although its plural is *zunūj*, the expression is used here in its collective sense to refer to a class of people. See Popovic, *Révolte*, 54–56, for a discussion of the origin of the word. The generally accepted view of the origin of the Zanj is that they were blacks imported from East Africa at a time that

who labored in removing the nitrous topsoil (*sibākh*)[118] of the marshland districts. Thereafter he crossed over the Tigris river and established himself in al-Dīnārī.[119]

An Account of [ʿAlī b. Muḥammad b. ʿAbd al-Raḥīm's] Expedition and What Determined Him to Revolt There

According to reports, his name and his origin were ʿAlī b. Muḥammad b. ʿAbd al-Raḥīm,[120] and he was descended from the ʿAbd al-Qays. His mother's name was Qurrah, a daughter of ʿAlī b. Raḥīb b.
[1743] Muḥammad b. Ḥakīm of the Banū Asad b. Khuzaymah, who were inhabitants of a village in the vicinity of al-Rayy called Warzanīn, where ʿAlī was born and grew up.

ʿAlī himself was reported to have said: "My ancestor Muḥammad b. Ḥakīm of al-Kūfah was one of those who took part in a rebellion against [the Caliph] Hishām b. ʿAbd al-Mālik with Zayd b. ʿAlī b. al-Ḥusayn.[121] But, when Zayd was slain, Muḥammad fled to al-Rayy, and finding refuge in Warzanīn, he remained there." ʿAlī's paternal grandfather, ʿAbd al-Raḥīm, who was of the ʿAbd al-Qays, was born in al-Ṭāliqān.[122] He went to Iraq and took up residence there and bought himself a concubine from Sind. She gave birth in Iraq to a son, Muḥammad, who was the father of our ʿAlī.[123]

---

cannot be determined. See Popovic, *Révolte*, 56–62; C. Pellat, *Le Milieu baṣrien et la formation de Ǧāḥiẓ*, 41.

118. See *EI*,[1] s.v. "Zandj"; Lane, *Lexicon*, s.v. *s-b-kh*.

119. The name of one of the canals in the environs of al-Baṣrah where the Zanj gathered to launch their first major attack on the city. See Popovic, *Révolte*, 90.

120. See Popovic, *Révolte*, 71–73, 187–90, for a discussion of his name(s) and genealogy.

121. The ʿAlid Zayd, known as Abū al-Ḥasan, led a revolt against the Umayyad Caliph Hishām in 112/730–31, and he was killed in the same year.

122. Ṭāliqān (or Ṭālaqān) was reputed to be one of the foremost towns of Upper Ṭukhāristān a district east of Balkh stretching along the southern side of the Oxus river. See Le Strange, *Lands*, 423.

123. There is another account of ʿAlī's origins that differs in many details from that of Ṭabarī's. In *al-Wāfī bi-al-Wafayāt*, al-Ṣafadī (d. 764/1363) recounts a tale told by ʿAlī's mother, Qurrah. While on pilgrimage to Mecca, her father would spend time in Medina with the family of a *shaykh* descended from ʿAlī b. Abī Ṭālib, the Prophet Muḥammad's cousin and son-in-law. The *shaykh* had a son called Muḥammad, who, after the death of his immediate family, was taken to Warzanīn by Qurrah's father. Qurrah and Muḥammad later married, and she bore him two daughters and a son,

[Earlier in Sāmarrā] ʿAlī was associated with a group attached to the family of the Caliph al-Muntaṣir, among them Ghānim al-Shiṭranjī (the Chessplayer), Saʿīd the Younger, and Yusr the Eunuch.[124] ʿAlī dervied his livelihood from them and from some of the Caliph's entourage and secretaries, seeking their favor by praising them in poetry.[125]

In the year 249/863–64, he reportedly left Sāmarrā for al-Baḥrayn. There he claimed that his genealogy was as follows: ʿAlī b. Muḥammad b. al-Faḍl b. Ḥasan b. ʿUbaydallāh b. al-ʿAbbās b. ʿAlī b. Abī Ṭālib.[126] At Hajar he summoned people to obey him, and a large number did so. However, others refused to do so. As a result, violent partisanship between them led to a number in each camp being killed. In the wake of these events ʿAlī left Hajar and moved to al-Aḥsāʾ.[127] There he took refuge with a section of the Banū Tamīm, a branch of the Banū Saʿd[128] called the Banū al-Shammās, among whom [1744] he made his residence. The people of Baḥrayn had regarded him as a prophet, so much so indeed that, according to report, taxes were collected in his name. He exercised judicial authority over them, and on his behalf they fought against the supporters of the central authorities. A substantial number, on the other hand, were afraid and, becoming embittered against him, caused him to withdraw into the desert. Even then, many in Baḥrayn joined him. Among them was a man from al-Aḥsāʾ, a grain weigher (*kayyāl*) called Yaḥyā b. Muḥammad al-Azraq, but known simply as al-Baḥrānī, who was a *mawlā* of the Banū Dārim.[129] Another was Yaḥyā b. Abī Thaʿlab, a merchant from Hajar. There was also a black *mawlā*[130] of the Banū

ʿAlī. See MS. British Museum Or. 6587, ff. 140b–43b. The passage is translated in Popovic, *Révolte*, 73. See also Popovic's article, "Quelques renseignements inédits concernant le maître de Zanj, ʿAlī b. Muḥammad," *Arabica*, XII/2, 1965, 175–87.

124. These three figures remain unidentified.

125. Popovic notes in *Révolte*, 74, that a later source, Ibn Abi al-Ḥadīd (d. 655/1257), in *Sharḥ nahj al-balāghah*, adds that ʿAlī also earned his living teaching children the arts of writing, grammar, and astronomy.

126. See reference n. 123, above.

127. See *EI*,[2] s.v. "al-Ḥasa."

128. The Tamīmite tribe of Saʿd resided in the Baḥraynī villages of al-Ẓahrān and Laḥsā, according to al-Masʿūdī, *Kitāb al-tanbīh wa-al-ishrāf*, 396–97.

129. These were descendants of Dārim b. Mālik b. Ḥanẓalah, a segment of the Banū Tamīm.

130. *Mawlā aswad*. See n. 4, above.

Ḥanẓalah named Sulaymān b. Jāmiʿ. This latter was a commander of ʿAlī's army. Thus ʿAlī moved about in the desert, from one tribe to another.

It was reported that ʿAlī used to say: "In the course of this period I received signs of my leadership as imām, which were manifest to the people." According to his own account, among such signs was this one: "I received sūrahs of the Qurʾān, which I had not learned by heart, and yet I was able to recite them in a flash. They included Subḥān, al-Kahf, and Ṣād."[131] He continued: "A further example was the time I was lying down, musing about the place I should be heading for to set up residence. The thought of the desert and its recalcitrant inhabitants dejected me, but then a cloud cast a shadow upon me; thunder crackled and lightning flashed. A thunderclap resounded in my ears, and a voice addressed me saying, 'Head for al-
[1745] Baṣrah.' I said to my companions who were assisting me, 'A voice from the thunder has commanded me to go to al-Baṣrah.'"

According to report, when ʿAlī had gone into the desert he caused people to believe that he was Abū al-Ḥusayn Yaḥyā b. ʿUmar, who had been slain in the neighborhood of al-Kūfah.[132] There he deceived some of them, and, as a consequence, a great many joined his ranks. He then made his way with them toward a place in al-Baḥrayn called al-Radm.[133] A major battle broke out among them, which swung against ʿAlī and his troops, and many were swiftly killed. The Arab tribesmen abandoned him in disgust and renounced any association with him. Once the tribesmen had left, ʿAlī found the desert wearisome, and he next set out for al-Baṣrah and settled among the Banū Ḍubayʿah. A group of them joined him there, among them ʿAlī b. Abān, known by the epithet of al-Muhallabī; included, too, were his brothers Muḥammad and al-Khalīl and others. ʿAlī arrived in al-Baṣrah in the year 254/868 at the time when Muḥammad b. Rajāʾ al-Ḥiḍārī was the Caliph's governor there. His arrival also coincided with the civil disturbances between the two rival Baṣran factions of al-Saʿdiyyah and al-Bilāliyyah.[134] ʿAlī's ambition was to secure the

---

131. Sūrahs 18, 38, and 17(?), respectively.

132. This apparently occurred during the reign of the Caliph al-Mustaʿīn. See Popovic, *Révolte*, 75.

133. See Yāqūt, *Muʿjam*, II, 774.

134. Precise identification of these two factions, who appear at a number of points in the story of the Zanj operations in al-Baṣrah, has proven elusive.

support of one of the factions. Thus he commissioned four of his associates, with whom he had been in league in al-Baḥrayn and who had campaigned on his behalf. Their names were Muḥammad b. Salm al-Qaṣṣāb al-Hajarī, Buraysh al-Quray'ī, 'Alī al-Ḍarrāb, and al-Ḥusayn al-Ṣaydanānī; they proclaimed their revolt in the 'Abbād mosque.[135] No one, however, responded to the appeal. Indeed, some soldiers chanced upon them, and they were forced to disperse without having won anyone over. 'Alī fled al-Baṣrah, with Ibn Rajā' in search of him, albeit in vain. Ibn Rajā' was informed of a number of Baṣrans who sympathized with Ali, and he had them arrested and imprisoned. [1746]

Among those jailed were Yaḥyā b. Abī Tha'lab, Muḥammad b. al-Ḥasan al-Iyādī, and the eldest son of the Zanj leader himself, 'Alī b. Muḥammad al-Akbar, together with his wife, the mother of their son, and another daughter of his and a pregnant servant girl. 'Alī, however, set out for Baghdad, accompanied by his associates Muḥammad b. Salm, Yaḥyā b. Muḥammad, Sulaymān b. Jāmi', and Buraysh al-Quray'ī.

When they had reached the marshlands (*al-baṭīḥah*)[136] one of the *mawlā*s of the Bāhilīs,[137] who administered the area, was on the lookout for them. His name was 'Umayr b. 'Ammār. He arrested them and conveyed them to the governor of Wāsiṭ, Muḥammad b. Abī 'Awn. 'Alī employed all his cunning and persuasion with Ibn Abī 'Awn until at last he and his companions were released. From there 'Alī traveled to Madīnat al-Salām, where he remained for a year. While in Baghdad he claimed to be related to Aḥmad b. 'Īsā b. Zayd.[138] He alleged that during his sojourn in the city signs appeared to him, allowing him insight into the minds of his companions and what each of them was doing. He besought his Lord for some token

135. See H. Halm, *Die Traditionen über den Aufstand 'Alī Ibn Muḥammads, des "Herrn der Zanǧ,"* 44–49, where he notes that, apart from the Shī'ite character of the revolt, the Zanj leader's following was comprised almost exclusively of *mawla*s.

136. See *EI*,[2] s.v. "al-Batīḥa." The word, which frequently occurs in the plural, *baṭā'iḥ*, applied to a very extensive area of swampland located on the lower course of the Tigris and Euphrates between al-Kūfah and Wāsiṭ in the north and al-Baṣrah, in the south. See also the articles in *EI*,[2] s.vv. "al-Fūrat," "Didjla"; Le Strange, "Ibn Serapion's Description of Mesopotamia and Baghdad," 297–99.

137. On this anxient Arabian tribe, see *EI*,[2] s.v. "Bāhila."

138. Ibn al-Athīr, *Kāmil*, VII, 208, lengthens the Zaydite connection, adding Muḥammad before Aḥmad.

revealing the true state of his own situation, and he saw on a wall a message being written to him by an invisible hand.

One of his followers reported that, during his stay in Madīnat al-Salām, ʿAlī won over to his side a number of persons. Among them were Jaʿfar b. Muḥammad al-Ṣūḥānī, who was a descendant of Zayd b. Ṣūḥān, Muḥammad b. al-Qāsim, and two servants[139] of Yaḥyā b. ʿAbd al-Raḥmān b. Khāqān,[140] who were named Mushriq and Rafīq.
[1747] He renamed Mushriq Ḥamzah and gave him his agnomen Abū Aḥmad. Rafīq he renamed Jaʿfar, his agnomen becoming Abū al-Faḍl.

During ʿAlī's stay this year in Madīnat al-Salām Muḥammad b. Rajāʾ was removed from his post in al-Baṣrah. When he left the leaders of the Bilāliyyah and Saʿdiyyah factions responsible for the civil disorder attacked and opened the prisons, releasing all the inmates. When the news reached ʿAlī that his family was among those freed, he departed for al-Baṣrah, returning there in the month of Ramaḍān 255 (August 11–September 9, 869). Accompanying him was ʿAlī b. Abān, who had joined up with him in Baghdad. Also with him were Yaḥyā b. Muḥammad, Muḥammad b. Salm, Sulaymān b. Jāmiʿ, and the two servants (*ghulāms*) of Yaḥyā b. ʿAbd al-Raḥmān, Mushriq, and Rafīq. A soldier called Abū Yaʿqūb, who later adopted the sobriquet Jurbān, met with the other six, and they all set off together. Finally arriving at a place called Barankhal,[141] they settled there in a castle called al-Qurashī,[142] which was located on a canal called ʿAmūd ibn al-Munajjim, as it was the Banū Mūsā b. al-Munajjim who had excavated it. Now ʿAlī gave out that he was acting as an agent on behalf of one of [the Caliph] al-Wāthiq's sons, handling the sale of *sibākh;* he thus ordered his companions to treat him as such, and there he remained.

---

139. On the various meanings of the word *ghulām* (plural *ghilmān*) see *EI*,[2] s.v. "Ghulām." The present narrative on the Zanj treats of a different context from that of the ruling circles in Baghdad or Sāmarrā; thus the renderings "attendant," "guard," "servant," and "page" are not always appropriate where the Zanj are concerned. See also *EI*,[2] s.v. "Djaysh," especially p. 507, for the term "young soldier." In what follows relating to affairs of the Zanj, unless otherwise noted, the word *ghulām* is translated loosely as "slave." See n. 59, above.

140. Yaḥyā, a cousin of the Caliph al-Mutawakkil's vizier ʿUbaydallāh b. Yaḥyā b. Khāqān, in 245/860 held a post in the public treasury, owing to ʿUbaydallāh's influence. See Ṭabarī, III, 1446.

141. The reading is uncertain. Halm, *Traditionen*, 76, adopts the reading Branhal.

142. Following Masʿūdī, *Murūj*, VIII, 32, Popovic, *Révolte*, 78, locates al-Qurashī at a place called Biʾr Nakhl.

It was reported from Rayḥān b. Ṣāliḥ, one of the slaves (*ghilmān*) of the Shūrajiyyīn,[143] who was the first of their number to join ʿAlī, that he said: "I was in charge of my master's slaves (*ghilmān*), transporting flour from al-Baṣrah to the Shūrajiyyīn and distributing it among them. I had conveyed a cargo to them as usual an on the way passed by the place where ʿAlī was staying, that is, at Barankhal in the castle al-Qurashī, when his supporters seized me and took me to him. I was ordered to greet him as *amīr,* which I did. He asked me where I had come from, and I told him that I had come from al-Baṣrah. He asked whether I had heard any news about them in al-Baṣrah, and I replied that I had not. He then asked me if there was any news of al-Zaynabī,[144] and I told him I knew nothing about him. Then he said: 'Tell me of the activities of the Bilāliyyah and Saʿdiyyah factions.' I replied that I had no information on them either. Finally, he inquired whether I knew anything of the slaves of the Shūrajiyyin and what each was doing in the business of transporting flour, *sawīq,*[145] and dates and also about those among both the freedmen (*al-aḥrār*) and slaves (*al-ʿabīd*)[146] who worked in the salt steppe (*shūraj*). I told him what I knew of these matters. He appealed to me to join him, to which I agreed. He then said to me, 'Induce as many slaves as you can to join, and bring them to me.' He promised to extend various benefits to me and make me their commander. He also made me solemnly vow that I would not disclose his whereabouts to anyone and that I would return to him. He then allowed me to proceed on my way. I delivered the flour tht I was carrying to its intended destination. I was away for the whole of that day and returned to Ali's camp the next morning." [1748]

When I arrived Rafīq, the servant of Yaḥyā b. ʿAbd al-Raḥmān, had also arrived at the camp. He had been sent to al-Baṣrah with

---

143. Ṭabarī, *Glossarium,* s.vv. *shūrajī, k-s-ḥ.* The Shūrajiyyīn were blacks engaged in the removal of the nitrous topsoil (*sibākh*) in the marshland. Although it is admittedly impossible to determine whether this group was comprised exclusively of freedmen or slaves, I have adopted the view that both were to be found in their ranks, though with the exception of certain explicit contexts (for example, see nn. 146 and 156, below) I have preferred for the purposes of this translation to indicate their status as servile.

144. His full name was Abū Manṣūr ʿAbdallāh b. Muḥammad b. Sulaymān al-Zaynabī, who will be noted on p. 752, below, leading a force of Baṣrans against the Zanj.

145. A prepared dish of parched barley meal often carried by travelers, as it can be reconstituted from its dried form by adding water or milk.

146. See n. 143, above.

some of his business goods. He arrived with Shibl b. Sālim, one of the slaves of the al-Dabbāsīn,[147] who had with him a piece of silk material, which ʿAlī had commissioned him to purchase to have it made into a banner (*liwā*ʾ).[148] Written upon it in red and green char-
[1749] acters were the following words: "God has purchased the souls of believers and their property, for they have attained to paradise fighting in the way of God," to the end of the verse.[149] ʿAlī's name and that of his father were also inscribed upon it, and the banner was fastened to the top of a barge pole.

In the early morning of Saturday, the 28th of Ramaḍān (September 9, 869), ʿAlī set out from [the castle al-Qurashī]. When he had reached the farthest end of the castle precinct, some slaves of one of the Shūrajiyyīn known as al-ʿAṭṭār met him as they were setting about their business. ʿAlī ordered them to be seized, along with their agent, who was placed in fetters. They numbered in all some fifty slaves. ʿAlī next proceeded to a place where al-Sanāʾī worked, and there around five hundred slaves were seized, among them one who was known as Abū Ḥudayd. Their agent was likewise bound with fetters and taken along as well. The place where this occurred was called Nahr al-Mukāthir. ʿAlī proceeded next to a place belonging to al-Sīrāfī and captured there another one hundred fifty slaves, among them an individual called Zurayq and another known as Abū al-Khanjar. Then, at a place belonging to Ibn ʿAṭāʾ, Ṭarīq, Ṣubayḥ al-Aʿsar, Rāshid al-Maghribī, and Rāshid al-Qarmaṭī were captured along with eighty more slaves. The next place was that of Ismāʿīl, who was known as a slave of Sahl al-Ṭaḥḥān. ʿAlī continued to operate in this fashion all day until he had amassed a large number of the Shūrajiyyīn slaves.

Assembling them together, ʿAlī rose and addressed them, raising their spirits by promising to lead and command them and to give them possession of property. He swore a solemn oath to them that
[1750] he would neither deceive nor betray them and that they would experience only kind treatment from him. ʿAlī then summoned their

---

147. Sellers of *dibs*, the juice pressed from fresh dates.

148. On the uses of banners and flags, see *EI*,[2] s.v. "ʿAlam."

149. Qurʾān 9:111. Although the symbolism of the Zanj revolt was ʿAlid, this verse has associations with the early Khārijite rebels, who may have referred to themselves as al-Shurāt (pl. of Shārī) "vendors," i.e., those who have sold their souls for the cause of God. See *EI*,[2] s.v. "Khāridjites."

masters and said to them: "I wanted to behead you all for the way you have treated these slaves, with arrogance and coercion and, indeed, in ways that Allāh has forbidden, driving them beyond endurance. But my companions have spoken to me about you, and now I have decided to set you free."

They replied that the slaves were merely habitual runaways, who would flee from ʿAlī [at the first opportunity], and then both he and they would be the losers. They said, "Turn them over to us, and let us pay you compensation for them." But ʿAlī ordered their slaves to bring whips of palm branches and, while their masters and agents were prostrated on the ground, each one was given five hundred lashes. ʿAlī extracted a vow from them, on penalty of having to repudiate their wives,[150] that they would neither divulge his whereabouts to anyone nor reveal the size of his following. They were then released and sent on their way to al-Baṣrah.

One of their number, a man named ʿAbdallāh and known as Karīkhā,[151] crossed over the Dujayl[152] and warned the Shūrajiyyīn to guard their slaves carefully. There were some fifteen thousand there at the time.

After performing the afternoon prayer ʿAlī ventured forth again, and upon reaching the bank of the Dujayl he found there boats laden with compost of dung and ashes (*samād*) entering port on the rising tide. Together with his partisans he traversed the river in them and then went on to the Nahr Maymūn.[153] He established his quarters in the mosque situated in the middle of the market that stretched along the Nahr Maymūn. He continued efforts to gather blacks (*al-sudān*)[154] to his camp right up to the time of the prayer breaking the fast of Ramaḍān (*ṣalāt al-fiṭr*).[155] On the day of the celebration of the feast he summoned his followers to assemble for prayer. When they

150. On the gravity of this oath, see *EI*,[1] s.v. "Ṭalaḳ."

151. Or, in an alternative reading, Karankha.

152. Literally, "Little Tigris," but here referring to the river Dujayl in al-Ahwāz, in order to distinguish it from the Dujayl canal of the Tigris to the north of Baghdad. See Le Strange, *Lands*, 232.

153. Yāqūt, *Muʿjam*, IV, 719. The Arabic word *nahr* can mean both "river" and "canal," and it is not always possible to distinguish them, given the nature of the primary sources; here, however, the term means canal.

154. See *EI*,[2] s.v. "ʿAbd." Although it is not entirely clear from Ṭabarī's usage, the term *sudān* (pl. of *aswad*) may be intended by him as synonym for the Zanj.

had done so, the pole flying his banner was set into the ground. ʿAlī
[1751] prayed with them, and in a sermon (*khuṭbah*) he recalled the wretched state from which, through him, God had rescued them. ʿAlī said that he wanted to improve their condition, giving them slaves (*al-ʿabīd*), money, and homes to possess for themselves, and that by them they could achieve the greatest things.[156] He then swore a solemn oath, and when his prayer and sermon were complete he ordered those who had followed his words to instruct those non-Arabic speakers among them who had not understood, in order [also] to raise their spirits. That was done, and ʿAlī entered the castle.

A day later he set out for Nahr Būr, where a detachment of his troops encountered a detachment of the [commander] al-Ḥimyarī and drove them off into the desert. The Zanj leader, accompanied by some more troops, joined forces with the others and defeated al-Ḥimyarī and his troops, driving them back as far as the Tigris flats. One of the superintendents of the blacks, called Abū Ṣāliḥ and known as "the Short," sought protection for himself and three hundred Zanj. ʿAlī graciously granted this and promised them good fortune. When the numbers of Zanj who had been thus gathered together increased significantly, he appointed leaders for them and said that, for each of them who brought another Zanj, he would be attached to him.

It is also said that ʿAlī did not appoint his commanders until after the battle of slaves (*al-khawal*)[157] in Bayān[158] and his move to Sabkhat al-Qandal.[159]

---

155. *EI*,[2] s.v. "ʿĪd al-Fiṭr."

156. M. A. Shaban, *Islamic History*, II, 101, argues that ʿAlī b. Muḥammad's movement was not a slave revolt but rather an ethnic Zanj or black revolt. He notes that some of the first to fight against ʿAlī were themselves employed in working the salt marshes (see, e.g., n. 163, below). In his view there were only a few runaway slaves, the vast majority of rebels being Arabs, with the support of free East Africans who had made their homes in the region. Certainly the interpretation of these events rests upon one's understanding of such highly ambiguous words as *ghulām*, *sudān*, *ʿabīd*, and *khawal*. Indeed Ṭabarī himself is far from consistent in his use of the word *ghulām*. In the present context ʿAlī's words and actions clearly suggest that those he was dealing with at this stage of his movement were of a relatively depressed, if not entirely servile, condition. Popovic in his detailed study of the revolt is unable to commit himself firmly on the question, and the truth most likely lies somewhere between Shaban's interpretation and the earlier view represented by T. Nöldeke in "A Servile War in the East."

157. See Lane, *Lexicon*, s.v. *kh-w-l*; n. 156, above.

158. A village situtated on a canal of the same name was located on the eastern side

Ibn Abī ʿAwn was transferred from the governorship of Wāsiṭ to that of al-Ubullah and the districts of the Tigris. On the day that [ʿAlī b. Muḥammad] appointed his commanders news reportedly reached him that al-Ḥimyarī and ʿAqīl, along with Ibn Abī ʿAwn's deputy, who had been stationed in al-Ubullah, had advanced toward him and were encamped at Nahr Ṭīn. ʿAlī ordered his troops to move to al-Razīqiyyah, which was located at the far side of al-Bā- [1752]
dhāward.[160] He reached there at the time of the midday prayer, which they performed and then prepared for battle. At the time where were only three swords in ʿAlī's so-called "army"—namely, his own, that of ʿAlī b. Abān, and that of Muḥammad b. Salm. Between the time of the midday and afternoon prayers, ʿAlī departed [from al-Razīqiyyah] with his troops and hastened back toward al-Muḥammadiyyah,[161] placing ʿAlī b. Abān in their rear with orders to report on anyone following them. He himself proceeded at the head of the company [of blacks] until they reached al-Muḥammadiyyah. He sat by the water's edge and ordered the company to quench their thirst. When the troops arrived, ʿAlī b. Abān said to him that they had seen swords glistening and heard the sounds of people moving behind them but that they could not tell whether they were moving away or heading toward them. He was still speaking when the enemy arrived. The Zanj called one another to arms and Abū Ṣāliḥ Mufarraj al-Nūbī hastened forth with Rayḥān b. Ṣāliḥ and Fatḥ al-Ḥajjām. Fatḥ had been eating [at the time], and so he went into the fray holding his plate. As his companions advanced, one of the Shūrajiyyīn called Bulbul encountered Fatḥ, who attacked him with his plate and beat him with it, causing Bulbul to drop his weapon, turn, and flee. He and four thousand other men were put to flight, some being killed and others dying of thirst on the way. A number, too, were

of the Tigris estuary, on the way to al-Ahwāz. See Le Strange, "Ibn Serapion's Description," 307–9.

159. The salt flat (*sabkhah*) situated by the Nahr al-Qandal (or al-Qandil), one of the nine major canals flowing into the estuary at al-Baṣrah. See Le Strange, "Ibn Serapion's Description," 304.

160. A town located between Wāsiṭ and al-Baṣrah. Yāqūt, *Muʿjam*, I, 318, vocalizes the word Bādhāward.

161. Ibn Serapion speaks of a great lagoon (*hawr*) called al-Muḥammadiyyah, the largest one of four in the swampland (*baṭaʾiḥ*) near al-Baṣrah. See Le Strange, "Ibn Serapion's Description," 297, 299.

taken captive and brought to the leader of the Zanj who ordered them
[1753] beheaded. Their heads were stacked on the backs of mules seized from the Shūrajiyyīn, who had used them for transporting the nitrous topsoil (*shūraj*). The procession set out and reached al-Qādisiyyah[162] by the time of the evening prayer.

A *mawlā* of the Hāshimites[163] attacked ʿAlī's company outside the village and killed one of the blacks. The news was brought to ʿAlī, and his companions asked him for permission to sack the village and search for the culprit who had killed their comrade. He replied saying, "That would be impossible without our knowing what the villagers intended and whether the killer acted with their consent. We will ask them to deliver him to us. If they do so, fine, but, if not, then it would be lawful for us to slay them."

ʿAlī urged them to prepare quickly for departure, and they returned to Nahr Maymūn, where he established himself in the same mosque that he had initially used. He ordered the heads [of the Shūrajiyyīn] to be brought as well and publicly displayed. He instructed Abū Ṣāliḥ al-Nūbī to make the call to prayer. This he did, saluting ʿAlī as the *amīr*. Then ʿAlī prayed the late evening prayer with his companions and spent the night there. The following morning ʿAlī set out again, first passing by the [village] of al-Karkh, before arriving at a village called Jubbā.[164] It was the time of the midday prayer. He crossed over the Dujayl (al-Ahwāz) by way of a ford he had been shown, but rather than entering the village he camped outside it. He sent a message to the inhabitants. Their elders, along with those of al-Karkh, came to meet him. He ordered them to provide hospitality for himself and his companions, which was done as he wished, and he spent that night among them.

The next day one of the inhabitants of Jubbā offered ʿAlī a bay horse,[165] but he could find neither bridle nor saddle for it; thus he had to make do with a rope and a cinch of palm fibers.[166] He set out and

162. A village in the marshlands (*baṭāʾiḥ*), not to be confused with a location of the same name north of Baghdad. See Le Strange, *Lands*, 50.

163. See nn. 139 and 156, above.

164. See Le Strange, *Lands*, 243. Situated to the east of the Dujayl, it was noted for its sugarcane.

165. *Faras kumayt*. See Lane, *Lexicon*, s.v. *k-m-t*.

166. Halm, *Traditionen*, 30–32, considers that this description conveys an eschatological sense — referring to the horse without saddle and bridle belonging to the Mahdī.

finally reached a place called al-ʿAbbāsī al-ʿAtīq, where he secured the services of a guide as far as al-Sīb,[167] a canal upon which was situated the village of al-Jaʿfariyyah. The villagers were alerted to his [1754] arrival and fled. ʿAlī entered and settled in the house of Jaʿfar b. Sulaymān,[168] which was located in the market, while his companions scattered thoughout the village. They brought to him a villager they had discovered, and ʿAlī asked him the whereabouts of the Hāshimites' agents. The man said they were in the thickets [outside the village]. ʿAlī sent the one nicknamed[169] Jurbān to fetch their headman, Yaḥyā b. Yaḥyā al-Zubayrī[170] a *mawlā* of the Ziyādiyyīn. He was asked whether he had any money, and the man replied that he did not. So ʿAlī ordered him beheaded. Fearing now for his life, the man confessed to having hidden some money away; he sent for it and brought to ʿAlī the amount of two hundred fifty dinars and one thousand dirhams, the first such booty he had gained. ʿAlī next asked the headman about the animals owned by the agents of the Hāshimites, and he pointed out three pack animals, one a bay, one chestnut, and one gray. One was given to Ibn Salm, another to Yaḥyā b. Muḥammad, while the third was given to Mushriq the servant of Yaḥyā b. ʿAbd al-Raḥmān. Rafīq rode upon a donkey, loaded with baggage. Some of the blacks discovered a cache of arms in a house belonging to one of the Banū Hāshim; they were seized. Al-Nūbī the Younger brought a sword, which the Zanj leader then gave to Yaḥyā b. Muḥammad. In this way there fell into the hands of the Zanj swords, spears, daggers, and shields.

That evening ʿAlī spent in al-Sīb, and in the morning he was given news of the arrival there of Rumays, al-Ḥimyarī, and ʿAqīl al-Ubullī. He despatched Yayāḥ b. Muḥammad with five hundred men, among them Sulaymān, Rayḥān b. Ṣāliḥ, and Abū Ṣāliḥ al-Nūbī the [1755] Younger. They engaged the enemy and routed them, seizing a galley[171] and arms in the process. After everyone had fled Yaḥyā b.

---

167. Yāqūt *Muʿjam*, III, 209; Le Strange, "Ibn Serapion's Description," 271, 274. The canal, which flowed through land (al-*jawāmid*, pl. of *jāmidah* "drained lands") reclaimed from the swamps, itself finally disppeared into the great swamp, al-Baṭāʾiḥ.

168. This refers to Jaʿfar b. Sulaymān b. ʿAlī al-Hāshimī; see Ṭabarī, III, 304–6.

169. See *EI*,[2] s.v. "Laḳab," on the meanings and application of sobriquets.

170. The reading of the *nisbah* is uncertain.

171. *Sumayriyyah*. See Lane, *Lexicon*, s.v. *s-m-r*.

Muḥammad returned to ʿAlī and told him the news. Remaining in al-Sīb that day, he set out the following morning for al-Madhār,[172] after reaching a pact with the inhabitants of al-Jaʿfariyyah that they would not engage in hostilities against him or aid or protect any of his enemies.

ʿAlī then traversed the [canal] al-Sīb and made for a village known as al-Yahūd, which lay along the Tigris. There he again encountered Rumays with a contingent of troops. Fighting between them continued throughout the day. A number of Rumays's troops were captured, while many others received arrow wounds. A servant belonging to Muḥammad b. Abī ʿAwn who had been with Rumays was killed. A galley with an oarsman aboard capsized; the man was seized and beheaded. Leaving the field of battle, ʿAlī continued toward al-Madhār. He reached the canal called Bāmdād[173] and crossed over it and into an open plain, where he saw an orchard and a small hill, known as Devils' Mountain.[174] He headed for the hill, positioned himself on the top, and settled his troops in the plain below while preparing for himself a scouting party.

Shibl b. Sālim reported that he had acted as scout for ʿAlī along the Tigris. "I sent word to him," he said, "that Rumays was on the bank of the Tigris, looking for someone to convey a message for him." So ʿAlī sent off ʿAlī b. Abān, Muḥammad b. Salm, and Sulaymān b.
1756] Jāmiʿ, and when they reached Rumays he said to them, "Convey greetings to your master, and tell him that he shall have safe-conduct to go anywhere without hindrance from anyone." In exchange, he should return the slaves (*al-ʿabīd*) to their owners (*al-mawālīhim*),[175] for which he would be paid five dinars per head. ʿAlī's men returned to him with Rumays's offer. ʿAlī became incensed at this and swore that he would come, rip open the belly of Rumays's wife, raze his home to the ground, and cause blood to flow everywhere. This response was duly delivered to Rumays, who then set off to station himself on the Tigris opposite ʿAlī's own camp.

That same day Ibrāhīm b. Jaʿfar al-Hamdānī[176] arrived to meet

172. The Nahr al-Madhār was the last reach of the easternmost course of the Tigris before it ran into the sea. The exact location of the town of al-Madhār is unknown; its surrounding district was called Jūkhā. See Le Strange, *Lands*, 42.

173. The reading is uncertain, an alternative being Bāṣdād.

174. Jabal al-Shayāṭīn.

175. See n. 156, above.

176. One of ʿAlī's future commanders.

ʿAlī with correspondence for him to read.[177] It was only at that moment that he joined ʿAlī's side. Following the last evening prayer, Ibrāhīm told ʿAlī that he did not think he should head for al-Madhār. When asked what he should do then, Ibrāhīm said that, as the inhabitants of ʿAbbādān, Mayān Rūdhān, and Sulaymānān[178] had rendered allegiance to him, he should return there. And he added, "You have also left behind a group of the Bilāliyyah at the mouth of the Qandal and at Abrasān[179] waiting for you."

Now when the blacks heard of Ibrāhīm's advice, along with what Rumays had proposed to ʿAlī that day, they feared that ʿAlī would betray them and hand them over to their masters. Thus some of them fled, while the rest became very disturbed. Muḥammad b. Salm reported their distress to ʿAlī and the fact that some had taken off. So that very night ʿAlī ordered them to be assembled together. Separating the Zanj of the Euphrates [from the others],[180] he summoned an interpreter to announce that none of them would be returned to his owner. ʿAlī swore a most solemn oath on this, adding, "Some of your number should watch me closely, and, if they sense any treachery on my part, they could kill me." Then ʿAlī assembled the remainder of the Zanj together — namely, the Furātiyyah, the Qarmāṭiyyūn, the Nūbah, and others who understood Arabic — and made the same solemn oath to them as well, which he personally pledged and confirmed. Moreover, he said that he had not revolted to achieve earthly goods and glory, but only for the wrath of God and against the corruption and decay of the faith that he saw among the people. He concluded saying, "I shall share personally in every battle with you and assume the same risks as you." The Zanj were pleased by these words and wished him well. [1757]

At dawn the next day ʿAlī commanded one of the slaves of the Shūrajiyyīn named Abū Manārah to blow the horn, as a signal for the

---

177. Ibrāhīm appears here for the first time in Ṭabarī's account without an indication of who he is (an agent?) or even a comment on the nature of the correspondence he carries.

178. See Le Strange, *Lands*, 44. The abrupt nature of the information in this paragraph, without prior reference to it, suggests that Ṭabarī's work as we have it may have been abridged from a longer text. See n. 217, below.

179. The reading is very uncertain, Abūsān, Anūshār being among other possibilities.

180. The text of the Leiden edition has al-Furātiyyah, but the critical apparatus notes the uncertain status of the reading; other manuscript copies provide al-Qawāniyyah, al-Maghāribah, and al-Fazzāniyyah as alternatives.

Zanj to assemble. He then set out again for al-Sīb, where he found al-Ḥimyarī, Rumays, and the associate of Ibn Abī ʿAwn. ʿAlī sent a secret message to them with Mushriq, who later returned with their reply. The leader of the Zanj reached the canal, and the associate of Muḥammad b. Abī ʿAwn approached, greeted [ʿAlī], and said, "It is no fit reward for our master from you that you cause his administrative district to be despoiled, given what you know he did for you in Wāsiṭ."[181] ʿAlī replied, "I have not come here to fight you, so tell your troops to make way for me so that I may pass by you."

[1758] ʿAlī departed from the canal [al-Sīb] and made for the Tigris. Shortly thereafter soldiers arrived accompanied by the inhabitants of al-Jaʿfariyyah, all fully armed. Abū Yaʿqūb, who was known as Jurbān, approached them and said, "People of al-Jaʿfariyyah! You are well aware that you have given us your solemn oath that you would neither fight against us nor provide assistance to anyone against us; indeed, you swore to assist any one of us if he came to you." They raised a great clamor and din, shouting as they fired stones and arrows at Jurbān.

There was a place nearby where there were some three hundred *zarnūqs*,[182] which Jurbān ordered dismantled and tied together like rafts.[183] They were launched onto the water, each with a single fighter astride it, and in this way battle with the enemy was joined.

Someone said that before the rafts were constructed, ʿAlī b. Abān swam across the canal. When the rafts had been made, the Zanj crossed the canal. They moved away from the bank of the canal and engaged the enemy with swords, killing a great number of them. Prisoners were first threatened, then released. One of the slaves of the Shūrajiyyīn called Sālim al-Zaghāwī was sent to bring back the troops who had entered the village of al-Jaʿfariyyah. He called out to them, "Anyone caught stealing anything from this village or taking any captives will have to answer for his actions and will be subject

---

181. That is, the governor of Wāsiṭ, Muḥammad b. Abī ʿAwn, had been persuaded to release ʿAlī and his companions from custody. See p. 33, above.

182. Lane, *Lexicon*, s.v. *z-r-n-q*, describes them thus: two pillarlike structures constructed by the head of a well, across which is placed a piece of wood, from which the pulley for drawing water is suspended. The plural is *zarānīq*. See also Ṭabarī, *Glossarium*, CCLXXVII; and S. Fraenkel, *Die aramaischen Fremdwörter im Arabischen*, 134, who calls it a *Wasseraufzug*.

183. *Al-shāshāt*, although the vocalization is uncertain. From the context "raft" seems a likely approximation.

to a painful punishment." ʿAlī b. Abān then recrossed the [al-Sīb] canal from the west to the east bank. After regrouping his troops under their chiefs, he had just passed beyond the village by the distance of a bowshot when he heard a great uproar coming from the direction of the canal. Carefully, the Zanj made their way back. [1759]

When Rumays, al-Ḥimyarī, and the associate of Ibn Abī ʿAwn, who, having heard of the situation at al-Jaʿfariyyah, had arrived on the scene, the blacks attacked them and seized four galleys, together with their crews and fighters. The personnel were disembarked and ʿAlī b. Muḥammad summoned the fighters for interrogation. They informed him that Rumays and Ibn Abī ʿAwn's associate had not let them go before compelling them to march on him and that the villagers had urged on Rumays, promising the two men large sums of money. The Shūrajiyyīn guaranteed to pay the associate in return for their slaves the sum of five dinars each. ʿAlī then inquired about a certain slave called al-Numayrī and another called al-Ḥajjām. They replied that al-Numayrī was being held as their prisoner, while the local people said that al-Ḥajjām had taken to robbing and murdering throughout their district, although evenutally he had been [caught] and beheaded, his body having been strung up publicly on the Abū al-Asad canal.[184] After ʿAlī had gleaned this information, he ordered the prisoners beheaded, all that is save one called Muḥammad b. al-Ḥasan al-Baghdādī, who swore that he had come with a safe-conduct, unarmed, and without hostile intent; he was set free. The severed heads and flags were borne away upon mules, while the ships were ordered destroyed by fire. ʿAlī then set out for Nahr Farīd, finally arriving at a canal named after al-Ḥasan b. Muḥammad al-Qāḍī, across which stretched a dam lying between al-Jaʿfariyyah and the cultivated area (*rustāq*)[185] of al-Qufṣ.[186]

Villagers from the Banū ʿIjl welcomed ʿAlī b. Muḥammad, offering him their lives and extending generously to him whatever they possessed. ʿAlī returned their kindness, ordering them to keep what they had offered.

---

184. One of the major canals flowing into the estuary (*fayḍ*) of al-Baṣrah. See Le Strange, "Ibn Serapion's Description," 303.

185. Spelled also as *ruzdāq*, *ruztāq*, and *rusdāq*, the word signifies a rural district consisting of cultivated lands with towns and villages. See Lane, *Lexicon*, s.v. *r-z-d-q*.

186. A town between Baghdad and ʿUkbarāʾ, but nearer the former, famous for its places of pleasure and entertainment, including fine wines. Yāqūt, *Muʿjam*, IV, 150.

[1760] He next proceeded to Nahr Bāqthā[187] and camped outside the village, which was on the canal itself and stretched along the bank of the Dujayl. The inhabitants of al-Karkh came to him, greeted him, prayed for his good fortune, and extended to him all the hospitality he required. A Jew from Khaybar called Māndawayh came to ʿAlī, kissed his hand, bowed before him, and then professed his gratitude for seeing him. Then he asked ʿAlī a number of questions, which he answered. The Jew claimed that he had found a description of him in the Torah and that he had foreseen fighting alongside him. He also queried ʿAlī about certain marks on his body, which he stated he knew about. The two men spent the evening discussing matters.

When ʿAlī set up his camp he [always] withdrew from his army with his six comrades. At that time wine[188] was not forbidden in his army. He had placed Muḥammad b. Salm in charge of watching carefully over the troops. Late that night one of the villagers of al-Karkh came and informed ʿAlī that Rumays, [leading] the inhabitants of al-Maftaḥ[189] and the adjoining villages, and ʿAqīl [accompanied by] the people of al-Ubullah, had arrived with fully armed Dabīlā.[190] Al-Ḥimyarī had also arrived that night with a group of Euphrates villagers at the Nahr Maymūn bridge, which they had destroyed to prevent ʿAlī's crossing. The following morning ʿAlī ordered it to be proclaimed to the Zanj to cross over the Dujayl. Then from the outskirts of al-Karkh he went to the Nahr Maymūn, where he found the bridge cut, with the enemy on the eastern side of the canal and gal-
[1761] leys containing the Dabīlā in the middle, while the villagers sailed in flat-bottomed vessels (*jarībiyyāt*) and reed boats (*mujawniḥāt*).[191]

---

187. The reading is conjectural.

188. *Nabīdh*. The word is a general term for various kinds of intoxicating beverages, which could be made from dates, raisins, barley, honey, or spelt. *Nabīdh* was considered synonymous with *khamr*, which is forbidden in he Qurʾān (2:219, 16:67, and 5:90, where it is described as the work of Satan). See *EI*,[1] s.v. "Nabīdh"; *EI*,[2] s.v. "Khamr."

189. See Le Strange, *Lands*, 48; Le Strange, "Ibn Serapion's Description," 299, 303; it was a village in the province of al-Baṣrah, lying between the city of al-Baṣrah and Wāsiṭ.

190. The critical apparatus of the Leiden edition notes, without supporting sources, that this was a group of Indian origin living in al-Baṣrah. See also Ṭabarī, *Glossarium*, CCXXXVI. The reference is probably to people from the Indian coastal trading port Daibul, located east of Mihran, who had extensive commercial links abroad. See Ibn Ḥawqal, *Configuration de la Terre*, II, 316.

191. On these types of rivercraft, see Ṭabarī, *Glossarium*, CLXII, CLXXII.

ʿAlī ordered his troops not to engage the enemy but to withdraw from the canal to protect themselves from arrows. ʿAlī retreated to a distance of about one hundred meters from the village. When the enemy saw that no one was about to attack them, a detachment left to make a reconnaissance. Now ʿAlī had commanded a group of his men to slip into the village and conceal themselves in ambush. When they spotted the enemy detachment, they attacked, and twenty-two prisoners were taken, while the remainder were pursued and a number of them were killed along the canal bank. They returned to ʿAlī with heads and prisoners and, after interrogating them, he had them beheaded as well. He ordered them to be guarded carefully, and for half the day their cries could be heard. A tribesman of the desert arrived seeking protection, and ʿAlī asked him about the depth of the river. The man told him he knew of a place that could be forded and informed him that the people were solidly against him and prepared to fight him. ʿAlī went with the man to the ford, about a mile[192] distant from al-Muḥammadiyyah, and he traversed the river with the rest of the company following behind him. Nāṣiḥ, known as al-Ramlī, supported ʿAlī, and he crossed over with the animals. Once on the eastern bank, ʿAlī turned again toward the Maymūn canal. Establishing himself there in the mosque, he gave orders for the heads [of the prisoners] to be planted on stakes. He remained there the whole day while Rumays's entire army traveled along the Dujayl and camped at a spot called Aqshā, opposite the Bard al-Khiyār canal.

ʿAlī b. Muḥammad sent out a scout, who returned with news of Rumays's location. Immediately, he despatched a thousand men to [1762] encamp on the salt marsh at the mouth of the [Bard al-Khiyār] canal, telling them to inform him if the enemy had not approached them by the time of the sunset prayer. He wrote to ʿAqīl, reminding him that he had formerly rendered him allegiance, along with a group of inhabitants from al-Ubullah. He wrote also to Rumays, reminding him of the pact that they had concluded at al-Sīb: that they would not fight each other and that he would send news of the central authorities to him. He entrusted these two letters to a peasant, after first exacting an oath from him to deliver them.

ʿAlī next moved from Nahr Maymūn and set out for the salt

192. One Arabic *mīl* equals two km., three *mīl* making six km., or one *farsakh*. See Hinz, *Islamische Masse*, 63.

marsh, where he had prepared a scouting party. Upon reaching the villages of al-Qādisiyyah and al-Shīfiyā, he heard a great commotion and saw shooting taking place; his practice when on the march was to give villages a wide berth. He commanded Muḥammad b. Salm to lead a party of men to al-Shīfiyā and ask the inhabitants to deliver to him the man who had murdered one of his troops as he was passing through. Muḥammad returned to inform ʿAlī that the villagers claimed they had no power to surrender the man, owing to his clientship with the Hāshimites and their protection of him. ʿAlī thus ordered his slaves to plunder the two villages, from which a great deal of currency in gold and silver, jewelry, ornaments, and gold and silver vessels were seized. On the same occasion slaves and women were captured, this being the first booty of its kind that they took. Muḥammad b. Salm's party happened upon a house in which there were fourteen Shūrajiyyīn slaves.[193] Their exit was blocked, and
[1763] they were captured. The Hāshimites' *mawlā* who had murdered the Zanj soldier was brought, and Muḥammad b. Salm ordered him beheaded. The execution was carried out.

At the time of the afternoon prayer Muḥammad left the two villages and set up camp by the salt marsh called Bard al-Khiyār. One of ʿAlī b. Muḥammad's six companions came to him at the sunset prayer time and told him that his soldiers were indulging in inebriating drink,[194] which they had discovered in al-Qādisiyyah. Accompanied by Muḥammad b. Salm and Yaḥyā b. Muḥammad, ʿAlī went to inform the troops that intoxicants were not permitted, and from that day he declared wine (*nabīdh*) illegal. He addressed them saying, "You will be engaging armies in battle, so cease this indulgence in drink!" And they assented to his demand.

The following day one of the slaves of the blacks[195] named Qāquwayh came and told ʿAlī that Rumays's troops had set out for the eastern side of the Dujayl and proceeded toward the riverbank. The leader of the Zanj summoned ʿAlī b. Abān to advance with the Zanj and attack Rumays. ʿAlī b. Muḥammad then summoned

193. *Ghilmān min ghilmān al-Shūraj*. See nn. 139, 146, 156, above.

194. The text refers to *khamr* and *nabīdh*, both of which could loosely be rendered by wine. See n. 188, above. The context here clearly intends intoxicating drink, although *nabidh* (and likely *khamr* as well) could be prepared in both alcoholic and nonintoxicating versions. See Ibn Sayyār, *Kitāb al-ṭabīkh*, 309–10.

195. The expression is *ghulām min al-sudān*.

Mushriq to bring him an astrolabe,[196] with which he took a reading of the sun, in order to determine the precise time. Then he, followed by his troops, crossed over the bridge[197] spanning the Bard al-Khiyār canal. When they had arrived on the eastern side, they overtook ʿAlī b. Abān and found that the forces of Rumays and ʿAqīl were on the river bank, while the Dabīlā were aboard boats from which they could shoot their arrows. The Zanj forces attacked and killed a great number of the enemy. Then a gust of wind from the western shore carried the boats to the nearest bank, and the blacks fell upon them, [1764] slaying all they found aboard.

Rumays and those with him retreated to Nahr al-Dayr[198] on the Aqshā road. He abandoned his boats without moving them, leaving the impression that he was staying there. ʿAqīl and Ibn Abī ʿAwn's associate left in haste for the Tigris without paying heed to anything. The Zanj leader ordered that the contents be removed from the boats that carried the Dabīlā; they were joined one to another. Qāquwayh went down to inspect them and found one of the Dabīlā. He tried to force him out, but the man resisted. Then he rushed the man with a trumpet (*ṣurnay*)[199] he was carrying and struck him a blow on the shoulder, severing one of the veins. A second blow cut a tendon in his leg. Then Qāquwayh grabbed the man and struck him on the crown of the head, and he collapsed. Seizing the man's hair, Qāquwayh cut off his head and took it to the Zanj leader, who ordered that he be given a dinar.[200] Then he commanded Yaḥyā b. Muḥammad to make Qāquwayh commander of one hundred blacks.

Thereafter the Zanj leader headed for the village of al-Muhallabī,[201] which lay opposite Qayyārān. The blacks, who had meanwhile been pursuing ʿAqīl and Ibn Abī ʿAwn's deputy, returned. They had captured a galley with two oarsmen still aboard. ʿAlī b.

---

196. See *EI*,[2] s.v. "Asṭurlāb," on the uses of this instrument.

197. *Qanṭarah*. This type of bridge was an arched or vaulted structure built with baked bricks or stones. See Lane, *Lexicon*, s.v. *q-n-ṭ-r*.

198. Yāqūt, *Muʿjam*, II, 660, IV, 839, states that a monastery called Dayr al-Dihdar had stood here from the days before Islam. The canal was one of the major waterways emptying into the estuary of al-Baṣrah. See Le Strange, "Ibn Serapion's Description," 303.

199. The reading is uncertain, but the meaning could be rendered either trumpet or bugle. See R. Dozy, *Supplément aux dictionnaires arabes*, I, 831, *ṣurnay*.

200. The expression is *dīnār khafīf*. See *EI*,[2] s.v. "Dīnār."

201. Written thus, the name does not appear in the *Index* and is otherwise unidentifiable. See n. 202, below.

Muḥammad asked the blacks for a report about it. They told him that, while [they were] chasing the galley, most of the crew had thrown themselves into the river and abandoned the craft, which they were then able to retrieve. ʿAlī then interrogated the oarsmen,
[1765] who informed him that ʿAqīl had coerced them into joining him, as he held their wives prisoner until they did so; he had used the same tactic with all the oarsmen. On the question of the arrival of the Dabīlā, the oarsmen said that ʿAqīl had promised them money, and so they followed him. Concerning the boats stationed at Aqshā, ʿAlī was informed that they belonged to Rumays, who had abandoned them, fleeing at the first light of day.

ʿAlī b. Muḥammad then returned to a position opposite the boats [at Aqshā], and the blacks were ordered to bring them to him across the canal. The boats were then plundered and set on fire.

The Zanj next proceeded to the village of al-Muhallabiyyah, also called T.n.gh.t.[202] ʿAlī camped nearby and gave the order for the place to be plundered and razed, which was done. As he moved along the Mādiyān canal, he found quantities of dates, which he also had burned.

After these events the Zanj leader and his followers perpetrated outrages in this region, which we have not mentioned since none was especially atrocious, considering that every act he committed was atrocious.[203]

Among the momentous encounters that he later had with the forces of the central authorities[204] was one against the Turk Abū Hilāl in Sūq al-Rayyān.[205] One of the Zanj commanders called Rayḥān reported that this Turk had arrived in Sūq al-Rayyān at the head of a force of some four thousand men or more. They were preceded by a group of people wearing bright clothes and sporting flags and drums. The blacks led a ferocious attack against the Turk. One of the

202. Popovic, *Révolte*, 88, locates this village on Nahr al-Mādiyān (not found in the *Index*); it is not to be confused with the similar place name mentioned in n. 201, above. The reading *t.n.gh.t* as an alternative designation is entirely conjectural.

203. By highlighting in his succeeding account only the major crimes and depredations of the Zanj, Ṭabarī is perhaps also pointing to a shift in their leader's policy toward plunder and destruction, rather than recruitment of forces.

204. The expression is *aṣḥāb al-sulṭān*, and Popovic, *Révolte*, 88 n. 3, observes that this almost certainly refers to a force of the local garrison and not to troops sent from Baghdad.

205. A large town on Nahr al-Rayyān in the region of al-Ahwāz.

blacks fell upon the people's standard-bearer, felling him with blows from the two cudgels he was carrying. The crowd fled, while the [1766] blacks pursued their onslaught on Abū Hilāl's troops, slaying nearly one thousand five hundred of them. One of the blacks chased after Abū Hilāl, who managed to save himself by escaping on a horse bareback. Then the darkness of night descended between the blacks and those who had escaped. In the morning the pursuit resumed, and the blacks returned with heads and prisoners, all of whom were then killed.

Following this engagement there occurred another involving the Zanj against the troops of the central authorities, in which ʿAlī b. Muḥammad was also victorious. According to what one of the Zanj leader's commanders[206] reported, the affair commenced as follows. The commander, whose name was Rayḥān,[207] said, "One night during the course of the year," (which we have mentioned was one in which his rebellion commenced) "ʿAlī b. Muḥammad heard the sound of a dog barking at the gates [of a dwelling owned by] ʿAmr b. Masʿadah.[208] He ordered an inquiry into the source of the barking and sent one of his followers to investigate. He later returned with the news that he had seen nothing at all, and then the barking resumed."

Rayḥān continued: "ʿAlī then called for me to go to the source of the barking, for it seemed as though the dog barked only at someone it could see. So I set out and suddenly came upon the dog, standing on a breakwater (*al-musannah*),[209] although I could see nothing else. And then I spied a man sitting on some steps. I spoke to him, and, when he heard me addressing him in Arabic, he replied, introducing himself as Sayrān b. ʿAfwiallāh. He said he had brought letters for ʿAlī b. Muḥammad from his partisans in al-Baṣrah; he had been one of his associates during ʿAlī's sojourn in al-Baṣrah. So I took him to ʿAlī, who read the correspondence he was carrying. ʿAlī asked

206. *Qāʾid li-ṣāḥib al-zanj min al-sudān*. Ṭabarī here seems to make a distinction between the Zanj as an ethnic/racial term and blacks (*al-sudān*) other than the Zanj.

207. Although it is not immediately apparent from the context here, this is the same Rayḥān b. Ṣāliḥ who has already appeared on p. 35, above, as one of the slaves of the Shūrajiyyīn.

208. Ṭabarī's editors identify this individual as ʿAmr b. Masʿadah al-Kātib al-Rāwī, about whom nothing else is known; see *Index*.

209. See Lane, *Lexicon*, s.v. *s-n-w(y)*.

[1767] Sayrān about al-Zaynabī and the numbers of men he had. He said that al-Zaynabī was mustering a large force of slaves, volunteers, and the factions of the Bilāliyyah and the Saʿdiyyah, which was going to be despatched against ʿAlī at Bayān. ʿAlī told Sayrān to lower his voice lest the slaves be frightened by his news. He then inquired who was to lead this army and was told that one Abū Manṣūr, a Hāshimite *mawlā*, had been selected for the post. Asked whether he had seen this force, Sayrān replied that he had and added that they were also equipped with ropes to bind the hands of any blacks they captured. ʿAlī then told Sayrān to return to the place where he was staying, and he wandered off to ʿAlī b. Abān, Muḥammad b. Salm, and Yaḥyā b. Muḥammad and engaged in discussing matters with them until the dawn broke."

The Zanj leader then set out to spy upon this new force. When he reached the far side of Tursā, Barsūna, and Sandādān Bayān,[210] a detachment came out to do battle with him. ʿAlī b. Abān was ordered to engage the enemy, and he routed them, capturing from among them one hundred blacks.

Rayḥān resumed: "I heard ʿAlī b. Muḥammad say to his followers that what they had witnessed was one of the signs of perfection of their mission—that is, the arrival of the detachment with their slaves, who were surrendered into their hands, God increasing thereby the numbers of his own forces. Then the Zanj proceeded until they reached Bayān."

Rayḥān continued: "'ʿAlī b. Muḥammad sent me, accompanied by a contingent of his troops to al-Ḥajar in search of transport boats (*al-kārawān*)[211] and [the rest of] their army in the palm belt on the western side of the [Nahr] Bayān.[212] We reached the designated spot and
[1768] there found one thousand nine hundred boats, protected by a detachment of volunteers. When they saw us they abandoned the boats and crossed over the Sulbān without their arms, heading toward Jūbak. We boarded the vessels and sailed them back to ʿAlī's camp. Also aboard these craft were a number of pilgrims who had intended to

---

210. Although the location of these places cannot be identified, the action of the narrative is moving toward the environs of al-Baṣrah.

211. Arabized from the Persian *kārabān*. See Ṭabarī, *Glossarium*, CDXLII, s.v. *qayrawān*.

212. A broad artificial channel that joined the estuary of the Tigris with the Dujayl. See Le Strange, *Lands*, 44, 48.

follow the road to al-Baṣrah. When we arrived with the boats ʿAlī had a carpet laid out on a rise of ground, and, seated upon it, he examined the pilgrims for the rest of the day until sunset, by which time they had begun to believe all that he told them. They said that, if they had had any spare resources, they would remain with him; with that he sent them back to their boats. In the morning ʿAlī fetched them from the boats and made them swear not to reveal to anyone the size of his forces; indeed they should, if asked, make as little of his circumstances as possible. The pilgrims presented ʿAlī with one of their carpets, and he reciprocated, giving them one of his own. ʿAlī also asked them to swear that they were carrying neither money nor commercial goods for the central authorities. However, they indicated that one man was a government agent, carrying dried fruits to al-Baṣrah. The master of the boat in which the man was found swore to ʿAlī that he was engaged only in ordinary commerce, and so he was released. The pilgrims were also free to leave."

The inhabitants of Sulaymānān appeared on the eastern bank of the Bayān opposite the Zanj, who were conversing with them. Ḥusayn al-Ṣaydanānī was among the inhabitants. He had been a close associate of ʿAlī b. Muḥammad in al-Baṣrah and one of the four persons who had declared their revolt in the ʿAbbād mosque. On this [1769]
day Ḥusayn rejoined ʿAlī[213]

ʿAlī asked Ḥusayn what had caused him to be absent for so long. He replied that he had been in hiding and that, when this army had left [al-Baṣrah], he had joined in with the masses of troops. ʿAlī then inquired about the army, its composition and numbers. Ḥusayn said that he had seen the army depart and tht it comprised one thousand two hundred slave fighters,[214] a thousand of al-Zaynabī's own troops, about two thousand from the Bilāliyyah and Saʿdiyyah factions, and two hundred cavalry. However, when this force had reached al-Ubullah a dispute had broken out between the army and the town's inhabitants, and each side had begun cursing and abusing the other. The slave troops had even vilified Muḥammad b. Abī ʿAwn. Ḥusayn continued, "I left them behind at Shāṭiʾ ʿUthmān, and I reckoned that they should arrive in the morning." ʿAlī asked what they intended to do upon arriving. Ḥusayn replied that they

---

213. See p. 33, above.
214. *Khawal*. See n. 156, above.

were intending to send the cavalry into Sandādān Bayān, while their infantry would approach from both banks of the canal.

The following morning ʿAlī sent out a scout to gather intelligence. He chose an old, feeble man, in order that attention would not be drawn to him. But the scout did not return. When he had been away a long time ʿAlī despatched Fatḥ al-Ḥajjām with three hundred men and Yaḥyā b. Muḥammad to Sandādān. He ordered Yaḥyā b. Muḥammad to pass through the market of Bayān. Fatḥ al-Ḥajjām reported to ʿAlī that the enemy was approaching en masse along both sides of the canal. ʿAlī inquired about the tide and was told that it had not yet come in. ʿAlī then observed that the enemy's cavalry could not have arrived as yet. He ordered Muḥammad b. Salm and ʿAlī b. Abān to lie in wait for them among the palm trees, while he occupied a higher vantage point on a hilltop overlooking them. Presently the [enemy] banners and foot soldiers came into view as they
[1770] approached the territory of Abū al-ʿAlāʾ al-Balkhī, situated on a bend of the Dubayrān canal.[215].

The Zanj raised the battle cry "Allāhu Akbar" and then launched their attack on the enemy, confronting them at Dubayrān. The enemy's slave contingent attacked under the leadership of Abū al-ʿAbbās b. Ayman, who was otherwise known as Abū al-Kubāsh and Bashīr al-Qaysī; the Zanj were forced to retreat to the hill were ʿAlī b. Muḥammad was stationed. The Zanj then counterattacked and this time held their position firm. Abū al-Kubāsh assaulted Fatḥ al-Ḥajjām and killed him. He also surprised one of the black slaves called Dīnār and delivered him several blows. Next the blacks charged the enemy facing them on the shore to the Bayān and were engulfed in sword fighting.

Rayḥān resumed: "I encountered Muḥammad b. Salm when he struck Abū al-Kubāsh a blow, causing him to fall into the mud, where one of the Zanj came across him and severed his head. ʿAlī b. Abān, however, claimed Abū al-Kubāsh's death for himself, as well as that of Bashīr al-Qaysī. Chatting about that day, ʿAlī (b. Abān) said, 'Bashīr al-Qaysī was the first person I encountered, and we struck each other blows. His blow landed on my shield, whereas mine caught him squarely in the chest and abdomen. I had pierced his ribs and slit open his stomach. He collapsed, and I slashed off his

---

215. The reading is conjectural.

head. Then I faced Abū al-Kubāsh, who gave me his full attention. One of the blacks came up behind him and struck his legs with a club, breaking them both. He fell and offered no resistance to my finishing him off and beheading him. I brought both heads to the leader of the Zanj.'"

Muḥammad b. al-Ḥasan b. Sahl said, "I heard the Zanj leader stating that ʿAlī had brought him the head of Abū al-Kubāsh and that of [1771] Bashīr al-Qaysī." Muḥammad added that he knew neither of them. Moreover, ʿAlī had told him that both men had been in the vanguard of their forces and, when he slew them, the troops had fled at the sight of their fallen leaders.

Rayḥān continued, according to what was reported from him, that the enemy fled using every avenue of escape while pursued by the blacks up to the Nahr Bayān. The water level in the canal had dropped, and, as the enemy attempted to cross, they sank in the mud, and most perished.

Some blacks passed by their comrade Dīnār, whom Abū al-Kubāsh had struck down. He was lying there wounded. The blacks mistook him for one of the enemy's slaves (*al-khawal*), and so they commenced to beat him with sickles, leaving him severely wounded. A passerby who recognized Dīnār carried him to the Zanj leader, who ordered his wounds attended to.

Rayḥān continued: "When the enemy had reached the mouth of the Nahr Bayān, they had lost many drowned and their boats with the animals aboard had been seized. Someone signaled us from a boat, and when we reached him he told us to enter the Nahr Sharīkān, where the enemy had set up an ambush. Yaḥyā b. Muḥammad and ʿAlī b. Abān set out along the canal, Yaḥyā taking the western and ʿAlī the eastern side, when they came across about a thousand Maghāribah[216] troops lying in wait. Ḥusayn al-Saydanānī was being held their prisoner.

When the enemy saw us, they fell upon Ḥusayn and cut him to pieces. They then advanced upon the Zanj with their spears extended, and fighting ensued until the time of the noon prayer. The blacks in their turn threw themselves upon the enemy, slaying them all and seizing their weapons. The blacks returned to camp and found their leader sitting on the bank of the Bayān. Some thirty-odd

216. Government troops of North African origin.

flags and about a thousand heads had been brought to him, among them heads of the brave and courageous slaves (*al-khawal*). That same day Zuhayr was brought to him as well."[217]

[1772] Rayḥān continued: "I did not know him, but Yaḥyā, who arrived while Zuhayr was standing before the leader of the Zanj, recognized him and said to me, 'This is Zuhayr the slave (*al-khawal*); why should you spare him?' And the order was given for Zuhayr to be beheaded."

The Zanj leader remained in his camp that day and night. The following morning he sent a scout to reconnoiter the Tigris shore. The scout returned to inform him that there were two barges[218] moored to the island, which was then located at the mouth of the al-Qandal canal. When the afternoon [prayer] was finished the scout set out again for the Tigris, to ascertain developments. At sunset Abū al-ʿAbbās came to ʿAlī b. Muḥammad; he was his wife's brother and was accompanied by a soldier called ʿUmrān, who was married to the mother of this same Abū al-ʿAbbās. ʿAlī placed his troops on parade for them and requested that they [review them]. ʿUmrān handed him a communication from Ibn Abī ʿAwn, demanding that he cross over the Bayān and leave the district of his jurisdiction. For his part, Ibn Abī ʿAwn informed ʿAlī that he had removed the barges blockading the way out. ʿAlī gave the command to take the boats from Jubbā, which could traverse the Bayān. His troops went to al-Ḥajar[219] and found in Sulbān two hundred boats loaded with flour. The boats were commandeered; clothing, some *barr.kanat*,[220] and ten Zanj were discovered on board. The troops were ordered to embark upon the boats and, when the tide came in at sunset, he crossed over [the Bayān] with them opposite the mouth of the Qandal canal. One of the boats carrying flour, which was in the charge of Abū Dulaf, was
[1773] blown off course by a strong wind. He arrived the next morning and reported to the Zanj leader that the wind had carried him as far as

217. The sudden introduction into the account of this individual, as if the reader were already familiar with him, suggests that the text we possess may contain lacunae or has been abridged. See Popovic, *Révolte*, 89; n. 178, above.

218. *Shadhah*, also *shadhawah*, a kind of war boat. See Ṭabarī, *Glossarium*, CCCVIII; Lane, *Lexicon*, s.v. *sh-dh-w*.

219. A location near al-Baṣrah.

220. Like Popovic, *Révolte*, 89 n. 5, I have been unable to identify this word, which is unvocalized in manuscripts B and O.

Ḥasak ʿImrān. There the villagers had shown an inordinate interest in him and the boat's cargo, and he had had to fend them off.

Fifty blacks joined ʿAlī's side, and, with their arrival and the acquisition of the boats, he entered the Qandal canal [district] and ventured as far as a village belonging to al-Muʿallā b. Ayyūb, where he set up camp. He spread out his troops up to Dubbā,[221] where they discovered three hundred Zanj, whom they brought back to ʿAlī. They also found an agent of al-Muʿallā b. Ayyūb, and, when they demanded money of him, he replied, "Let me cross over to Bursān, and I will bring you money." So he was released, and he went. He failed, however, to return, and when his absence became prolonged ʿAlī gave the order to plunder the village. And this was done.

Rayḥān continued this report: "On that day I saw the leader of the Zanj taking part in plundering with the rest of us. My hand and his fell at the same time upon a quilted woolen jacket; we each had hold of a part of it, tugging it toward us, when I finally let him have it."

Later ʿAlī b. Muḥammad set out for al-Zaynabī's garrison, situated on the western bank of the Qandal canal. The defenders were defiant, and, although they believed they could resist, they actually did not possess sufficient strength to do so, and all, some two hundred persons, were killed, to the last man. ʿAlī b. Muḥammad remained in the castle that night and set out on the morning tide for the salt flat of al-Qandal. His troops proceeded along both sides of the canal and, arriving at the village of Mundhirān, they entered and [1774]
plundered it. A number of Zanj were found in the village, and ʿAlī had them apportioned among his commanders. From there ʿAlī reached the far end of the Qandal [canal] and directed his boats into a canal called al-Ḥasanī, which opened onto another canal called al-Ṣāliḥī, which led directly to Dubbā. He camped there on the flats.

One of his followers reportedly said that it was there that ʿAlī b. Muḥammad named his commanders, and he denied his having done so previously.

ʿAlī b. Muḥammad dispersed his troops among the canals until they converged upon the main square of Dubbā. They found there a man belonging to the harbor dwellers in al-Baṣrah who sold dried dates. His name was Muḥammad b. Jaʿfar al-Muraydī. He was

221. The name of one of the subdistricts of al-Baṣrah, through which ran many canals. Yāqūt, *Muʿjam*, II, 544.

brought to ʿAlī who, recognizing Muḥammad, greeted him. He asked him about the Bilāliyyah faction [in al-Baṣrah]. The man replied, "I was bringing you a message from them when the blacks met me and brought me to you. The Bilāliyyah are seeking certain conditions from you; if you grant them, they will follow and obey you." ʿAlī consented to the conditions. He also authorized the man to be responsible for them until they were able to reach him. ʿAlī then let Muḥammad go and sent with him an escort that would take him as far as al-Fayyāḍ[222] and then return. For four days the Zanj leader waited in vain for Muḥammad's return. On the fifth day ʿAlī disbanded the boats he had with him on the canal and proceeded by land between the canal called al-Dāwardānī and the Nahr al-Ḥasanī and the Nahr al-Ṣāliḥī. He had scarcely moved from one canal to the next, when he saw about six hundred horsemen approaching from the direction of the Nahr al-Amīr.[223] His troops hastened along the Dāwardānī, with the horsemen proceeding upon the western bank.
[1775] A lengthy discussion took place, and it transpired that the horsemen were Arab tribesmen, among whom were ʿAntarah b. Ḥajanā and Thumāl.

ʿAlī sent Muḥammad b. Salm to talk to ʿAntarah and Thumāl, and they in turn inquired who the Zanj leader was. Muḥammad pointed out ʿAlī, and the two Arabs said they wished to talk with him. Muḥammad returned to report to ʿAlī what they had said. He added, "If you would speak to them . . . ," but ʿAlī interrupted him abruptly and said, "This is a trap." He ordered the blacks to attack the tribesmen. When the blacks crossed the canal, the tribesmen turned away from them and raised the black flag.[224] Then there appeared in their midst Sulaymān, the brother of al-Zaynabī, who had been with them all the time. The Zanj troops returned, while the tribesmen withdrew. ʿAlī said to Muḥammad b. Salm, "Did I not tell you that they had set a trap for us?"

The Zanj arrived in Dubbā, and ʿAlī scattered his troops among the palm groves. They had found sheep and cattle, which they pro-

---

222. Yāqūt, *Muʿjam*, III, 926, describes this as an ancient, broad canal in al-Baṣrah, with villages and cultivated fields along its banks.

223. A canal in al-Baṣrah (not to be confused with another of the same name in Wāsiṭ) dug by order of the ʿAbbāsid Caliph al-Manṣūr and thus originally known as Nahr Amīr al-Muʾminīn. See Yāqūt, *Muʿjam*, IV, 835.

224. Indicating their support for the government.

ceeded to slaughter and gorge themselves on, spending the entire night there. The following morning they reached the narrow waterway (*al-arkhanj*)[225] called al-Muṭahhirī, which joined the Nahr al-Amīr opposite al-Fayyāḍ from both sides. There they encountered Shihāb b. al-ʿAlāʾ al-ʿAnbarī with a detachment of slaves (*al-khawal*). In the ensuing action Shihāb escaped with a small troop, but many of his forces were slain. Shihāb was pursued into the center of al-Fayyāḍ. There the Zanj came across six hundred slaves of the Shū- [1776]
rajiyyīn; they captured them and brought them to ʿAlī's camp, while their agents were killed. ʿAlī advanced as far as a castle called al-Jawharī, situated on the salt flats of the Barāmikah, and spent the night there. In the morning he reached the flats that began at the Dīnarī canal and the farthest reaches of which extended to the Nahr al-Muḥdath. ʿAlī reunited his troops and ordered them not to press on toward al-Baṣrah until the signal was given. Thereafter they were set loose to plunder the countryside, while ʿAlī spent the night there.

An Account of the Zanj Leader's Advance upon al-Baṣrah with His Army

After the Zanj leader had mustered his troops, they reportedly set out for al-Baṣrah from the salt flats stretching beside the Dīnārī canal, the farthest reaches of which extended to the Nahr al-Muḥdath. When they had arrived opposite the Nahr al-Riyāḥī, a party of blacks arrived and informed him that they had seen armed men in the al-Riyāḥī area itself. Moments later the Zanj assembled at a call to arms, and the Zanj leader ordered ʿAlī b. Abān to cross the canal against the foe, who were on the eastern side of the Dīnarī canal. ʿAlī b. Abān took about three thousand men with him while the Zanj leader collected together his remaining troops, telling ʿAlī [at the same time] that, if he required reinforcements, he need only ask for them. After ʿAlī b. Abān had left, the Zanj called for their weapons, for they had spotted another movement [of troops] from a direction different from the one ʿAlī had taken. The Zanj leader inquired about the troop movement and was told that they were com- [1777]
ing from the direction of the village of al-Jaʿfariyyah, which lay be-

225. See Ṭabarī, *Glossarium*, CXI.

side the Nahr Ḥarb. So he despatched Muḥammad b. Salm in that direction.

It was reported from Rayḥān (b. Ṣāliḥ), one of ʿAlī b. Muḥammad's followers, that he said, "I was among those accompanying Muḥammad (b. Salm) when we set out at the time of the noon prayer. We confronted the enemy in al-Jaʿfariyyah, and a fierce battle developed between us, which lasted until the late afternoon." The blacks next led a ferocious assault, forcing the enemy to turn heel and flee. Around five hundred persons were killed from among the soldiers, the Arab tribesmen, and the Baṣran factions of the Bilāliyyah and the Saʿdiyyah. Among the enemy that day was one Fatḥ, a slave of Abū Shīth, and he too fled, with Fayrūz the Elder in pursuit. When Fatḥ realized that Fayrūz could not be shaken off, he flung his metal helmet at him, albeit in vain. He next threw his shield at Fayrūz, but this also did not cause him to retreat. Finally, he heaved a metal oven[226] he had been carrying at Fayrūz, again without the desired effect. They reached the Nahr Ḥarb, and Fatḥ jumped into the canal and escaped, leaving Fayrūz to return to the Zanj leader bearing the weapons that Fatḥ had discarded.

Muḥammad b. al-Ḥasan — Shibl said, "It was related to us that Fatḥ had leaped across the Nahr Ḥarb that day." Shibl continued, "I related this tale to al-Faḍl b. ʿAdī al-Dārimī, and he said that he had been with the Saʿdiyyah that day and that Fatḥ had not been carrying a metal oven[227] with him. In fact, he was wearing only a yellow-silk tunic. He fought until there remained no one else in the battle, and then he made his way to the Nahr Ḥarb and leaped across it to the western bank." He seems not to have known Rayḥān's story about Fayrūz.

[1778] Rayḥān said, "I met Fayrūz before he had returned to the Zanj leader, and he told me the story of his encounter with Fatḥ and showed me the weapons. The Zanj had resorted to recovering spoils as I made my way along the Nahr al-Dīnārī. Suddenly I came across

---

226. The expression is *tannūr ḥadīd*, which suggests an implement designed for battlefield conditions or a journey, as the common domestic *tannūr* was constructed of baked earth or clay. If the implement was shaped like the Beduin metal cooking implement, the *sāj*, round and concave as a shield, it could have easily been carried. This interpretation seems confirmed by another occurence of the term, at n. 374, below.

227. See n. 226, above.

a man sitting under a palm tree. He was wearing a silk hat (*al-qalansuwah*), red shoes, and a woolen tunic (*al-durrāʿah*). I seized him, and he showed me letters he was carrying, which he said were from a group of people in al-Baṣrah who had sent them with him. I threw a turban (*al-ʿamāmah*) around his neckand led him to the Zanj leader and reported the man's news. ʿAlī b. Muḥammad asked the man's name, and he replied, 'I am Abū al-Layth Muḥammad b. ʿAbdallāh from Iṣfahān, and I have only come to you from a strong desire to be in your company.' ʿAlī accepted him."

Moments later the cry "God is greatest" was heard, and ʿAlī b. Abān appeared in possession of the head of one of the Bilāliyyah called Abū al-Layth al-Qawārīrī (Muḥammad b. al-Ḥasan — Shibl said that Waṣīf al-Zuhrī was the person who killed Abū al-Layth al-Qawārīrī, one of the celebrated members of the Bilāliyyah) and [in possession of] the head of another Bilāliyyah member named ʿAbdān al-Kasibī who had a voice among them, as well as the heads of a number of others from them. ʿAlī b. Muḥammad queried ʿAlī b. Abān about the incident, and he told him that no one had fought him more tenaciously than these two men, meaning Abū al-Layth and ʿAbdān. ʿAlī b. Abān forced them to flee and finally drove them into the Nahr Nāfidh, where they had a barge, which he capsized.

Muḥammad b. Salm later arrived with a prisoner from the Bilāliyyah whom Shibl had captured. His name was Muḥammad al-Azraq al-Qawārīrī. Muḥammad was also carrying a number of heads. ʿAlī b. Muḥammad called the prisoner over and asked him about the commanders of these two armies. The man replied that those in al-Riyāḥī were commanded by Abū Manṣūr al-Zaynabī and [1779]
the others along the Nahr Ḥarb were commanded by Sulaymān, the brother of al-Zaynabī, who stationed himself on their rear flank in the outlying areas. To a query about their numbers, he replied that he did not know the figures, only that they were a considerable force. ʿAlī then had Muḥammad al-Qawārīrī released and attached to Shibl's group.

ʿAlī and the Zanj next made for the salt flats of al-Jaʿfariyyah. He remained there that night among the slain. The following morning he gathered together his troops and cautioned them [again] against their entering al-Baṣrah. Regardless, some of them, including Ankalwayh, Zurayq, Abū al-Khanjar — who had not yet been made a commander — Salīm and, Waṣīf al-Kūfī hastened on ahead. When they reached the Nahr al-Shādhānī, a number of Baṣrans came out to meet them, the number swelling quickly into a multitude. ʿAlī b. Muḥammad received news of this and sent off Muḥammad b. Salm, ʿAlī b. Abān, and Mushriq, Yaḥyā's slave, with a large contingent. He went along with them, accompanying the boats that were loaded with pack animals and the wives of the slaves. He established camp at the bridge on the Nahr Kathīr.[228]

Rayḥān continued: "I joined ʿAlī b. Muḥammad, having received a wound on my leg from a rock. He asked about developments and I told him that the battle was well underway. He then ordered my return and accompanied me until I reached the high ground overlooking the Nahr al-Sabābijah. He said to me, 'Go to our troops and tell them to disengage and fall back.' I told him that he should get as far
[1780] away from the place as possible, for I was unsure of his safety from the enemy's slave troops. So he withdrew.

I myself went and informed the commanders of his orders, and they retreated. The Baṣrans pressed the Zanj hard, and a complete rout was the result. That happened in the late afternoon. Many fell into the Kathīr and Shayṭān[229] canals. ʿAlī b. Muḥammad called to his followers to come back, but they could not return. A number of them drowned in the Nahr Kathīr and many were slain on the canal bank as well as on the Shādhānī. Among the commanders who drowned that day were Abū al-Jawn, Mubārak al-Baḥrānī, ʿAṭāʾ al-Barbarī, and Salām al-Shāmī. The slave of Abū Shīth,[230] Ḥārith al-Qaysī, and Suhayl caught up with ʿAlī b. Muḥammad, and together they mounted the arched bridge (*qanṭarah*) over the Nahr Kathīr. ʿAlī then turned back to [challenge] them, and they retreated before him until they were back on the ground.[231] On this day ʿAlī was wearing a woolen tunic, a turban, sandals, and a sword, and he carried a shield. When he had left the bridge, the Baṣrans mounted it again in pursuit. ʿAlī turned back and killed a man on the fifth step of the bridge. He called out to his men to alert them to his position,

228. A canal in al-Baṣrah named after Kathīr b. ʿAbdallāh al-Salmī, who, as governor of the city, had it dug during the last years of the Umayyad period. See Yāqūt, *Muʿjam*, IV, 843–44.

229. A canal in al-Baṣrah named after a client of Ziyād b. Abīhi, the Umayyad governor of Iraq. See Yāqūt, *Muʿjam*, IV, 840.

230. Named Fatḥ; see p. 60, above.

231. That is, off the bridge.

but none of them remained in that spot save for Abū al-Shawk, Muṣliḥ, and Rafīq, Yaḥyā's slave."

Rayḥān said, "I was with ʿAlī b. Muḥammad at the time. He fell back to al-Muʿallā[232] and camped on the western side of the Shayṭān canal."

Muḥammad b. al-Ḥasan said that he had heard the leader of the Zanj himself relate the following: "That day I had found myself at one point completely out of touch with my troops and they with me. Only Muṣliḥ and Rafīq remained with me. I was wearing a pair of Sindī sandals and a turban, a twist of which had become unraveled [1781] and trailed along the ground. I was in too much of a hurry to pick it up, as I was carrying a sword and shield. Muṣliḥ and Rafīq hurried ahead on foot, and as I lagged behind they disappeared from sight. I spotted two Baṣrans behind me, one carrying a sword, the other with a rock in his hand. They saw me and recognized me and redoubled their efforts to catch me, so I turned upon them and they backed off. I finally made it back to the spot where my troops were gathered. They had become perturbed at my loss, and seeing me again calmed them down."

Rayḥān continued: "ʿAlī b. Muḥammad returned to al-Muʿallā on the western side of the Nahr Shayṭān and camped there. He discovered upon inquiry that many of the men had fled and, after an inspection, he found there were a total of only five hundred men left. A horn was blown, the sound of which used to be the signal for the slaves to assemble, but no one returned. ʿAlī b. Muḥammad spent the night there, in the course of which Jurbān arrived. He had escaped in the general flight, taking with him thirty slaves. ʿAlī asked him where he had vanished to, and he replied that he had made a reconnaissance of al-Zawāriqah."

Rayḥān continued: "ʿAlī b. Muḥammad sent me to find out for him who was still at the Nahr Ḥarb bridge. I found no one around. The Baṣrans had plundered the boats that ʿAlī had brought there, removing the pack animals and taking possession of his other goods, his letters and astrolabes. The following morning, when ʿAlī b. Muḥammad inspected the troops again, he discovered that a thousand [1782] men had made their way back during the night."

---

232. Probably the same village as that belonging to Muʿallā b. Ayyūb. See p. 57, above.

Rayḥān said that Shibl was among those who had fled, but Nāṣiḥ al-Ramlī denied that.

Rayḥān continued: "Shibl returned [to camp] in the morning with ten slaves. ʿAlī b. Muḥammad rebuked him harshly. He demanded to know what had happened to a slave called Abū Naʿjah Nādir and another, ʿAnbar al-Barbarī. Shibl reported that they had both fled with the others. The leader of the Zanj remained stationed where he was and gave the order for Muḥammad b. Salm to venture to the arched bridge of the Nahr Kathīr and there preach to the people, informing them of the reasons for his revolt. Muḥammad set out, accompanied by Sulaymān b. Jāmiʿ and Yaḥyā b. Muḥammad; they stopped [by the river] while Muḥammad crossed over and made his way into the midst of the troops of al-Baṣrah.[233] As he commenced to address them, they caught him off guard, fell on him, and killed him."

Al-Faḍl b. ʿAdī said that when Muḥammad b. Salm crossed the river to preach to the Baṣrans, they were assembled at a spot called al-Faḍl b. Maymūn. Fatḥ, the slave of Abū Shīth, was the first person suddenly to confront and strike him down with a sword; then Ibn al-Tūmanī al-Saʿdī severed his head. Sulaymān and Yaḥyā returned to report to ʿAlī b. Muḥammad, who ordered them to say nothing to the Zanj until he had a chance to do so himself. Following the afternoon prayers, he announced the death of Muḥammad b. Salm to those troops who had not heard the news. He said to them, "Tomorrow you shall slay ten thousand Baṣrans to avenge him." He sent Zurayq and
[1783] his slave Saqlabtūyā[234] with orders to prevent anyone from crossing the river. That was on Sunday, the 13th of Dhū al-Qaʿdah in the year 255 (October 23, 869).

Muḥammad b. al-Ḥasan — Muḥammad b. Simʿān al-Kātib: On Monday, the 14th of Dhū al-Qaʿdah (October 24, 869), the people of al-Baṣrah[235] assembled together and went forth in the wake of what they regarded as a triumph over the Zanj the previous day. The man

233. The expression is *ahl al-Baṣrah,* which could signify either the populace or troops; the latter seems preferable here. See n. 235, below. Clearly this incident did not take place in al-Baṣrah itself but rather on the outskirts of the city. See Popovic, *Révolte,* 92.

234. The reading is conjectural.

235. The expression once again is *ahl al-Baṣrah.* See n. 233, above. Here, however, Ṭabarī indicates a much broader participation in the expedition against the Zanj than just military personnel.

selected to lead the expedition was a Baṣran by the name of Ḥammād al-Sājī, a sailor experienced in operating and fighting from barges. The force comprised volunteers, archers, people from the main mosque, those from the Bilāliyyah and Saʿdiyyah factions prepared to follow Ḥammād, and onlookers from the Hāshimites, Qurayshites, and other sections of the populace. Three barges were loaded with archers who crowded on board, eager to get to the scene of battle. A mob proceeded on foot, some bearing arms while others were mere spectators without weapons. The barges and boats entered the Umm Ḥabīb canal on the tide after sunset that same day. The procession of foot soldiers and spectators along the canal bank was so dense and numerous that they blocked from view everything in front of them. The Zanj leader had stationed himself on the canal known as al-Shayṭān.

Muḥammad b. al-Ḥasan said the Zanj leader told him that, when his scouts had arrived and he knew of the approaching crowd, he sent off Zurayq and Abū al-Layth al-Iṣbahānī with a detachment of troops along the east bank of the [Shayṭān] canal, and Shibl and Ḥu- [1784]
sayn al-Ḥammāmī with another detachment along the western bank. Both parties were to set up ambushes. ʿAlī b. Abān was ordered to take the remainder of his troops to intercept the enemy. They should, however, crouch down facing the enemy, guarding themselves with their shields, allowing no one to attack until the adversaries were close enough to brandish swords at them. When the situation had developed in this way, the Zanj attacked the enemy. The Zanj leader gave orders to the two ambuscades that when the throng [on the banks] were abreast of them and they heard their own troops on the attack, they should emerge on both sides of the canal shouting at the enemy. The Zanj women were ordered to gather bricks and keep the men supplied with them.

Muḥammad b. al-Ḥasan said that after this incident the leader of the Zanj told his followers, "That day, as I beheld the mob approaching, I was gripped by a terrible fear, such an overwhelming terror that I appealed [to God] for help. I was accompanied by only a few troops, among them Muṣliḥ, and there was not one among us who did not imagine that he was going to meet his doom. Muṣliḥ marveled at the size of the multitude and I motioned to him to contain himself. As the enemy neared, I cried out, 'Oh God, this is the hour of trial, so come to my aid!' I had scarcely finished saying this when I saw white

[1785] birds sweep down upon the enemy, and one of the galleys overturned, and all on board were drowned.[236] The barges met the same fate. My troops then fell upon the enemy they were heading for, shouting at them." The ambushers emerged from their hiding places on the canal banks behind the boats and the foot soldiers, clubbing those among them and onlookers on shore who tried to flee. A group here was drowned, a group there was killed, while others who fled toward the canal seeking rescue were overtaken by the sword. Those who resisted were slain, while those who ventured into the water were drowned. The foot soldiers on the canal's edge who sought escape in the water were either killed or drowned until most of the enemy forces had been annihilated. None but the odd fugitive was saved. The numbers of Baṣrans missing soared as their wives raised a chorus of lament.

People spoke of this day as the Day of the Barges (*yawm al-shadhā*).[237] They were horrified by the number killed that day. Among the innumerable host killed were a number of sons of the Hāshimite Jaʿfar b. Sulaymān and forty famous archers.

The abominable one[238] had the heads [of the slain] collected. He displayed them so that relatives of the deceased who came to him could claim those they recognized. For the rest, which no on claimed, he put aboard a flat-bottomed boat (*jarībiyyah*), filling it up. The boat was released on the falling tide from the Umm Ḥabīb
[1786] canal, where it drifted toward al-Baṣrah, stopping at Mashraʿah[239] al-Qayyār. People came and recovered the heads of those they recognized.

After this day the enemy of God became ever more powerful as fear of him gripped the Baṣrans' hearts. They abstained from further battle with him, but the central authorities were informed of his escapades, and Juʿlān al-Turkī was sent with reinforcements to the

236. On this incident, see Halm, *Traditionen*, 26.

237. *Shadhāh* being the name of the type of vessel employed by the Baṣrans.

238. Ṭabarī suddenly changes his tone toward the Zanj leader, employing the epithet *al-khabīth* here for the first time. On the following page he calls him "enemy of God." Lane, *Lexicon*, s.v. *kh-b-th*, gives a rich variety of words to choose from, among them "base, corrupt, artful, cunning, and wicked"; "abominable one" has been used here consistently to render *khabīth*.

239. *Mashraʿah*, as part of the place name, signifies a place to which people come to drink or draw water, and where animals are also watered. See Lane, *Lexicon*, s.v. *sh-r-ʿ*.

Başrans. Juʿlān ordered Abū al-Aḥwaṣ al-Bāhilī to proceed to al-Ubullah as governor, sending as support a Turk called Jurayḥ.

The abominable one alleged that his followers had boasted to him in the wake of this [recent] battle that they had slaughtered the entire fighting force of al-Başrah save for the weak and incapacitated. "Give us permission to storm the city," they demanded. ʿAlī b. Muḥammad berated them and decried their request. "On the contrary," he scolded, "get as far away from al-Başrah as possible; we have instilled fear and terror in them, and now you are safe. The thing to do now is forsake war with them until they come looking for you." Then he withdrew his forces to a salt flat at the farthest edge of the network of canals and then went on to the al-Ḥājir canal.

Shibl said that this place was the salt flats of Abū Qurrah, which lay between the Nahr Abū Qurrah and the Nahr al-Ḥājir. ʿAlī b. Muḥammad stationed himself there and gave the command to his troops to construct huts from the reeds (*akwākh*).[240] These salt flats were surrounded by palm groves, villages, and cultivated fields. The Zanj soldiers spread out right and left, raiding the villages, murder- [1787] ing the farmers, stealing their property, and leading their livestock away.

Such was the news of ʿAlī b. Muḥammad and of the people who were affected by his rebellion this year.

Al-Ḥasan b. Muḥammad b. Abī Shawārib al-Qāḍī[241] was imprisoned on the 28th of Dhū al-Qaʿdah (November 7, 869), and ʿAbd al-Raḥmān b. Nāʾil al-Başrī was appointed to the judgeship of Sāmarrā in Dhū al-Ḥijjah (November 10–December 8, 869) of this year.

Leading the pilgrimage this year was ʿAlī b. al-Ḥasan b. Ismāʿīl b. al-ʿAbbās b. Muḥammad b. ʿAlī.[242]

---

240. See G. Young, *A Reed Shaken by the Wind*, for a modern account of life among the marsh Arabs.

241. See n. 6, above.

242. He had led the pilgrimage the previous year as well.

The Events of the Year 256

(December 9, 869–November 28, 870)

Among the significant events of the year was the arrival in Sāmarrā of Mūsā b. Bughā. Ṣāliḥ b. Waṣīf was driven into hiding, while some of Mūsā's military commanders transferred al-Muhtadī under escort from the Jawsaq palace to the palace of Yājūr.[243]

It was reported that Mūsā b. Bughā entered Sāmarrā with those accompanying him on Monday the 11th of al-Muḥarram of this year (December 19, 869). Upon his arrival, Mūsā commenced a review of his troops, the left and right wings and the central sector presented
[1788] together with their arms, which took place in al-Ḥayr, and continued up to the point where they reached the Gate of al-Ḥayr adjacent to the Jawsaq palace and the Qaṣr al-Aḥmar. This was on the very day that al-Muhtadī was holding a session of the court of appeal (*maẓālim*). Aḥmad b. al-Mutawakkil b. Fityān[244] was among those summoned to attend that day, because of the court. He was still there at

243. The copyist of manuscript C reads for Yājūr the name of another Turkish commander, Yārjūkh.

244. The future Caliph al-Muʿtamid; see p. 115, below, for his accession date. His patronymic was Abū al-ʿAbbās, though he was also known by his mother's name, Fityān, or, according to Ibn al-Athīr (*Kāmil*, VII, 235), Qityān or Qinīn.

the palace when the *mawlas* (of Mūsā b. Bughā) entered and took al-Muhtadī off to the palace of Yājūr. Aḥmad b. al-Mutawakkil followed and continued the court of appeal session, deputizing for al-Muhtadī, in the tent of Mufliḥ, until the business with al-Muhtadī was cleared up and he had been returned to al-Jawsaq and released.

Bāyakbāk had been in charge of affairs in the caliphal palace and had been replaced a few days previous by Sātikīn. This was owing, people thought, to al-Muhtadī's confidence in him, which meant Sātikīn would also control both the palace and the Caliph's person at the moment of Mūsā (b. Bughā's) arrival. On that day Sātikīn remained in his own quarters, leaving the palace vacant. Mūsā arrived at the palace while al-Muhtadī was in session of the court of appeal; he was informed of Muhtadī's arrival but delayed giving him permission to enter for a while. When he and his company were finally allowed an audience, there first occurred a discussion like that on the day that [Mūsā's] delegation and messengers had arrived.[245] However, when such discussion became prolonged, the Turks began to mutter impatiently among themselves in their own tongue. Al-Muhtadī was then forced to leave the assembly and he was borne away on one of the animals of the Shākiriyyah, while the Turks plundered what was available in the Jawsaq palace in the way of riding beasts belonging to the elite. They then headed for al-Karkh[246] and upon reaching the Gate of al-Ḥayr in the fiefs attached to the palace of Yājūr, they brought him into the palace itself.

One of the *mawlās* who was present that day recounted the rea- [1789]
son for their seizure of al-Muhtadī. One *mawla* had remarked to another that the delays [created by al-Muhtadī] were merely a device to allow Ṣāliḥ b. Waṣīf to take them by surprise with his forces. This prospect frightened them and caused them to remove al-Muhtadī to another spot.

---

245. As described p. 28, above.

246. This is the Karkh of Sāmarrā, also known as Karkh Fīrūz, to distinguish it from the southern quarter of Baghdad of the same name. It lay ten miles north of Sāmarrā. See Le Strange, *Lands*, 52; also Yāqūt, *Muʿjam*, III, 17. The Caliph al-Muʿtaṣim constructed al-Karkh beyond the built-up area of Sāmarrā, where the Turkish military personnel held lands (*qaṭāʾiʿ*), in order to keep them separated from the ordinary population of the city and from certain other contingents of the army that were housed there. See D. Ayalon, "Preliminary Remarks on the Mamluk Military Institution in Islam," especially 55, quoting al-Yaʿqūbī.

Someone reported that he had heard al-Muhtadī say to Mūsā, "What do you wish? Mercy on you! Honor God, and fear Him, for it is a momentous matter that you undertake." Mūsā replied, "We desire nothing but good. I swear by the grave of al-Mutawakkil, absolutely no harm will befall you from our part." The one who had overheard this remark was prompted to say to himself that, had Mūsā really sought only [the Caliph's] good, he would have better sworn on the grave of either al-Muʿtaṣim or al-Wāthiq.[247]

When al-Muhtadī had been transferred to Yājūr's palace, the *mawlās* extracted vows and promises from him that he would not side with Ṣāliḥ against them and that he would not harbor toward them ulterior intentions different from the way he treated them openly. Al-Muhtadī agreed, and the *mawlas* renewed their oath of allegiance to him on Tuesday the 12th of al-Muḥarram (December 20, 869). Later the same morning they sent for Ṣāliḥ to come to them for discussions, and Ṣāliḥ promised to appear.

One of the chiefs of the Farāghinah[248] reported that, when he was asked what they were demanding of Ṣāliḥ b. Waṣīf, he replied, "The blood of the government secretaries and their property and the blood of al-Muʿtazz and his entourage and property."[249]

The commanders accepted after pondering these matters, while their troops remained outside by the Gate of al-Ḥayr next to the palace of Yājūr. Then, on the Tuesday evening, Ṣāliḥ went into hiding.[250]

Ṭalmajūr recounted the following. "On the evening of Tuesday we assembled together with Ṣāliḥ. After he had ordered the distribution of periodic payments (*arzāq*) to those assigned to guard duty (*aṣḥāb*
[1790] *al-nawbah*), he ordered one of the company present to review[251] the

247. Both al-Muʿtaṣim and al-Wāthiq had died of natural causes while al-Mutawakkil had been murdered by Mūsā's father in league with Waṣīf, the father of Ṣāliḥ. For brief accounts of these events, see Kennedy, *Age*, 171–75; Sourdel, *Vizirat*, I, 271–86.

248. A regiment of soldiers from the province of Farghanah, a large area lying on the north and south sides of the upper Jaxartes river. The region first supplied soldiers as guards for the Caliph al-Muʿtaṣim (d. 227/842). See Le Strange, *Lands*, 476–80, *EI*,[2] s.v. "Farghana."

249. Ṭabarī here means that the chief was seeking recompense for the blood of those mentioned, that is, vengeance. The Caliph al-Muʿtazz had been killed some five months previously.

250 That is, within a day of Mūsā b. Bughā's arrival in Sāmarrā.

251. On the formal procedures of the military review, see Bosworth, "Recruitment," especially 70–77.

number of troops at hand. That morning their number had been some five thousand. Returning to Ṣāliḥ, the man said that there were now only eight hundred men, most of whom were his freedmen (*ghilmān* and *mawlas*).[252] For a while Ṣāliḥ was silent, then he rose and left us without any further instructions. This was his last act."

It was reported from someone who had overheard that Bukhtīshūʿ (b. Jibrīl)[253] said, alluding to Ṣāliḥ before Mūsā's arrival, "First we roused this unruly force and incited them; then, when finally they did come to us, we were preoccupied with drinking and playing backgammon. It was as if we were here one moment, then just vanished when he (Mūsā) reached al-Qāṭūl."

In the early hours of Wednesday morning, Ṭughtā[254] arrived at the door of Yājūr's palace, where Mufliḥ confronted him and delivered him a blow with his battle-ax, striking him on the right temple. Those who remained with Ṣāliḥ the night he went into hiding included, from among the senior army commanders, the said Ṭughtā b. al-Ṣayghūn, Ṭalmajūr who was al-Muʾayyad's associate, Muḥammad b. Turksh, Khamūsh, and al-Nūshurī, while from among the ranking secretaries there were Abū Ṣāliḥ ʿAbdallāh b. Muḥammad b. Yazdād, ʿAbdallāh b. Manṣūr, and Abū al-Faraj.[255]

On the Wednesday morning, which was the 13th of al-Muḥarram (December 21, 869), Ṣāliḥ had already gone into hiding, while Abū Ṣāliḥ made for the palace of Yājūr. ʿAbdallāh b. Manṣūr arrived there too with Sulaymān b. Wahb,[256] who disclosed to those present that he had drafts for five thousand dinars, which Ṣāliḥ had wanted him to handle. He refused to do so until the whole affair [concerning Ṣā- [1791]

252. On the interchangeability of these terms, see the discussion by Ayalon, "Preliminary Remarks," especially 51.

253. Bukhtīshūʿ was the name of a famous Christian family, originally from Jundaysābūr, which supplied a number of physicians to the caliphs throughout the third/ninth century. Bukhtīshūʿ b. Jibrīl died in exile in Baḥrayn in the year 256/870. His connection with Ṣāliḥ's forces is, however, unclear. On the family, see *EI*,[2] s.v. "Bukhtīshūʿ."

254. The reading is conjectural.

255. Abū al-Faraj was the son of Najāḥ b. Salamah, who had been in charge of the government department of the seal (*tawqīʿ*), with control as well over the fiscal prefects during the reign of al-Mutawakkil. In 245/858 both father and son were arrested and Najāḥ put to death; the property of both men was confiscated. See Ṭabarī, III, 1440–43; Sourdel, *Vizirat*, I, 262–63, II, 733–34.

256. See Sourdel, *Vizirat*, II, 300–2. A former secretary of Mūsā b. Bughā, he was at this time al-Muhtadī's vizier.

liḥ and Mūsā] was settled. On this same day, Kanjūr was given a robe of honor[257] and entrusted with searching Ṣāliḥ's palace. Yājūr, Mūsā's associate, brought al-Ḥasan b. Makhlad from the palace of Ṣāliḥ, where he had been imprisoned.

On the same day of the month, Sulaymān b. ʿAbdallāh b. Ṭāhir was made governor of Madīnat al-Salām and the Sawād. Robes of honor were sent to him, more indeed than had been bestowed upon ʿUbaydallāh b. ʿAbdallāh b. Ṭāhir.[258]

This same day as well al-Muhtadī was returned to al-Jawsaq, while ʿAbdallāh b. Muḥammad b. Yazdād was sent to al-Ḥasan b. Makhlad.[259]

A public proclamation was issued against Ṣāliḥ b. Waṣīf, and on the 22nd of Ṣafar (January 29, 870) he was killed.

An Account of Ṣāliḥ's Discovery in Hiding and His Death

The cause of this was as follows. On Wednesday, the 27th of al-Muḥarram of the year 256 (January 4, 870), al-Muhtadī publicly disclosed the contents of a letter. He said that Sīmā al-Sharābī claimed a woman had brought it from somewhere near al-Qaṣr al-Aḥmar and given it to Kāfūr, a eunuch (*khādim*)[260] in charge of the harem. She had told him that it contained some valuable information and mentioned also where she lived, should anyone wish to make contact with her. The letter was then delivered to al-Muhtadī. When in fact it became expedient to question the woman about the letter, she was
[1792] not to be found at the address she had given, and no one had any news about her.

It was reported that al-Muhtadī himself had discovered the letter but did not know who was responsible for delivering it.

Al-Muhtadī then summoned Sulaymān b. Wahb to attend him,

---

257. *Khilʿah.* This was generally not a single item of clothing but a variety of fine garments; see n. 447, below. See also *EI*,² s.v. "Khilʿa."

258. See p. 14 and n. 52, above. Here Sulaymān is officially awarded the position his brother had passed on to him.

259. Although Ṭabarī does not say so, the implicit sense here is that Ibn Yazdād was given permission to deal with al-Ḥasan b. Makhlad as he wished.

260. On this class of servant, see D. Ayalon, "On the Eunuchs in Islam," also *EI*,² s.vv. "Khādim," "Khaṣī."

along with a group of the *mawlas*, among whom were Mūsā b. Bughā, Mufliḥ, Bāyakbāk, Yājūr, Bakālabā, and others. He showed the letter to Sulaymān and asked him if he recognized the handwriting. Sulaymān replied that it was the hand of Ṣāliḥ b. Waṣīf, whereupon al-Muhtadī ordered Sulaymān to read the letter to the assembled company.

Ṣāliḥ stated in it that he had gone to ground in Sāmarrā. He had done so preferring safety for himself but also to spare the *mawlas* and in fear that skirmishes between them might erupt into full-scale hostilities. His intention was that everyone should sleep on the matter, so that whatever happened would be after reflection upon what he had set out in his letter. Ṣāliḥ went on to detail what he had seized of the secretaries' property. He said that al-Ḥasan b. Makhlad had that information, and he was one of the secretaries still in their custody. Next he noted who had delivered money to him and to whom he had entrusted its distribution. He remarked upon the affair of Qabīḥah and indicated that information on that was possessed by Abū Ṣāliḥ b. Yazdād and Ṣāliḥ al-ʿAṭṭār. Among other matters that he touched upon Ṣāliḥ attempted to justify his behavior for certain actions, while apologizing for others. In any event, his words expressed the strength of his feelings.

When Sulaymān had finished reading the letter, al-Muhtadī followed by urging upon the company reconciliation, harmony, and agreement, as he sought to stimulate an aversion for dissension, mutual hatred, and destruction. This only caused them to suspect that al-Muhtadī knew of Ṣāliḥ's whereabouts and that he might deliver them into [Ṣāliḥ's] hands. This suspicion created much discussion [1793]
among them and lengthy examination of the matter. On Thursday morning, the 28th of al-Muḥarram 256 (January 5th, 870), the Turkish commanders went together to the residence of Mūsā b. Bughā inside the Jawsaq compound, muttering and discussing matters among themselves. News of this reached al-Muhtadī.

Aḥmad b. Khāqān al-Wāthiqī reported that he had been the one to bring this news to al-Muhtadī's attention. He said that he had heard someone present at the meeting of commanders say, "The troops are unanimous in their decision to depose this man." Aḥmad continued: "I went to his brother Ibrāhīm (al-Muwaffaq) and informed him of developments, and he in turn passed on the information from me to al-Muhtadī. I nevertheless feared that the Commander of the Faithful might hasten to inform the Turks about me; but God granted me security."

Aḥmad reported further that the brother of Bāyakbāk addressed the assembly[261] once they had disclosed to him the course of action they had decided upon. He said: "You have slain the son of al-Mutawakkil, who was handsome, generous, and kind, and now you want to murder this man, who is a good Muslim who fasts, does not drink forbidden wine (*nabīdh*), and had done no wrong. By God, if you do kill him, then I shall take off for Khurāsān and spread notice of this whole affair of yours far and wide."

When news of this meeting reached al-Muhtadī, he entered his audience chamber girt with sword, dressed in clean robes, and perfumed. He then summoned the Turks into his presence, but for a while they refused. When finally they stood before him he said to them, "I have heard what you intend to do with me. I am not like my predecessors, such as Aḥmad b. Muḥammad al-Mustaʿīn, or even like the son of Qabīḥah. By God, I have not come to confront you without being prepared to die. I have already entrusted my brother
[1794] with my son to succeed me. This is my sword, and by God I shall fight with it so long as I can hold onto it. And by God, if one hair of my head is touched, the lot of you shall surely perish. Have you no religion? Have you no shame? Have you no piety? How long will this dissension against the caliphs, this boldness and effrontery against God, go on? It is all the same to you whether one wants to spare you or, hearing such a tale as this about you, calls for gallons of drink to celebrate joyously your misfortune and rejoices in your ruin! Tell me from what you yourselves know: Are you aware of any of this wealth of yours that has reached me? You, O Bāyakbāk, don't you realize that just one of your company is more fortunate than all of my own family? If you really want to know, just take a look! Will you see in any of their residences furniture, servants, and slaves or whether they possess estates and revenues (*ghallāt*)?[262] Fie on you! And now

261. This meeting, according to Ibn al-Athīr (*Kāmil*, VII, 219), took place in the apartment of Mūsā b. Bughā, which was located in the Jawsaq palace. Ibn al-Athīr, however, puts the words into the mouth of Bābakiyāl, rather than Bāyakbāk's brother.

262. The word *ghallah* (pl. *ghallāt*) means the produce, revenue, or income from a wide variety of sources: produce of the land or income from its rent, rental of a house, or hire of a slave. See Lane, *Lexicon*, s.v. "*gh-l-l*."

you come and say that I know what Ṣāliḥ is up to! Is he not just another *mawlā* like yourselves? How then would I put up with him, if you all think ill of him? If you should choose to make peace, that is what I heartily desire for all of you. But, if you persist in pursuing this course, that is your business.[263] Seek out Ṣāliḥ, and satisfy your blood lust! But, as for myself, I have no knowledge of his whereabouts."

They demanded that he swear an oath upon that, to which al-Muhtadī replied, "I will give you my right hand on it, but I shall postpone doing so until tomorrow when I perform the Friday prayers in the presence of the Hāshimites, religious judges, conciliators, and other men of rank."

The Turks seemed to relent a little at this. Al-Muhtadī sent for the Hāshimites, and they arrived in the evening. When al-Muhtadī gave them permission to enter and greetings were exchanged, he made no mention to them of these matters and simply ordered them to be at the palace for the Friday prayers, and they departed. The next morning, Friday, they (the Turks) had made no move. Al-Muhtadī performed his prayers; everyone was calm and departed in peace. [1795]

Someone who had overheard the quarrel on Wednesday reportedly said that, when Ṣāliḥ had been denounced as a traitor, al-Muhtadī had observed that Bāyakbāk had also been around when Ṣāliḥ was embroiled in the affair of the secretaries and the wealth of Qabīḥah's son (al-Muʿtazz). Thus, if Ṣāliḥ had gained anything from the business, Bāyakbāk must have profited as well. This remark infuriated Bāyakbāk.

Someone else who had heard this remark reported that al-Muhtadī had also observed that Muḥammad b. Bughā, too, had been around and was fully cognizant of what had happened and indeed had participated in the whole affair. This gibe provoked Abū Naṣr (Muḥammad b. Bughā's) anger.

It has been said that for a long time[264] the Turkish commanders held their counsel about the insult implicit [in al-Muhtadī's words] but that in their hearts they harbored rancor against him, though they were prevented from doing anything from fear of disorder and the lack of financial resources. When, however, the revenue arrived

263. That is, "I won't try to stop you."
264. Literally, from the time of the age of Moses.

from Fārs and al-Ahwāz on Wednesday, the 27th of al-Muḥarram (January 4, 870), they were roused to action. The total amount of these revenues was 17.5 million dirhams.

On Saturday, news spread among the populace that the army was about to depose and murder al-Muhtadī, an end they sought by provoking him to anger. They had leaflets written and distributed in the congregation mosque and in the streets. Someone who claimed to have read one said it contained, in part, the following words:

> In the name of God the Compassionate, the Merciful. O community of Muslims! Pray to God for your Caliph, the just, the favored, the second ʿUmar b. al-Khaṭṭāb. Pray that God grant him victory over his enemies, that He spare him the trouble of [enduring] his oppressor, and that He fill him
> [1796] and this community with bounty by extending his life. The *mawlā*s have been urging al-Muhtadī to abdicate, and for some days he has been submitted to torture. Those conducting this campaign are Aḥmad b. Muḥammad b. Thawābah and al-Ḥasan b. Makhlad. May God show mercy upon those with pure intentions and pray for Muḥammad (may the peace and blessings of God be upon him).

On Wednesday, the 4th of Ṣafar of this year (January 11, 870), the *mawlā*s in al-Karkh and al-Dūr[265] became agitated. They despatched a spokesman, ʿĪsā, to tell al-Muhtadī that they needed to discuss certain matters with him. They requested that the Commander of the Faithful send one of his brothers to them. So al-Muhtadī sent his oldest brother, Abū al-Qāsim ʿAbdallāh, along with Muḥammad b. Mubāshir al-Karkhī, and they set out to inquire what was troubling the *mawlā*s. First, the *mawlā*s professed their obedience and loyalty to the Commander of the Faithful. They had heard that Mūsā b. Bughā, Bāyakbāk, and a number of their commanders were seeking to depose al-Muhtadī. While they would freely sacrifice their lives, they would not do so for that.

The *mawlā*s continued, saying that they had read the leaflets distributed in the main mosque and in the streets. In this regard they complained of their straitened circumstances, the delay [in the pay-

265. Another settlement for the Turkish soldiery, lying farther to the north of al-Karkh. See Le Strange, *Lands*, 52.

ment of their] allotments, and the damage done to estates and the land tax as a result of the commanders' acquisition of fiefs (*iqṭā'*).[266] Moreover, most of the revenue from the land tax had been swallowed up by their chiefs and their bonuses and extras from previously established practices, as well as allotments for women and other interlopers.[267] They talked at length in this vein. Abū al-Qāsim ʿAbdallāh b. al-Wāthiq finally said to them, "Write all this down in a letter to the Commander of the Faithful, and I will ensure that it is delivered to him on your behalf." So a letter was drafted. The secretary [1797] responsible for writing it was Muḥammad b. Thaqīf al-Aswad, who acted as a secretary for ʿĪsā, on occasion master of al-Karkh.

Abū al-Qāsim and Muḥammad b. Mubāshir left and delivered the letter of al-Muhtadī, who replied in his own hand, sealing the letter with his own seal. On the following morning Abū al-Qāsim went to al-Karkh, where he met the *mawlās*. They went together to the palace of Ushnās, which had been turned into a congregational mosque for them. In the public square they halted, the assembled *mawlās* comprising some one hundred fifty cavalry and about five hundred infantry. Abū al-Qāsim read out Muhtadī's greetings to them, saying, "The Commander of the Faithful says that this is his personal letter to you, written and sealed by himself, so listen to it, and weigh carefully what it says." Abū al-Qāsim then handed the epistle to their secretary, who read it out:

> In the name of God, the Merciful, the Compassionate. Praised be God, and His manifold blessings be upon Muḥammad the Prophet and his family. May God guide us and you rightly, and be to us and to you both friend and protector. I have taken note of your message and rejoice in your expression of loyalty and obedience. May God reward you and protect you well. It distresses me greatly to hear of your misery and your needs. By God, would that I could arrange for your welfare by eating and feeding my children and household only the necessary minimum amount of food and clothing my children only in what suffices to hide their modesty. But

266. See *EI*,[2] s.v. "Iqṭāʿ."

267. The system of military payments was open to abuse by the commanders' inclusion in the registers of persons not entitled to such stipends. The formal military reviews were occasions intended to weed out such interlopers (*al-dukhalā*), although this did not always work in practice. See Bosworth, "Recruitment," especially 71.

no, by God! May He protect you! Since I accepted rule over you, I have had only fifteen thousand dinars for my own needs and those of my household, children, servants, and retinue. You have access to what [amounts] have arrived and shall arrive, and everything has been disbursed to you with
[1798] nothing held back. As for what you mention hearing and reading about in the leaflets distributed in the mosques and streets and about your unstinting service, this is indeed worthy of you. So why apologize for bringing the matter up? We and you are as one. May God compensate you well for your pledges and your fidelity. But the situation is not as you have heard; knowing this, act accordingly, God willing. As for what you mention about fiefs, bonuses, and other matters, I shall examine these questions and, God willing, shall earn your affection in doing so. Peace be upon you. May God rightly guide us and you, and be protector to us both. Praised be God, Lord of the worlds. Manifold blessings be upon Muḥammad the Prophet and his family.

When the man who was reading the letter reached the point where al-Muhtadī had said that he had only received a sum of fifteen thousand dinars, Abū al-Qāsim motioned to the man, and he stopped. And then he (Abū al-Qāsim) said, "What is this [paltry sum]? During his reign, the Commander of the Faithful has deserved more than this amount for a shorter period for [expenditure] on his allotments, provisions, and assistance. Surely you know what previous caliphs have spent on gifts for effeminates, singers, musicians, building villas and such like! So pray to God for the Commander of the Faithful!"

The man resumed reading the letter, and when he had finished there was much discussion. Then the *mawlās* made a statement of their own. Abū al-Qāsim replied, advising them to express their views in a letter, commencing it in the customary manner of correspondence to caliphs and addressing it from "the commanders, their deputies, and chiefs[268] in al-Karkh, al-Dūr and Sāmarrā."

They did so, first praying to God for the Commander of the Faithful. Then they requested the following: that all matters pertaining

268. *Al-quwwād wa-khulafā'ihim wa-al-ʿurafā'*. For the use of these ranks, see p. 79, below.

to rank, both high and low, be referred back to the Commander of the Faithful without interference from anyone else; that arrangements of military administration revert to what they had been in the days [1799] of al-Mustaʿīn, namely, that every nine men be under a chief,[269] every fifty men under a deptuy (*khalīfah*), and every hundred men under a commander (*qāʾid*); that women, extras, and bonuses be excised from the register; that a *mawlā* not be included as part of a *qabālah* contract[270] or any other; that they be paid regularly every two months; that the practice of granting the fiefs be discontinued; and, finally, that the Commander of the Faithful be able to increase [the pay] of whomsoever he wished and promote whom he liked.

The *mawlā*s added that immediately following their letter they were going to proceed to the residence of the Commander of the Faithful and remain there until their needs were met. Moreover, if they heard of anyone interfering with him concerning these matters, they would have his head. If anyone touched a hair of the Commander of the Faithful's head, they would kill Mūsā b. Bughā, Bāyakbāk, Mufliḥ, Yājūr, Bakālabā, and others. And with that they prayed to God for the Commander of the Faithful.

They gave the letter to Abū al-Qāsim and he departed and delivered it. In Sāmarrā the *mawlā*s became unsettled and the commanders very disturbed. Al-Muhtadī had already taken his seat in the court of appeal, and the jurists and judges were allowed to enter and take theirs. The commanders stood according to their ranks while Abū al-Qāsim entered ahead of the plaintiffs. Al-Muhtadī read the letter and withdrew with Mūsā b. Bughā. The caliph next ordered Sulaymān b. Wahb to endorse their copy of the letter, approving what they had requested. When Sulaymān had done this in a paragraph or two, Abū al-Qāsim said, "O Commander of the Faithful,

269. *ʿĀrif*. As a term applied to certain military and civilian offices, see *EI*,[2] s.v. "ʿĀrif."

270. On the nature of the juridical term "guarantee" as used in the practice of fiscal contracts, see *EI*,[2] s.v. "Ḳabāla"; Sourdel, *Vizirat*, II, 585–86. Military commanders sought such contracts in anticipation of benefits accruing from speculation on the differential between the sum contracted by a guarantor with the central treasury and the amount the guarantor was actually able to collect from taxes levied on the harvest. Here the intention seems to be a limitation of the abuse of the system by exclusion of *mawlā*s as guarantors. Ibn al-Athīr, *Kāmil*, VII, 222, however, has *lā yudkhal mawlā fī mālihi*, which suggests that *mawlā*s were not to be included as part of their commanders' property. Neither reading provides an entirely satisfactory understanding of the passage.

only your endorsement in your own hand will satisfy them." So al-Muhtadī took the paper and struck out what Sulaymān had written, endorsing each article of their requests with his approval, stating that each would be fulfilled. He then composed a separate commu-
[1800] nication in his own hand, sealing it himself, and gave it to Abū al-Qāsim. The latter spoke to Mūsā, Bāyakbāk, and Muḥammad b. Bughā, "Send messengers accompanying me to them, to plead your excuses before them concerning what has reached them about you." So each of them appointed a man to go along with Abū al-Qāsim. He found the *mawlā*s assembled in their usual places, numbering around a thousand cavalry and three thousand infantry. The time was noon on Thursday, the 5th of Ṣafar (January 12, 870) of this year.

He read to them greetings from the Commander of the Faithful, saying, "The Commander of the Faithful has responded to everything you have asked for. So pray to God for him." He handed the letter over to their secretary who first read out al-Muhtadī's endorsements, then read them the second letter from the caliph. It went as follows:

> In the name of God the Compassionate, the Merciful. Praised be God, He alone. God's blessings and peace be upon Muḥammad the Prophet and his family. May God guide you aright and protect you. May He give you plenty and restore your circumstances and through you and by means of you those of Muslims as well. I have taken note of your despatch and I also read it to your chiefs. They reported the same things as you have and have asked for the same things as you have. I have already consented to everything that you requested, out of love for your welfare and friendship, and to rally your support. I have ordered your allotments to be so stipulated that they will accrue to you on a regular basis; thus, there is no need for you to be unsettled. Be of good heart. Peace! and may God guide you aright and protect you; may He provide you with plenty and restore your circumstances and, through you and by means of you, those of Muslims as well.

When the man reading the letter had finished, Abū al-Qāsim said to them, "These men are messengers from your chiefs who have come to plead their excuses before you for what you may have heard about them. They say that your are all brothers and belong to each other." Then the messengers spoke along the same lines. The *mawlās* themselves engaged in lengthy discussion and at the end of it drafted a [further] communication to the Commander of the Faithful, setting forth in it the same kind of justification as they had in their first letter. They dissociated themselves from what they had [1801] asserted in the previous communication. Now, they would be satisfied with nothing less than the Caliph's endorsement of five points. These were to reduce the increases; the restoration of fiefs to their former conditions [of tenure]; the demotion of *mawlās* who were gatekeepers from the status of the "elite" to that of the lower-ranking palace guards (*barrāniyyīn*);[271] reversion to the military administrative practices of the days of al-Mustaʿīn; and, finally, restoration of *talājī* properties,[272] so they could be placed in control of someone to whom were attached fifty men from the troops of al-Dūr and fifty from Sāmarrā, all of which could be successfully carried out by the *dīwāns*. In addition, the Commander of the Faithful should turn over the army to one of his brothers, or someone else [of his choice] who could act as intermediary between them in their affairs; but this person should not be from among the ranks of the *mawlās*. Ṣāliḥ b. Waṣīf and Mūsā b. Bughā should each be held responsible for his wealth. Thus, nothing would content them short of having all the requests in their communications dealt with; this, as well as having their pay (*al-ʿaṭāʾ*) expedited, their regular pay (*arzāq*)[273] being made every two months. The *mawlās* also informed the Caliph that they had written to the troops of Sāmarrā and the Maghāribah troops to join them, and that they would be going to the res-

---

271. Ṭabarī, *Glossarium*, CXXX.

272. Dozy, *Supplément*, II, 524. These properties referred to ownership of land ceded to another person, who undertook to protect the original owner's right to work the land; see also Lane, *Lexicon*, s.v. *l-j-ʾ*, for a variant meaning.

273. The difference between the two terms for pay or stipend, as explained by Lane, seems to be founded upon the time between payments; whereas, for example, the *ʿaṭāʾ* could be an allowance paid once a year, the *rizq* (pl. *arzāq*) was paid more frequently, the period stipulated being two months. In both instances payment appears to have been made both in money and in provisions and equipment. See Lane, *Lexicon*, s.v. *ʿ-ṭ-w*. The word *ʿaṭāʾ*, which means "gift," was originally applied to pensions paid to Muslims and then became the term for troops' pay, where it could also be an ad hoc payment. See *EI*,[2] s.vv. "ʿAṭāʾ," "Djaysh."

idence of the Commander of the Faithful to seek fulfillment of their demands.

Their letter of demands was given to Abū al-Qāsim, the Caliph's brother. Meanwhile they wrote another to Mūsā b. Bughā, Bāyakbāk, Muḥammad b. Bughā, Mufliḥ, Yājūr, Bakālabā, and the other commanders, reporting their communication with the Caliph, and its contents.

[1802] They noted, moreover, that the Commander of the Faithful had accepted their request so long as the commanders did not interfere with his decisions; were the commanders in fact to do so and oppose the *mawlās*, then no agreement could be arranged with them on anything. The letter added that, if the Commander of the Faithful were wounded or if a hair of his head was disturbed, they the *mawlās* would have the heads of all of them. They would now only be satisfied with the reappearance of Ṣāliḥ b. Waṣīf who would, together with Mūsā b. Bughā, examine the matter of the whereabouts of the [disputed] wealth; for before he vanished Ṣāliḥ had promised to pay them their allotments (*arzāq*) for six months.

This letter was given to Mūsā's messenger, while the *mawlās* despatched several of their colleagues with Abū al-Qāsim to deliver the other letter to the Commander of the Faithful and to await his response.

When Abū al-Qāsim returned, Mūsā sent some five hundred horsemen to stand by the al-Ḥayr Gate situated between al-Jawsaq and al-Karkh. Abū al-Qāsim turned aside to them along with the soldiers' messengers and those of Mūsā's forces. Mūsā's messenger gave him the *mawlās*' letter intended for himself and his associates. Among this group were Sulaymān b. Wahb and his son, Aḥmad b. Muḥammad b. Thawābah, and some other secretaries. When Mūsā had read the letter to them, Abū al-Qāsim said that he bore another letter from the *mawlās*, this one of the Commander of the Faithful; he did not, however, disclose it to them. They then all rode off together to al-Muhtadī whom they found seated on a carpet in the sun, having just finished his prayers. In the palace he had destroyed every musical instrument and gadget of pleasure and amusement. Once the letters were delivered, he was left alone for a while. Later, he instructed Sulaymān b. Wahb to compose replies to the matters raised by the *mawlās* in five brief notes. Al-Muhtadī passed these on, enclosing them in a letter of him own, and gave [the roll] to his brother.

The commanders also composed a reply to the *mawlās* and gave it [1803]
to Mūsā's associate. By sunset Abū al-Qāsim had returned to the Turks with al-Muhtadī's greetings and he read out to them the Caliph's letter:

> In the name of God the Compassionate, the Merciful. May God find us worthy to obey and please Him. I have noted your letter, May God protect you. I have sent to you the five endorsements meeting the terms that you stipulated. So now delegate agents to those in the government bureaus who will successfully execute the promises, God willing. As for your request to turn your affairs over to one of my brothers so that your news may be brought to my attention and your needs conveyed to me, by God I would have been content to review these matters personally, and observe every matter that concerns your welfare. However, I shall, God willing, select for you one of my brothers or someone else suitable, as you have asked for. But do keep me informed as to your needs and also what you deem appropriate for yourselves, and I shall do what I can to meet your wishes. God willing. May God find us worthy to obey and please Him.

Then Mūsā's messenger delivered the epistle from Mūsā and his colleagues. In it he said:

> In the name of God, the Compassionate, the Merciful. May God preserve and keep you, and perfect His bounty upon you. We have noted your letter. You are brothers to us and our cousins, and we are set upon meeting what you desire. The Commander of the Faithful, may God strengthen him, has ordered your wishes in all that you seek to be dealt with, and he has sent the endorsements concerning them to you. As for the matter you mention concerning Ṣāliḥ, the *mawlā* of the Commander of the Faithful, and our change of attitude toward him, [be assured that he is to us] as a brother and cousin, and we did not seek anything on this matter that you would find objectionable. If he had promised you six
> months payment of allotments, then [know] that we have [1804]
> raised the matter in messages to the Commander of the

> Faithful seeking the very terms that you have requested. As for what you have stated regarding not obstructing the Commander of the Faithful, leaving him with full authority to govern, we ourselves are obedient and loyal to the Commander of the Faithful. Sovereign power is God's alone; He is our Master and we His slaves, and we are in no way recalcitrant toward Him in the governance of affairs. You state that we wish the Commander of the Faithful misfortune. May God surround whoever wishes that with a ring of misfortune and humiliate him in both this world and the hereafter. May God preserve and keep you and perfect his bounty upon you.

When Abū al-Qāsim had read these letters to the Turks, they said to him that, as it was evening, they would consider their situation during the night and return to him in the morning with their decision. At which point they split up and Abū al-Qāsim returned to the Commander of the Faithful.

The following day was Friday. Mūsā b. Bughā rode out in the early morning from the palace of the Commander of the Faithful accompanied by one thousand five hundred troops. He camped outside the al-Ḥayr Gate, which was adjacent to the fiefs of al-Jawsaq and al-Karkh. Al-Muhtadī's brother, Abū al-Qāsim left with al-Karkhī,[274] reaching the assembled Turks, who numbered around five hundred horsemen and three thousand foot soldiers.

Now when Abū al-Qāsim had gone the previous night to address the Turks, he had with him the Caliph's endorsements. Upon arriving, he extracted a message from al-Muhtadī, the copy of which resembled the letter containing the endorsements rolled inside it. So when Abū al-Qāsim read the message, his audience went into an uproar of conflicting views. The crowd increased with numbers of *mawlā* infantry from around the district of Sāmarrā joining them in al-Ḥayr.

Abū al-Qāsim kept waiting, expecting to go off with a response
[1805] that he could write up and then convey to the Commander of the Faithful. Nothing had happened, however, by four o'clock. They then broke up. One group said they wished that God would

274. This is Muḥammad b. Mubāshir al-Karkhī, mentioned p. 76, above.

strengthen the resolve of the Commander of the Faithful to provide the full amount of the allotments owed them, as they had suffered great hardship because of the delays. Another faction stated that they would not be content until the Commander of the Faithful appointed his brothers over them, one in al-Karkh, another in al-Dūr, and a third in Sāmarrā; they did not want any of the *mawlās* to govern them. A third party stated that they wanted Ṣāliḥ b. Waṣīf to reappear. They were the smallest party of the three.

As the debate dragged on, Abū al-Qāsim left for al-Muhtadī with all the news, first picking up Mūsā where he had camped and setting off with him. After completing his Friday prayer, al-Muhtadī transfered the army to Muḥammad b. Bughā, with orders to go with his brother Abū al-Qāsim to the *mawlās*; they rode out with about five hundred cavalry. Mūsā meanwhile returned to the camp he had set up that morning. Abū al-Qāsim and Muḥammad b. Bughā reached the *mawlās* and mingled with them in their midst. Abū al-Qāsim spoke to them, saying that the Commander of the Faithful had issued documents endorsing everything they had asked for. There now remained none of their requests that the Commander of the Faithful had not gone all out to fulfill. In addition, a safe-conduct was issued for Ṣāliḥ b. Waṣīf to come out of hiding. Abū al-Qāsim then announced the safe-conduct for Ṣāliḥ, which Mūsā and Bāyakbāk had sought from the Commander of the Faithful, who had responded to [1806]
them with his firmest assurances.

Abū al-Qāsim then asked, "What are you agreed upon?" Discussion intensified and when Abū al-Qāsim departed, the agreed-upon demands were stated by them as follows: Mūsā should hold the same rank of Bughā the elder; Ṣāliḥ should hold the rank that Waṣīf (his father) had held in the days of Bughā (the Elder); and Bāyakbāk should be restored to his previous rank. Moreover, the army should remain in its present hands until Ṣāliḥ b. Waṣīf emerged from hiding. And finally, an allowance (*ʿaṭāʾ*) should be assigned to them, as well as their periodic allotments (*arzāq*)[275] expedited according to the Caliph's agreement. To these points they all assented. The *mawlās* departed but had scarcely gone a hundred fifty cubits' distance before they were quarreling again, some saying they were satisfied, others claiming they were not. Al-Muhtadī's messengers de-

275. Ibn al-Athīr, *Kāmil*, VII, 224, mentions only the allowance (*al-ʿaṭāʾ*).

parted to him, as the soldiers had split up and were about to depart [for Sāmarrā]. Mūsā at that point returned as well, and the troops dispersed to their usual places in al-Karkh, al-Dūr, and Sāmarrā.

The next morning was Saturday. The Waṣīf clan along with a group of their freedmen (*mawlās* and *ghilmān*) rode forth calling out, "Arms!" Foot soldiers belonging to Ṣāliḥ b. Waṣīf's troops stole pack animals of the public infantry and proceeded to camp in Sāmarrā at the edge of the river valley of Isḥāq b. Ibrāhīm beside the mosque of Lujayn, the mother of al-Mutawakkil's children. Abū al-Qāsim had set out at the same time heading for al-Muhtadī's palace. On his way to al-Muhtadī's palace he passed Ṣāliḥ's forces; they joined him, his accompanying retinue, and pages and asked Abū al-Qāsim if he would take a message from them to the Commander of the Faithful. He told them to state their message but their response was such a confused babble that all he understood was that they wanted Ṣāliḥ [to return]. And so this was what he passed on to the Commander of the Faithful as well as to Mūsā in the presence of a group of commanders.

[1807] It was reported from someone present at this assembly that Mūsā b. Bughā said, "They demand that I give up Ṣāliḥ as though he were with me and I were the one who had hidden him away! If they have him, they should bring him forth!"

News of the gathering of the Waṣīf clan was confirmed and also that [Mūsā and his troops] broke out from the palace of the Commander of the Faithful and rode fully armed into the quarter of al-Ḥayr, assembling finally in the area between al-Dakkā and the rear of the main mosque. News [of this] reached the Turks and those who had taken refuge with them, and they ran helter-skelter, horseman, foot soldier, young, and old, none waiting for the other, until they reached the narrow streets and alleyways and the safety of their homes. Mūsā and his troops marched forward in a body toward the Caliph's palace, every commander in Sāmarrā riding with him. Proceeding steadily through the quarter, they left where the two city walls adjoined it. Mufliḥ and Wājin[276] and those attached to them went along Baghdad street until they reached the sheep market; they then turned into Abū Aḥmad street, where they met up with Mūsā's army. Mūsā and the commanders accompanying him, including Yā-

276. The reading is uncertain.

jūr, Sātikīn, Yārjūkh, and ʿĪsā al-Karkhī, headed along Abū Aḥmad street as far as the river and then made their way toward the Jawsaq palace. The estimated size of Mūsā's army that day, which was Saturday, was four thousand horsemen armed with bows at the ready, breastplates,[277] spears, and battle-axes[278]. Most of the commanders who in al-Karkh had demanded Ṣāliḥ were now with Mūsā's army, prepared to take on anyone else who demanded him.

Someone who had inquired into these events reported that most [1808] of those riding with Mūsā were sympathetic toward Ṣāliḥ. There was no commotion that day among the troops of al-Karkh or al-Dūr. The first thing the troops did upon arriving at the Jawsaq palace was to issue a proclamation to the following effect: Anyone on the following morning, which was Sunday, from among all of Ṣāliḥ's commanders, his family, servants, and supporters who had not presented himself at the palace of the Commander of the Faithful would have his name dropped from the payroll and his house destroyed; and he would be flogged and led in chains to the Maṭbaq [prison].[279] Whoever emerged after having been in hiding after three days would be liable to the same punishment. Whoever stole an animal from a civilian or molested such a one in the public way would likewise be liable to a painful punishment. Mūsā and his company spent Sunday night, the 8th of Ṣafar (January 15, 870) still pursuing this matter.

On Monday morning al-Muhtadī received intelligence that the rebel Musāwir had been committing murder in and setting fire to Balad.[280] In his council meeting, al-Muhtadī proclaimed a call to arms and ordered Mūsā, Mufliḥ, and Bāyakbāk to leave [for Balad]. Mūsā evacuated his camp, but on Wednesday, the 11th of Ṣafar (January 18, 870), the order to Mūsā, Muḥammad b. Bughā, and Mufliḥ was canceled. They said, "We should all stay until our business and Ṣāliḥ's is settled." On that they were all agreed, fearing that Ṣāliḥ would cause them mischief in their absence.

---

277. *Al-jawāshin* (sg. *jawshan*). See Lane, *Lexicon*, s.v. *j-w-sh-n*.

278. *Al-ṭabarzīnāt*, an Arabized word from the Persian *ṭabarzad*. See Lane, *Lexicon*, s.v. *ṭ-b-r-z-d/l-/n*.

279. The *Index* does not list a place by this name in Sāmarrā, though the context clearly indicates that this city is intended. The duplication of Baghdad place names in Sāmarrā was perhaps not uncommon (e.g., al-Karkh).

280. A town on the road from Mosul to Naṣībīn, some seven leagues from the former. See Le Strange, *Lands*, 99.

One of the *mawlās* reportedly said, "I saw one of the Waṣīf clan who had got together soldiers who were playing polo[281] with Mūsā and Bāyakbāk in the hippodrome of Bughā the Younger, on Wednesday the 11th of Ṣafar [January 18, 870]."

The search for Ṣāliḥ b. Waṣīf was intensified and for this reason raids were made upon many of those who had formerly been connected with him or else were suspected of giving him refuge.
[1809] Among these were Ibrāhīm b. Saʿdān al-Naḥwī, Ibrāhīm al-Ṭālibī, Hārūn b. ʿAbd al-Raḥmān b. al-Azhar al-Shīʿī, Abū al-Aḥwaṣ b. Aḥmad b. Saʿīd b. Salm b. Qutaybah, Abū Bakr, an in-law of Abū Harmalah al-Ḥajjām, Shāriyah the singer, al-Sarakhsī, chief of the special security police, and many others.

Ibrāhīm b. Muḥammad b. Ibrāhīm b. Muṣʿab b. Zurayq reported that the owner of the Rabʿ al-Qubbah, which was opposite the palace of Ṣāliḥ b. Waṣīf, had related to him, saying, "On Sunday while we were sitting around, a slave boy suddenly emerged from a small alleyway and I could see that he was very frightened. We did not know him and wanted to ask him what the matter was, but he vanished. Moments later a *mawlā* of Ṣāliḥ b. Waṣīf arrived, a ruffian (*ʿayyār*)[282] called Rūzbah; he was with three or four others whom we also did not know, and they disappeared into the alleyway. Shortly after, they reemerged with Ṣāliḥ b. Waṣīf and we then asked what was going on. It seems that the slave boy had gone into a house in the alleyway wanting a drink of water, when he heard someone say in Persian, 'O commander, hide quickly, for a slave boy has come asking for a drink of water.' Now the lad had heard these words and, as he was acquainted with this ruffian (Rūzbah), he went and told him what had happened. The ruffian rounded up three other men and they captured Ṣāliḥ."

This same ruffian who had led the attack on Ṣāliḥ reportedly said, "This slave lad told me what he had heard, and when I arrived at the house with these three men, there was Ṣāliḥ with mirror and comb

---

281. The text reads *ṣawālijah*, which is the plural of *ṣawlajah*, Arabized from the Persian *chawgan*. Lane, *Lexicon*, s.v. *ṣ-w-l-j*, describes the *ṣawlajah* as a kind of golf stick, with which a ball is struck by men on horseback, an accurate enough description of the game of polo.

282. See *EI*,² s.v. "ʿAyyār"; cf. the lengthy study by C. Cahen, "Mouvements populaires et autonomisme urbain dans l'Asie musulmane du Moyen Âge," especially 25–56, 233–65.

in his hands attending to his beard. When he saw me, he ran into the house, and I was afraid he might be going for his sword or some [1810] weapon, and I held back. Then I cautiously spied upon him and discovered that he was huddled in a corner, so I approached and brought him out, and he did no more than implore me. When he did, I told him there was no way I could let him go; but I would take him past the residences of his family, his companions, his commanders, and hirelings, and if two of them were to meet me I would turn him over to them. However, I met no one on the way who was not eager to help me to abuse him."

It was reported that the two of them had gone a distance of some two miles accompanied by fewer than five government soldiers.

It was further reported that, when Ṣāliḥ was captured, he was wearing a shirt, a half-silk lined garment,[283] and drawers; his head was bare, and he walked barefoot.

Ṣāliḥ was borne away upon a mustard-colored pack animal, the crowd running behind him, while five special security men tried to prevent their attacking him. Having arrived with Ṣāliḥ at the palace of Mūsā b. Bughā, Bāyakbāk, Mufliḥ, Yājūr, Sātikīn, and other commanders joined them there. Ṣāliḥ was then taken, riding a saddled mule, through the Ḥayr Gate, which was next to the *qiblah*[284] side of the main mosque as they made their way to the Jawsaq palace. Just as they reached the edge of the minaret,[285] one of Mufliḥ's soldiers struck Ṣāliḥ a blow to the shoulder from behind, which nearly killed him. His head was then severed and the corpse left behind. At length they came to al-Muhtadī's palace a little before sunset. Ṣāliḥ's head, wrapped in a garment of one of Mufliḥ's pages, was dripping with [1811] blood. Al-Muhtadī was at that moment at prayer, and he did not see them bring in the head, which was then taken away to be cleaned up. After al-Muhtadī had finished his prayers, he was informed that they had killed Ṣāliḥ and brought his head to him. His only reaction was to say "Cover it up," and he began to repeat "Praise the Lord!"[286] The

283. *Mubaṭṭanah mulḥam*. See Lane, *Lexicon*, s.v. *b-ṭ-n*.

284. The *qiblah* is the direction the Muslim faces when performing the prayer, i.e., the direction of Mecca. See *EI*,² s.v. "Masdjid."

285. This could be the minaret (*al-minārah*) of the mosque, which Yāqūt says could be seen from the countryside for miles around. See *Muʿjam*, III, 17.

286. *Tasbīḥ*. The word also signifies the act of praying. Lane, *Lexicon*, s.v. *s-b-ḥ*, notes that it meant to perform the supererogatory morning prayer.

news reached Ṣāliḥ's residence, at which a wailing lament was raised and continued thoughout the night. On Monday the 22nd of Ṣafar (January 29, 870), the head of Ṣāliḥ b. Waṣīf was carried around town upon a lance, while proclamation was made: "This is the recompense for slaying one's master." It was hung up at the Public Gate for an hour and then removed, a practice followed for three successive days. The head of Bughā the Younger was removed at the same time as Ṣāliḥ's head was publicly displayed on the Monday.[287] Then it was given to Ṣāliḥ's family, and they buried it.

One of the *mawlās* reportedly said that he saw Mufliḥ crying when he had looked at Bughā's head, saying, "May God slay me if I do not avenge his death." On Thursday the 25th of Ṣafar (February 1, 870), Mūsā sent Ṣāliḥ's head to his sister Umm al-Faḍl, al-Nūshurī's wife, who had previously been married to Salamah b. Khāqān. One of the Hāshimites reportedly said, "I congratulated Mūsā b. Bughā for killing Ṣāliḥ, and he said, 'He was an enemy of the Commander of the Faithful and deserved to die.'" He also congratulated Bāyakbāk, who retorted, "I had nothing to do with this. Ṣāliḥ was my brother!"

Al-Salūlī recited these lines to Mūsā after Ṣāliḥ b. Waṣīf had been killed:

You have avenged yourself on the Pharaoh when he acted tyrannically.
    And you have come when you did, O Mūsā, as ordained.[288]
[1812] Three; each of them is an oppressor, a brother of envy,
    accusing you of oppression and aggression out of hate.
Waṣīf is in Karkh, of whom an example was made, and Bughā
    is at the bridge, burning in the embers and flames.
And Ṣāliḥ, son of Waṣīf, his body lies tossed in the dust
    in al-Ḥayr, and his soul is in hell.

On the 1st of Jumādā I of this year (Thursday, April 6, 870), Mūsā b. Bughā and Bāyakbāk set out against the Khārijite Musāwir. Muḥammad b. al-Wāthiq bade them farewell.

Also in this same month of Jumādā I (April 6–May 5, 870), Musāwir b. ʿAbd al-Ḥamīd and the Khārijite ʿUbaydah al-ʿUmrūsī met

287. Bughā's death had been reported by Ṭabarī earlier, in the year 254/868, and his head was publicly displayed first in Sāmarrā and then in Baghdad. See III, 1694–95.

288. Reference to Qur'ān 20: 40.

in battle at al-Kuḥayl. They each held opposing views.[289] In his victory Musāwir killed ʿUbaydah.

In this month of Jumādā I Musāwir and Mufliḥ met each other in battle. I was told that Musāwir returned from al-Kuḥayl after he had killed al-ʿUmrūsī, with many of his men wounded, whose injuries had not yet healed. Indeed the battle [against al-ʿUmrūsī] had left them exhausted by the time they reached Mūsā's army and those who had joined him. As Musāwir attacked, Mūsā was in a defensive position. Their encounter took place at Jabal Zaynī,[290] and, when the victory Musāwir sought did not occur, he and his troops held fast to the mountain side and made their way to the top. There they lit fires [1813]
and stuck their spears into the ground. Mūsā was camped farther down on the lower slopes of the mountain. Later Musāwir escaped by leading his troops down the far side of the mountain away from Mūsā's position and left them thinking that he was still on top.

On the 14th of Rajab of this year (June 17, 870), al-Muhtadī was deposed, and he died on the 18th (June 21, 870).

An Account of [al-Muhtadī's] Removal and Death

It was reported that on the 2nd of Rajab (June 5, 870) the dwellers of al-Karkh, Sāmarrā, and al-Dūr were aroused to demand their allotments. Al-Muhtadī sent their chief Ṭabāyaghū[291] and his own brother ʿAbdallāh to talk to them, but they were not well received; instead they insisted on talking directly to the Commander of the Faithful himself.

Abū Naṣr (Muḥammad) b. Bughā left that night for his brother's army camp, which was at al-Sinn in the vicinity of the Khārijite (Musāwir). Meanwhile, a group of soldiers went to the Jawsaq palace on Wednesday and al-Muhtadī spoke to them for some time. Their allowance was not forthcoming on Wednesday and Thursday, but they were prepared to refrain from any action until they knew what Mūsā b. Bughā was prepared to do. Now Mūsā had paid the allowance to his army for a month since his troops had been patient while

289. Ibn al-Athīr, *Kāmil*, VII, 226, explains that the feud was over whether or not a sinner's repentance can be accepted; Musāwir argued that it should be, while ʿUbaydah claimed it could not.

290. Ibn Ḥawqal, *Kitāb al-masālik wa-al-mamālik*, 110.

291. The reading is conjectural.

he was engaged in fighting (Musāwir) the Khārijite. But then disagreements broke out and Mūsā set off for the Khurāsān Road.

Explanations differed as to why these disagreements occurred,
[1814] why Mūsā left for the Khurāsān Road, and why al-Muhtadī had openly confronted certain Turks (*al-atrāk*) engaged in battle against him.

Some said that Mūsā had withdrawn from the conflict with the Khārijite (Musāwir) and had headed for the Khurāsān Road because al-Muhtadī was well disposed toward Bāyakbāk, who was still with Mūsā's army confronting Musāwir. The Caliph wrote to Bāyakbāk, ordering him to take command over Mūsā's army and either to dispose of Mūsā b. Bughā and Mufliḥ or else to bring them back in chains. When this despatch reached Bāyakbāk he took it to Mūsā b. Bughā and said, "I am not at all happy with this, as it appears to be only a plot against the lot of us. If you are treated this way today, then tomorrow I could be treated in the same manner. What do you think?" Mūsā replied, "In my view you should return to Sāmarrā and tell the Caliph that you will loyally assist him against Mufliḥ and myself. In this way he will feel at ease about you, and then we can plan to kill him." After returning from battle against the rebel they made for their homes, while Bāyakbāk went to see al-Muhtadī. Confronting him angrily, al-Muhtadī said, "I ordered you to kill Mūsā and Mufliḥ, so how could you leave the army and treat this matter so lightly?" Bāyakbāk asked how he could have dealt with them and managed to kill them when they had superior forces and were more powerful than he. Moreover, he said, "Once something or other happened between Mufliḥ and myself, and I did not avenge myself then; but I have in any case brought my army, companions, and those obedient to me to assist and reinforce your rule, and this has left Mūsā with fewer supporters." Al-Muhtadī said to him, "Lay down your weapons," and he ordered him brought into the palace.
[1815] Bāyakbāk replied, "O Commander of the Faithful, this is no way to treat me, as I have come to you in good faith; I must first return home and leave instructions for my companions and family." Al-Muhtadī refused to allow that, as it was essential to check Bāyakbāk's story. And so Bāyakbāk was relieved of his weapons.

When Bāyakbāk's companions had not heard from him for a while, his chamberlain Aḥmad b. Khāqān quickly urged them to search for their leader before something happened to him. Seething with anger, the Turks surrounded the Jawsaq palace. At the time al-Muhtadī was with Ṣāliḥ b. ʿAlī b. Yaʿqūb b. Abī Jaʿfar al-Manṣūr.[292] When he perceived these developments, al-Muhtadī asked him for advice on what he should do. Ṣāliḥ replied, "O Commander of the Faithful, none of your ancestors could match you for courage and daring. Abū Muslim's[293] hold over the Khurāsānīs was far more powerful than this Turk's position[294] among his followers. But no sooner had [Abū Muslim's] head been thrown to them than they quieted down, even though some of them worshiped him and regarded him as their lord. So if you were to do that, they would [similarly] be appeased; for you are much bolder and stouthearted than al-Manṣūr."

So al-Muhtadī summoned Muḥammad b. Mubāshir al-Karkhī, a blacksmith who had made tent pegs and poles in al-Karkh and then had become very devoted to al-Muhtadī in Baghdad, and the Caliph trusted him. Now he ordered him to kill Bāyakbāk, which deed was done while the Turks were lined up armed in the Jawsaq palace demanding to see Bāyakbāk. Al-Muhtadī gave the order to the commander ʿAttāb b. ʿAttāb to throw them Bāyakbāk's head. He did so and, after a brief delay, the Turks broke into a rage, and one of them attacked and killed ʿAttāb. Al-Muhtadī then sent for contingents of the Farāghinah, the Maghāribah, the Ūkashiyyah,[295] the Ushrūsaniyyah,[296] and Turks who had rendered allegiance to him for the sum of two dirhems and some barley meal (*sawīq*). After they arrived, many among their ranks were killed, about which people have had [1816]
many [different] things to say. It was said that some four thousand Turks who took part in the fighting were killed; others put the number at two thousand, while others said only a thousand. That was Saturday, the 13th of Rajab (June 16, 870).

On Sunday the numbers of Turks gathered together had swollen to some ten thousand men united by their common cause. The brother

292. A descendant of the second ʿAbbāsid Caliph, al-Manṣūr.

293. One of the leading commanders of the ʿAbbāsid revolt against the Umayyads in Khurāsān; his rising power was perceived as a threat to the new dynasty, and he was murdered by the Caliph al-Manṣūr. On his role and significance, see Shaban, *The ʿAbbāsid Revolution*, 153–68; *EI*,² s.v. "Abū Muslim."

294. That is, Bāyakbāk.

295. The reading is uncertain, a variant being al-Ubkasiyyah.

296. Troops drawn from the province of Ushrusānah, which lay to the east of Samarqand between the rivers of Sughd and the Jaxartes. See Le Strange, *Lands*, 474–76.

of Bāyakbāk, Ṭaghūtyā,[297] and Aḥmad b. Khāqān, Bāyakbāk's chamberlain, had arrived with around five hundred men, plus the Turks and Persians brought by Ṭaghūtyā. Al-Muhtadī went out with Ṣāliḥ b. ʿAlī, who was wearing a Qurʾān tied around his neck; he pleaded with people to come to the aid of their Caliph. But the final straw was when the Turks accompanying al-Muhtadī sided with their fellows who supported Bāyakbāk's brother. Al-Muhtadī was left with the Farāghinah and the Maghribah and some of the populace, who were of little use to him. Thirsting for vengence, Ṭaghūtyā, Kāyakbāk's brother, launched a bitter attack, broke up their battle order, and routed them. Large numbers were killed while the rest turned and fled. Al-Muhtadī, sword in hand, fled from the scene, crying out, "O you people, come to your Caliph's assistance!" He finally managed to reach the place of Abū Ṣāliḥ ʿAbdallāh b. Muḥammad b. Yazdād, which was located next to Khashabat Bābak. Aḥmad b. Jumayl, the commandant of police, was there. Al-Muhtadī entered
[1817] and, setting aside his weapon, he donned a [plain] white garment, in order to slip from the roof of one palace to another and make his escape. A search for him failed.

Then Aḥmad b. Khāqān arrived with thirty horsemen, making inquiries of al-Muhtadī's whereabouts and learned news of him at the palace of Ibn Jumayl. Aḥmad promptly rushed his men to the rooftops and al-Muhtadī was struck at last by an arrow and wounded by a sword. Aḥmad b. Khāqān had him carried on a pack horse, or mule, with a groom riding behind until they returned to the [Jawsaq] palace. His enemies gathered and began cuffing him and spitting in his face. They sought information as to the value of goods and furnishings he had sold, and al-Muhtadī confessed to a sum of six hundred thousand [dinars], which al-Karkhī had deposited for him with various people in Baghdad. They took his written pledge for that amount and then handed him over to someone who [tortured him] by kicking him in the testicles until he died.[298]

---

297. The reading is conjectural.

298. *Fa wuṭiyaʾ ʿalā khuṣyatihi ḥattā qatalahu.* Ibn al-Athīr adds that he was also struck by sword blows and that afterward his executioners bore witness that he had died without a mark on him. He was buried in the tomb of the Caliph al-Muntaṣir. *Kāmil,* VII, 230. See also Ṭabarī's account, p. 99, below.

Other Accounts of al-Muhtadī's Death

Someone else said that the beginning of the whole dispute occurred when the sons of the Turks met together and stated that they were not content to allow anyone to be their chief except the Commander of the Faithful. They wrote to Mūsā b. Bughā and Bāyakbāk to that effect, while the two were still engaged with the Khārijite (Musāwir). On Friday Mūsā arrived with his men at a bridge in the district of al-Wazīriyyah. Al-Muhtadī was camped with his army in al-Ḥayr; he approached them but then turned away and proceeded armed to the Jawsaq palace. On Saturday, the 13th of Rajab (June 16, 870), Bāyakbāk came [to al-Muhtadī] as an obedient subject, while Mūsā headed for the district of the Khurāsān Road with about two thousand men. One of the *mawlās* came to tell al-Muhtadī that Bāyakbāk had promised Mūsā he would assassinate him in the Jawsaq palace. Al-Muhtadī had Bāyakbāk disarmed and imprisoned. This [1818] was on Saturday, about the time of the afternoon prayer. Later the inhabitants of al-Karkh and al-Dūr went out in search of Bāyakbāk. The search was resumed the following morning, and everyone joined in either walking or riding, each one carrying a weapon. Al-Muhtadī had just finished the noon prayer when the crowd reached the Jawsaq palace. He confronted them with the Farāghinah and Maghāribah, but the Turks forced them back and then mounted a full attack upon them. Pursuing al-Muhtadī's forces, the Turks had laid a trap for them and many of the Farāghinah and Maghāribah were slain. Al-Muhtadī himself fled and as he passed the residence of Abū al-Wazīr, one of his servants shouted out, "O you people, here is your Caliph!"

With the Turks in hot pursuit behind him, al-Muhtadī managed to reach the palace of Aḥmad b. Jumayl and, by scaling the walls, he moved from one residence to another. The Turks spread throughout the entire district and finally trapped him in the house of a servant belonging to ʿAbdallāh b. ʿUmar al-Bāzyār. Wearing only a shirt and drawers and wounded in the side, he was taken away on an emaciated pack animal. The residences of [Muḥammad b. Mubāshir] al-Karkhī, the Banū Thawābah, and a number of others were sacked. On Monday Aḥmad b. al-Mutawakkil, who was known as Ibn Fityān, was brought to the palace of Yārjūkh, while the Turks circulated the streets praising the populace for not having opposed them.

Others said that the cause of these events was quite different. On Monday, the 2nd of Rajab (June 5, 870), the troops of Dūr Sāmarrā and al-Karkh became agitated and began to congregate in al-Karkh
[1819] and the area beyond it. Al-Muhtadī despatched to them Kayghalagh, Ṭabāyaghū b. Ṣūl Artakīn and his own brother ʿAbdallāh, who remained with them until the crowd calmed down, whereupon the men returned to the [Jawsaq] palace. Word reached Abū Naṣr Muḥammad b. Bughā the Elder that al-Muhtadī had been speaking to the *mawlās* about him and Mūsā, telling them that the [Bughā] brothers possessed money. This stirred fear in Abū Naṣr, and he fled on Tuesday night, the 3rd of Rajab (June 6, 870). Al-Muhtadī sent four letters to Abū Naṣr granting him safe conduct for himself and those with him. Two letters arrived while he was in al-Muḥammadiyyah[299] with Artakīn b. B.r.n.m. kātakīn[300] and the others while he was with Faraj the Younger. Abū Naṣr put his trust in the safe-conduct and returned to the [Jawsaq] palace, together with his other brother, Ḥabshūn, and Bakālabā. They were imprisoned along with Kayghalagh, Abū Naṣr being isolated from the others. Money was demanded of him and fifteen thousand dinars was received from his agent. On Tuesday, the 3rd of Rajab (June 6, 870), Abū Naṣr was put to death and his body tossed into a well of the underground canal system (*al-qanāt*). The corpse was removed on Monday, the 16th of Rajab (June 19, 870), and taken to his house. It reeked of decay. Three hundred *mithqāls*[301] of must and six hundred of camphor were purchased to apply to the body, but the odor could not be checked. Al-Ḥasan b. al-Ma'mūn said the funeral prayer over him.

Al-Muhtadī had corresponded with Mūsā b. Bughā at the time of Abū Naṣr's imprisonment and ordered Mūsā to surrender the army to Bāyakbāk and to bring his *mawlās* to Sāmarrā. He also wrote Bāyakbāk about delivering the army into his command and ordering
[1820] him to continue the fight against the Khārijite [Musāwir]. Bāyakbāk took the letter to Mūsā; he read it, and they then agreed to return to Sāmarrā. Word reached al-Muhtadī that they had disobeyed him. He

299. The place of that name in the marshlands (*baṭā'iḥ*) seems intended here.

300. The first part of the name is unpointed in the text, and therefore the first three consonants are conjectural.

301. For details of the variations in the use of this term of measurement, see Hinz, *Islamische Masse*, 1–2.

called the *mawlās* together, exhorting them to obedience, urging them to attend him in the palace and leave off neglecting him. For each of the Turks and those of similar status al-Muhtadī arranged a stipend of two dirhems per day to be paid, and a dirhem for each of the Maghāribah. From these two groups and their friends he rounded up some fifteen thousand men in the Jawsaq palace and other apartments. Among the Turks was a man called al-Kāmilī. In charge of administration of the palace after Kayghalagh had been imprisoned was Masrūr al-Balkhī; the chief commander was Ṭabāyaghū, and ʿAbdallāh b. Takīn was put in charge of prisoners.

Mūsā, Mufliḥ, and Bāyakbāk learned of the incarceration of Abū Naṣr, Ḥabshūn, and the others and were hence on their guard. On Thursday messengers and despatches flowed between them and al-Muhtadī. The same day, which was the 11th of Rajab (June 14, 870), al-Muhtadī ventured forth with his force to await the arrival of the enemy. No one, however, appeared. On the Friday, the 12th of Rajab (June 15, 870), news was confirmed that al-Muhtadī and Mufliḥ had turned off the Sāmarrā road toward the district of al-Jabal and halted there. On Saturday Bāyakbāk, Yārjūkh, Asātakīn, ʿAlī b. Bāris, Sīmā the Tall, and Khuṭārish presented themselves at the Jawsaq palace. Bāyakbāk and his deputy Aḥmad b. Khāqān were imprisoned, while the rest were dismissed. Bāyakbāk's followers and some of the other Turks met together and asked themselves why their commander had been imprisoned and why Abū Naṣr had been killed. Al-Muhtadī confronted them on Saturday, but, as no conflict [1821] occurred, he returned [once again] to the palace. On Sunday the two sides met again, al-Muhtadī with his force of Maghāribah, Turks of the lower-ranking guards,[302] and the Farāghinah. He placed Masrūr al-Balkhī on the right flank and Yārjūkh on the left, with himself, Asātakīn, Ṭabāyaghū, and some other commanders occupying the heart of the battle line.

As the day grew hotter, the combatants approached each other, and battle ensued. The men demanded Bāyakbāk, and al-Muhtadī threw his severed head into their midst. ʿAttāb b. ʿAttāb had pulled it out of his tunic. When they saw it, Bāyakbāk's brother Ṭaghūtyā and a group of his elite soldiers intensified the attack against al-Muhtadī's forces. The right flank turned, followed by the left, while the re-

302. *Al-atrāk al-barrāniyīn*. See n. 271, above.

mainder of the army fled from al-Muhtadī. There were many slain on the two sides.

Ḥabshūn b. Bughā reportedly said that seven hundred eighty men had been killed. The fighters dispersed and al-Muhtadī returned to the palace, locking behind him the gates through which he had entered and making his exit from the al-Maṣāff Gate, evenutally through the Iṭākh Gate into the little market of Masrūr and along al-Wāthiq street until he finally reached the Public Gate. There he cried out, "O you people, I am the Commander of the Faithful. Fight to defend your Caliph!" But none of the people heeded him. As he passed thus, crying out in the street but seeing no one prepared to help him, he reached the prison gate and ordered the release of all the inmates, thinking that they would come to his aid. Instead, they all fled. Not one responded to him.

After this al-Muhtadī made his way to the palace of Abū Ṣāliḥ
[1822] ʿAbdallāh b. Muḥammad b. Yazdād, where the commandant of police, Aḥmad b. Jumayl, was staying. They broke in on him, and he was taken out by way of the Bureau of Estates and taken to al-Jawsaq, where he was imprisoned along with Aḥmad b. Khāqān. Ibn Jumayl's palace was then plundered.[303]

Among the commanders of the Maghāribah who were killed during the battle was Naṣr b. Aḥmad al-Zubayrī, and of the commanders of the Shākiriyyah ʿAttāb b. ʿAttāb was killed bringing back Bāyakbāk's head. According to some al-Muhtadī killed a considerable number with his own hands in the course of the fighting.

Later, after al-Muhtadī was imprisoned, strong words were exchanged between him and his captors. They wanted him to abdicate but he refused, surrendering himself instead to death. They said that he had, in his own hand, made a written agreement with Mūsā b. Bughā, Bāyakbāk, and a number of the other commanders that he would neither deceive, harass, nor murder any of them, or even think of doing so, and, [if] he actually treated them in this manner, either collectively or individually, and they found out, they would be free to break their oath of allegiance to him, take charge of affairs, and depose whomsoever they pleased. On this basis they felt free to break their compact.

303. Which presumably explains why he was staying elsewhere at the time of al-Muhtadī's final hours.

After the rout of the Caliph's forces, Yārjūkh had gone to the [Jawsaq] palace and taken some of al-Mutawakkil's sons back to his own palace. There, on Tuesday[304] the 13th of Rajab (June 16, 870), the oath of allegiance was rendered to Aḥmad b. al-Mutawakkil, known as Ibn Fityān, who took the regnal name of al-Muʿtamid ʿalā Allāh. On Thursday,[305] the 18th of Rajab (June 21, 870), the death of Muḥammad b. al-Wāthiq al-Muhtadī was witnessed. The only marks [1823] on his body were the two wounds he had received on the Sunday during the fighting; one of these was an arrow wound, the other was sustained by a sword blow. Jaʿfar b. ʿAbd al-Wāḥid and a number of the Caliph's brothers recited prayers at his funeral. He was buried in the tomb of al-Muntaṣir. Mūsā b. Bughā and Mufliḥ entered Sāmarrā on Saturday, the 20th of Rajab (June 23, 870); Mūsā saluted al-Muʿtamid, who granted him a robe of honor. Mūsā returned to his residence, and calm settled upon the populace.

Someone who reportedly had witnessed these events said that on Saturday evening, the 1st of Rajab (June 4, 870), the whole population of al-Karkh and al-Dūr was stirred up and began to congregate. Whenever the people became agitated, al-Muhtadī would send his brother ʿAbdallāh to them, just as he did on this occasion. When ʿAbdallāh got there, he found them making their way to the Jawsaq palace. He addressed them and guaranteed them action to meet their needs. They, however, refused [this promise], insisting instead on returning with him to the Commander of the Faithful to plead their case with him directly. Now when ʿAbdallāh returned, there were present in the palace at that time Abū Naṣr Muḥammad b. Bughā, Ḥabshūn, Kayghalagh, Masrūr al-Balkhī, and others. ʿAbdallāh conveyed to al-Muhtadī what had transpired between him and the crowd, and he was ordered to go back and bring some of them to the palace. Encountering the crowd now quite near the Jawsaq palace, he directed them to stay where they were and send some of their number to accompany him. This they also rejected.

When the news of the crowd's approach reached Abū Naṣr and the others in the palace, they all left by way of the al-Nazālah Gate. No [1824] one was left in the palace except Masrūr al-Balkhī and Alṭūn, the deputy of Kayghalagh, and among the secretaries only ʿĪsā b. Far-

304. Actually, a Friday.
305. Wednesday, in fact.

rukhānshāh. The *mawlās* entered the palace near the gate of the Qaṣr al-Aḥmar, filling it with about four thousand men. They reached al-Muhtadī and complained to him of their situation. Chiefly, they were counting on the removal of their amīrs from responsibility for them, so that their affairs could be handled by the Commander of the Faithful's own brothers. Moreover, they wanted the amīrs and secretaries admonished for extorting sums from the central treasuries, the amount mentioned running to one hunded fifty million.[306] Al-Muhtadī promised to examine the matter and respond to their requests. So they remained in the palace for the rest of the day and al-Muhtadī sent Muḥammad b. Mubāshir al-Karkhī to purchase quantities of barley meal for them to eat.

At that, Abū Naṣr b. Bughā moved promptly to set up camp in al-Ḥayr a short distance from the racecourse. Around five hundred men joined him there, but during the night most slipped away, leaving behind fewer than a hundred. So Abū Naṣr decamped and moved to al-Muḥammadiyyah.[307]

On Thursday morning the *mawlās* resumed their original demands. They were told that what they wanted was difficult to achieve. Dislodging power from the hands of the amīrs would not be smooth sailing for them; all the more difficult when combined with attempts to seize their money. "Consider your own positions. If you think that you have the patience to see this affair through to its end,
[1825] then the Commander of the Faithful has responded positively. But if it be otherwise, the Commander of the Faithful will do his best for you." They refused, however, to accept anything other than what they had sought in the first place. So they were invited to take oaths of allegiance and obedience that they would stand by their word and not go back on it, that they would fight against anyone who attacked them, and that they would be loyal to the Commander of the Faithful and protect him. To all these conditions they consented. Solemn oaths were administered and about one thousand men swore to them that day.

ʿĪsā b. Farrukhānshāh,[308] who was in charge of affairs, assuming

306. It is not specified whether the sum mentioned is in dirhams or dinars.

307. This location is clearly the one in close proximity to Sāmarrā. In the *Index* it is mistakenly placed in the marshlands of the south.

308. See Sourdel, *Vizirat*, I, 303–4; ʿĪsā did not actually hold the title of vizier.

the responsibilities of vizier, wrote to Abū Naṣr on behalf of the *mawlās*, mentioning their objection to his leaving the palace without cause and also that they had come to the Commander of the Faithful only to plead their needs and that when they found the palace empty they remained. Were he to return, they would restore his position, having had no wish to provoke him.

ʿĪsā also wrote in the same vein to Abū Naṣr on behalf of the Caliph. Between late afternoon and early evening Abū Naṣr approached from al-Muḥammadiyyah and entered the [Jawsaq] palace with his brother Ḥabshūn, Kayghalagh, Bakālabā, and a group of other commanders. The *mawlās* stood before them, armed. Abū Naṣr and the others joined al-Muhtadī where he was seated. Saluting him, Abū Naṣr drew near and kissed his hand, his feet, and the carpet. He then backed up, and al-Muhtadī addressed him, saying, "O Muḥammad, what do you think about what the *mawlās* are saying?" "What are they saying?" asked Abū Naṣr. Al-Muhtadī said, "They report that you all have expropriated wealth and usurped posts and that you give no thought to their affairs or to what could restore their welfare." Abū Naṣr Muḥammad replied, "O Commander of the Faithful, what have I to do with finances? I was not secretary of a bureau nor did administrative districts fall into my hands." Al-Muhtadī asked him, "So where is all the wealth if it is not in your possession [1826]
and your brother's or in the possession of your secretaries and your companions?"

The *mawlās* now came closer. ʿAbdallāh b. Takīn and a group of them stepped forward and, seizing Abū Naṣr by the hand, cried out, "Here is the enemy of the Commander of the Faithful, standing before him armed with a sword." They relieved him of his sword. One of Abū Naṣr's pages named Thītal, who was then present, drew his sword and made a move to prevent them from harming Abū Naṣr. As Thītal had moved next to the Caliph, ʿAbdallāh b. Takīn reacted instinctively and struck him a blow on the head with his sword. No one in the room was without his sword drawn. Al-Muhtadī rose and entered a nearby apartment. Muḥammad b. Bughā was taken away and placed in a compartment in the palace, while the rest of his companions were imprisoned. The *mawlās* wanted to kill Abū Naṣr's page, but al-Muhtadī restrained them, saying he would handle the matter in his own way. He ordered the page given a [clean] shirt from the wardrobe and his head cleansed of blood; then he should be put in prison.

By Thursday morning the numbers of *mawlās* had increased and oaths of loyalty and obedience sworn. Later on ʿAbdallāh b. al-Wāthiq gave the order for a thousand men of the Shākiriyyah, Farāghinah, and others to depart for al-Rafīf. Among the Khurāsānian commanders instructed to go with them were the following: Muḥammad b. Yaḥyā al-Wāthiqī, ʿAttāb b. ʿAttāb, Hārūn b. ʿAbd al-Raḥmān b. al-Azhar, Ibrāhīm the brother of Abū ʿAwn, Yaḥyā b. Muḥammad b. Dāʾūd, a son of Naṣr b. Shabath, ʿAbd al-Raḥmān b. Dīnār, Aḥmad b. Farīdūn, as well as others.

Afterward ʿAbdallāh b. al-Wāthiq learned that these commanders
[1827] were saying to each other how improper it was to send them to the district [of al-Rafīf], so he abandoned the venture. They had a mind to correspond with Mūsā and Mufliḥ about leaving [for Sāmarrā] and handing the army over to one of the other commanders. Finally, they agreed to write Mūsā and Mufliḥ about the matter, and word was also sent to some of the commanders concerning their assumption of the army management in place of the two. Notes were sent as well to lower-ranking officers about what their troops in Sāmarrā had asked and what [positive] responses they received. Copies were made [for them] of the letters that had been sent to the commanders, and they were told to wait and see. If Mūsā and Mufliḥ swiftly did as they had been ordered, coming with their freedmen to the Caliph's palace and handing over the army to whomever had been charged with the task, well and good. Otherwise they were to shackle the two of them, taking them by force to the Caliph. These letters were despatched by means of thirty men, who left Sāmarrā on the night of Friday, the 5th of Rajab (June 8, 870).

Meanwhile in the palace each one who swore an oath of obedience was paid the sum of two dirhems per day. ʿAbdallāh b. Takīn was the person in charge of distributing the money to the oath takers; he was Kanjūr's brother-in-law. When Mūsā and his companions learned of this, Mūsā, who was then in al-Sinn, became alarmed about Kanjūr and had him beaten and imprisoned. Bāyakbāk heard the news while he was in al-Ḥadīthah and he went to al-Sinn[309] and had Kanjūr re-

309. Two locations on the Tigris south of Mosul, al-Ḥadīthah lying at the junction with the Upper Zāb river, al-Sinn near the junction with the Lower Zāb river. For both, see Le Strange, *Lands*, 90, 91.

moved from prison. The messengers arrived in al-Sinn with the commander's despatches while the army was assembled there. One of the despatches was read out to the troops. They responded by swearing an oath of support and departing for the bridge at al-Rafīf, where they established camp. This was Thursday, the 11th of Rajab [1828]
(June 14, 870).

The same day al-Muhtadī set out for al-Ḥayr. He reviewed the troops, marched around a bit, and then returned [to the Jawsaq palace], giving the order to have tents and pavilions[310] pitched for them in al-Ḥayr. On Friday morning around a thousand men from Mūsā's army had left [deserting him]. Among them were Kūtakīn and Khushanaj.[311] Once again al-Muhtadī made for al-Ḥayr. He placed Kūtakīn in charge of the right flank of his forces and Khushanaj in charge of the left, while he himself took the middle sector. Next the messengers began again to shuttle between the two armies. What Mūsā b. Bughā wanted was to be made governor of some district and allowed to proceed to it, while what the men wanted Mūsā to do was to come with his freedmen in order to negotiate with them. Nothing, however, was settled that day.

On Friday evening those who wanted to leave Mūsā had done so and Mūsā together with Mufliḥ had turned again toward the Khurāsān Road with about one thousand men. The same night Bāyakbāk and a group of his commanders joined ʿĪsā al-Karkhī and spent the night with him. The following morning, Saturday, Bāyakbāk and his company came to the Jawsaq palace, where he, Yārjūkh, Asātakīn, Aḥmad b. Khāqān, Khaṭārimush, and others were relieved of their swords. They appeared together before al-Muhtadī and saluted him. All were ordered to withdraw save Bāyakbāk who was commanded to remain standing before al-Muhtadī while he enumerated his many transgressions against Muslims and Islam. After this the *mawlā*s abused him and locked him up in one of the palace chambers. Just five hours later, at sunset on Saturday, he was killed. Thus [1829]
was the matter settled. There was no unrest and only a few who disapproved of Bāyakbāk's treatment bothered to talk about it, and even they did not seem especially concerned.

On Sunday the Turks expressed their objection to the Farāghinah

---

310. *Al-khiyām wa-al-maḍārib.*

311. The Arabized form of the Persian Khushank.

being treated as their equals in the palace, their admission to it altogether, [for] it became clear to them that the plot to murder the Turks' own leaders was designed to give the Farāghinah and the Maghāribah the upper hand. The Turks then abandoned the palace entirely to them. Protestations at that were voiced from al-Karkh and also included a demand for Bāyakbāk, as his troops had joined with theirs. Al-Muhtadī instructed a group of the Farāghinah to attend upon him, and he informed them of the Turks' objections. He said to them, "If you are sure you are up to taking care of the Turks, the Commander of the Faithful would not be displeased to have you by his side. If you feel yourselves unable to cope with them, we will be willing to do what they wish before things come to a head." The Farāghinah said they could cope and that, if they were combined with the Maghāribah, they could overcome them (the Turks); and they listed a number of reasons for their priority over the Turks. The Farāghinah sought to induce al-Muhtadī to go after the Turks and discussion about this continued until noon. Finally, when al-Muhtadī marched forth, most of his cavalry was comprised of Farāghinah and most of his infantry of Maghāribah. The Turks, who numbered around ten thousand men, were located between al-Karkh and the district of the fiefs. Al-Muhtadī and his forces numbered only six thousand, fewer than a thousand of whom were Turks, these being the troops of Ṣāliḥ b. Waṣīf and a contingent accompanying Yārjūkh.

As the two sides advanced toward each other, Yārjūkh and his con-
[1830] tingent broke off, while the troops of Ṣāliḥ b. Waṣīf fled in retreat to their homes. Ṭāshtimur emerged from behind al-Dakkah, where his troops had been waiting in ambush, and against stiff resistance hand-to-hand fighting raged for a time during the day until al-Muhtadī's forces were beaten. Al-Muhtadī held on trying to rally his troops around him; he continued fighting until he despaired of their return and then rode off in a hasty retreat. He carried an embossed sword[312] and was wearing a breastplate covered by a garment of patterned white-silk material.[313] He reached Khashabat Bābak, all the while urging people to help him and stand against the enemy. However, only a party of riffraff (*al-ʿayyārūn*)[314] decided to follow him.

312. *Sayf mushaṭṭab*. See Lane, *Lexicon*, s.v. *sh-ṭ-b*.
313. *Ḥarīr abyaḍ muʿayyan*. See Lane, *Lexicon*, s.v. *ʿ-y-n*.
314. See references in note 282, above.

When they got as far as the prison, they seized his horse's bridle and demanded he release the prison inmates. He turned his face from them, but they did not leave him until he had given the command to open the prison; then they abandoned him and busied themselves at the prison gate. Al-Muhtadī was left entirely alone.

He found his way to the palace of Abū Ṣāliḥ b. Yazdād where Aḥmad b. Jumayl was staying. Upon entering he had the doors locked behind him and shed his clothes and weapons. He had received a hip wound, and requested a [clean] shirt and pantaloons, which Aḥmad b. Jumayl gave him. After cleaning the wound, he drank some water and then said his prayers. A party of around thirty Turks led by Yārjūkh approached the palace of Abū Ṣāliḥ and beat upon the door until they were admitted. Al-Muhtadī heard them and, grabbing his sword, he made his way as quickly as possible up a flight of steps to the palace roof. One of the Turks wanted to go up after al-Muhtadī and, lunging at him with his sword, he missed and tumbled down [1831] the stairs. The Turks fired arrows at him, one of which struck his chest. It was only a slight wound but al-Muhtadī nevertheless knew he was finished. So he surrendered and descended, throwing away his sword. Seizing al-Muhtadī the Turks put him on a pack animal, with one of them in charge, and made their way back along the road he had come from to Yārjūkh's palace in the district of the fiefs.

The Jawsaq palace was plundered by the Turks who stripped it clean. Aḥmad, known as Ibn Fityān, b. al-Mutawakkil, imprisoned at the time in al-Jawsaq, was released by the Turks. They wrote to Mūsā b. Bughā asking him to come to [Sāmarrā]. Al-Muhtadī remained in their care, but no one did anything more to him. On Tuesday, in the district of the fiefs, they rendered the oath of allegiance to Aḥmad, the son of al-Mutawakkil, taking him on Wednesday to the Jawsaq palace, where the Hāshimites and the court elite also rendered their allegiance.

During these days, attempts to persuade al-Muhtadī to abdicate were made, but he refused and would not consent. He died on Wednesday. The following day, Thursday, his body was produced for the Hāshimites and the court elite; then his face was uncovered and his body washed. Ja'far b. 'Abd al-Wāḥid recited the funeral prayers over him on Thursday, the 18th of Rajab 256 (June 21, 870).

On Saturday, the 20th of Rajab (June 23, 870), Mūsā b. Bughā arrived [in Sāmarrā], and Aḥmad Ibn Fityān rode to the Public Audience Hall[315] on Monday, the 22nd of Rajab (June 25, 870); the public oath of allegiance was rendered there.

Muḥammad b. ʿĪsā al-Qurashī reportedly said that, when al-Muhtadī fell into the hands of the Turks, he refused to abdicate. So they removed his fingers and toes, causing the palms of his hands and his feet to become swollen. After that they did several other things to him, until he died.[316]

Muḥammad b. ʿĪsā also[317] reported, on the cause of the death of
[1832] Abū Naṣr Muḥammad b. Bughā, that he had set out from Sāmarrā to meet his brother Mūsā. Al-Muhtadī sent his brother ʿAbdallāh after Abū Naṣr with a contingent of the Maghāribah and Farāghinah, who caught up with him in al-Rafīf and brought him back to be imprisoned.

Once, before the conflict with al-Muhtadī, Abū Naṣr had visited the Caliph, greeting him. Al-Muhtadī said to him, "O Muḥammad, your brother Mūsā came [to Sāmarrā] with his army and slaves (*ʿabīd*) only to slay Ṣāliḥ b. Waṣīf and leave again." Abū Naṣr replied, "O Commander of the Faithful, may God protect you from thinking that! Mūsā is your loyal servant, engaged in fighting a vile enemy." Al-Muhtadī said, "Ṣāliḥ was more useful to us than Mūsā, and his policies better suited the empire. Now this ʿAlawī[318] has returned to al-Rayy." Abū Naṣr replied, "O Commander of the Faithful, what can he [Mūsā] do? He had defeated him and slain his companions and scattered his forces in every direction. But, whenever he goes away, he [al-Ḥasan] always returns. My God, he [al-Ḥasan] will do so again unless you order him [Mūsā] to remain in al-Rayy forever." The Caliph said, "Enough of that! Your brother has accomplished nothing more than stealing and expropriating property for himself."

---

315. *Dār al-ʿāmmah.* Bosworth, "Recruitment," 63, notes that this term indicated the outer sections and annexes of the Caliphs's palace, where troops other than palace guards were quartered and workshops, storehouses, and stables were located. Bosworth is, however, referring to Baghdad during the Caliph al-Muʿtaḍid's reign (279–89/892–902); in Sāmarrā, Public Audience Hall seems an appropriate designation for the Arabic phrase.

316. The critical apparatus notes an additional phrase taken from *ʿUyūn al-akhbār:* Al-Dūlābī related that the brother of Bāyakbāk arrived with Khanjar and drank from the [Caliph's] blood.

317. Ṭabarī does not mention the name of the transmitter, but it seems plausible to assume that it is a continuation of Muḥammad b. ʿĪsā's account.

318. That is, the rebel al-Ḥasan b. Zayd.

At this Abū Naṣr replied rudely, "Let what he and his family have acquired since you became Caliph be assessed and restored to their owners, and then do the same for what you and your brothers have acquired!" Al-Muhtadī ordered him arrested, beaten, and imprisoned; his palace was plundered along with that of Ibn Thawābah. A bounty was put on the heads of al-Ḥasan b. Makhlad, Ibn Thawābah, and Mufliḥ's secretary, Sulaymān b. Wahb al-Qaṭṭān, who fled in consequence; their palaces were also stripped bare.

Following this, al-Muhtadī brought together the various groups of Farāghinah, the Ushrūsaniyyah, the Ṭabariyyah, the Daylamites, the Ishtākhaniyyah, and the remnants of the Turks of al-Karkh and the clan of Waṣīf and sought their support against Mūsā and Mufliḥ. He argued that they had expropriated much wealth and monopolized the tax revenue, and moreover that he was afraid they were plotting [1833] to kill him. "If you help me," he said, "I shall pay all that is owing to you and increase the level of your allotments." At this they agreed to assist him against Mūsā and his forces. As they remained in the Jawsaq palace, they renewed their oath of allegiance to him. Al-Muhtadī ordered barley meal and sugar to be purchased for them and each man was paid a daily rate of two dirhams, and given a frequent ration of bread and meat. The army command was entrusted to Aḥmad b. Waṣīf and ʿAbdallāh b. Bughā al-Sharābī.

The Banū Hāshim rallied to them, and together with al-Muhtadī they set out riding through the markets appealing to people for help saying, "These godless ones who slay caliphs and maltreat their own *mawlā*s are the same who have appropriated the tax revenue for themselves; so support and aid the Commander of the Faithful." Ṣāliḥ b. ʿAlī b. Yaʿqūb b. al-Manṣūr and other members of the Banū Hāshim spoke to people in a similar fashion. Al-Muhtadī later wrote to Bāyakbāk with orders to take over as commander of the whole army and to arrest Mūsā and Mufliḥ.

After al-Muhtadī's death, people searched for Abū Naṣr [Muḥammad] b. Bughā, thinking he was still alive. When they were at last led to the spot where he was buried and he was disinterred, his body was found to have been butchered. The remains were taken to his family for Bāyakbāk's body was also taken and buried. The Turks broke a thousand swords over Muḥammad b. Bughā's grave in accordance with their custom when a chief died.

It was said that when al-Muhtadī refused to abdicate, his testicles were ordered crushed until he died.

It was also said that, when al-Muhtadī faced his executioners, he uttered these words:

"Were I able, I would be determined,
but there was an obstacle between intent and execution of the act."[319]

[1834] The day that Muḥammad b. Bughā was imprisoned nothing [else] was done to him. Restitution was demanded and he paid nearly twenty thousand dinars. After ripping open his belly and wringing his neck, they put him to death. His body was thrown into a well of the underground canal system, remaining there until the day after they took al-Muhtadī into custody when the *mawlās* extracted it for burial.

Al-Muhtadī's caliphate, to the very end of his reign, lasted exactly eleven months and twenty-five days.[320] He was then thirty-eight years old. He was a man of wide and elegant forehead, and austere gray-blue eyes, short and rotund, broad-shouldered, and with a long beard. He was born in al-Qāṭūl.[321]

In this year Juʿlān arrived in al-Baṣrah to take on the leader of the Zanj.[322]

News of [the] Encounter [between Juʿlān and the Zanj]

Following his arrival in al-Baṣrah, Juʿlān reportedly advanced with his army from the city until he was just a *farsakh*[323] distant from the Zanj army. There he had a trench excavated to enclose his forces where he remained for six months. Al-Zaynabī, Burayh, the Banū Hāshim, and other Baṣrans who were prepared to fight the abominable one were sent forth on the day that Juʿlān promised them he would attack the Zanj. But, when the two sides met, they only threw

---

319. Literally "a barrier between the wild ass and escape."

320. Ibn al-Athīr, *Kāmil*, VII, 233, has fifteen days.

321. See Le Strange, *Lands*, 57.

322. Popovic, *Révolte*, 93. Popovic observes that at this point, with the Caliph's despatch of a Turkish officer commanding government troops, the Zanj revolt had lost its local character and had become "an affair of state."

323. About 6 km.

stones and shot arrows at each other, and Juʿlān found he could not proceed owing to the dense stand of palm trees and undergrowth, which allowed no room for the horses upon which most of his troops were mounted.

Muḥammad b. al-Ḥasan reported that after Juʿlān had spent some time thus entrenched, the Zanj leader said he had decided to conceal some of his troops along the approach roads to the trench and then [1835] launch a night attack upon him. The result of the attack was that a number of Juʿlān's men were killed and the rest were gripped with such terror that Juʿlān left the camp to return to al-Baṣrah. Now prior to the abominable one's nocturnal attacks against Juʿlān, al-Zaynabī had collected fighters from the Bilāliyyah and Saʿdiyyah factions and despatched them to Juʿlān from the districts of the Nahr Nāfidh and Hazārdar, so as to confront the Zanj from two sides. However, they offered no resistance when they encountered the Zanj whose victory left many of them dead while the rest fled in disarray. Juʿlān escaped to al-Baṣrah and remained there, which made his weakness apparent to the central authorities.

Thus, Juʿlān was removed from responsibility for fighting the abominable one, and Saʿīd al-Ḥājib was ordered to proceed to undertake the task.

In this year the Zanj leader transferred [his headquarters] from the salt flats where he had established himself on the western side of the Nahr Abī al-Khaṣīb.[324]

In this year as well the Zanj leader reportedly seized fourteen seacraft, which had formed part of a convoy heading for al-Baṣrah. When news of the Zanj raids on the waterways reached the boats' owners, they proposed binding their boats one to the other so as to form a kind of island linking the first craft to the last, which they could then sail along the Tigris. The abominable one got wind of this and detailed some of his troops to capture the flotilla, encouraging them by saying it was easy prey.

Abū al-Ḥasan said that he has heard the Zanj leader comment, "When news of the approaching boats reached me, I went to say my [1836] prayers. I had begun my humble petition for God's assistance when

324. See Le Strange, "Ibn Serapion's Description," 304. It was at this place around this time that the Zanj leader built his capital, al-Mukhtārah. The canal takes its name from a freedman of the Caliph al-Manṣūr who was granted lands here in fief. According to the *Index*, it was also known as Nahr al-Atrāk.

a voice addressed me, saying that I had been granted a great victory. Scarcely a moment later, I turned round and caught sight of the boats and my troops heading toward them in flat-bottomed craft. They quickly overwhelmed the boats, killed the fighters on board, captured slaves, and plundered vast treasure, the extent of which could not be counted or even estimated." For three days the Zanj were allowed to carry on in this fashion, after which their leader ordered anything left to be delivered to him.

On the 25th of Rajab (June 28, 870) of this year the Zanj occupied al-Ubullah, killing many of the inhabitants and burning the city.

An Account of the Zanj Occupation of al-Ubullah[325]

At the time Juʿlān had withdrawn from the trench he had constructed in Shāṭiʾ ʿUthmān and returned to al-Baṣrah, the Zanj leader reportedly harassed the inhabitants of al-Ubullah with several brigades of troops, attacking them with infantry from the direction of Shāṭiʾ ʿUthmān and from the commandeered boats from the Tigris. His troops then turned toward the Nahr Maʿqil.[326]

The Zanj leader reportedly said that he hestitated whether to head for ʿAbbādān[327] or al-Ubullah but decided in favor of the former. He entrusted the task to some of his men but was then told that the nearest enemy with regard to abode and the most fitting one to concentrate on to the exclusion of anything else were the inhabitants of al-Ubullah. "Therefore," he said, "the army that I had despatched against ʿAbbādān I recalled and redirected to al-Ubullah."

The Zanj continued fighting the populace of al-Ubullah until Wednesday evening, the 25th of Rajab (June 28, 870). That night the
[1837] Zanj stormed the city from the Tigris side and the Nahr al-Ubullah. Abū al-Aḥwaṣ and his son were killed in the fighting, while the city was put to the torch. As the buildings were constructed of teakwood and built close together, the fire swept through the city, causing a violent wind, while the sparks of the conflagration spread as far as

325. Popovic, *Révolte*, 94–96; Ibn al-Athīr, *Kāmil*, VII, 236–37.

326. The chief waterway of the nine canals lying on the western side of the Tigris estuary and the one through which ships reached al-Baṣrah from the north. It was named after a Companion of the Prophet. See Le Strange, "Ibn Serapion's Description," 303, 305.

327. See Le Strange, *Lands*, 43, 44.

Shāṭi' ʿUthmān and engulfed it. Many were slain and many others drowned. Much booty was secured but more goods perished in the flames than were plundered. That evening ʿAbdallāh b. Ḥumayd al-Ṭūsī and one of his sons, who were aboard a barge on the Nahr Maʿqil with Abū Ḥamzah Nuṣayr, were killed.

This year the inhabitants of ʿAbbādān also surrendered to the Zanj leader and yielded their citadel to him.

The Account of [the Zanj Leader's] Summons for [the] Surrender [of the Inhabitants of ʿAbbādān]

The reason for this was that when the Zanj had dealt with the inhabitants of al-Ubullah in the manner they had, the ʿAbbādānians' resolve weakened, and they feared for their lives and their families. Therefore they gave themselves over to the Zanj and surrendered their city to the abominable one. His troops occupied it and seized the slaves (*al-ʿabīd*) and weapons they found there; the abominable one distributed among his troops the weapons that they brought to him.

In this year as well the Zanj occupied al-Ahwāz and captured Ibrāhīm b. al-Mudabbir.[328]

An Account of [the Occupation of al-Ahwāz]

The reason for this was that following the actions of the Zanj in al-Ubullah and the surrender of the inhabitants of ʿAbbādān to the abominable one,[329] he next set his ambitions on al-Ahwāz. He had attached the ʿAbbādānians' slaves (*mamālīk*) to his own Zanj troops, while distributing among them as well the weapons that had been seized from the city.

The Zanj troops eagerly set off for Jubbā. The population offered [1838]
no resistance and fled from the Zanj, who entered the town, killing,

---

328. Ibrāhīm b. al-Mudabbir was the brother of the celebrated Aḥmad b. al-Mudabbir, financial administrator under the Ṭūlūnids in Egypt. See *EI*,[2] s.v. "Ibn al-Mudabbir."

329. Ibn al-Athīr, *Kāmil*, VII, 237, who has consistently referred to ʿAlī b. Muḥammad as "the Zanj leader," avoiding the pejorative epithets used by Ṭabarī, calls him here al-ʿAlawī al-Baṣrī, the Baṣran ʿAlid, as though conferring an honorific title of conqueror upon him.

burning, and pillaging. They also laid waste the environs of Jubbā, arriving at last before al-Ahwāz. The governor there at the time was Saʿīd b. Yaksīn, who was also in charge of defense matters; Ibrāhīm b. Muḥammad b. al-Mudabbir was in charge of the bureaus of taxes and estates. The population of al-Ahwāz also fled from the Zanj, and almost no one offered resistance. Saʿīd b. Yaksīn withdrew with his soldiers, but Ibrāhīm b. al-Mudabbir remained behind with his pages and servants. The Zanj entered and occupied the city. Ibrāhīm b. Muḥammad, who had received a blow to the head, was captured and all his possessions, including money, furnishings, and slaves (*raqīq*), were seized. This was on Monday the 12th of Ramaḍān in the year 256 (August 13, 870).

Following these events in al-Ubullah and al-Ahwāz the Baṣrans were in such a state of dread that many evacuated the city for various other places, as disquieting rumors spread among the common people.

In Dhū al-Ḥijjah (October 30–November 28, 870) of this year the Zanj leader sent an army commanded by Yaḥyā b. Muḥammad al-Baḥrānī to fight Shāhīn b. Bisṭām.[330] But, as Yaḥyā failed to achieve his objective, he returned from the campaign.

In Rajab (June 4–July 3, 870) of this year Saʿīd b. Ṣāliḥ al-Ḥājib arrived in al-Baṣrah to wage war against the Zanj on behalf of the central authorities.

In this year as well there occurred a battle between the troops of
[1839] Mūsā b. Bughā who had gone with him to the district of al-Jabal in revolt against Muḥammad b. al-Wāthiq and Musāwir b. ʿAbd al-Ḥamīd the Khārijite. The battle took place in Khāniqīn.[331] Musāwir greatly outnumbered Mūsā and his two hundred men, yet they were able to rout Musāwir and slay a large number of his troops.

---

330. He was the secretary attached to Ibrāhīm b. Sīmā who had replaced Saʿīd b. Yaksīn in his post in al-Ahwāz. For the account of Shāhīn's death, see pp. 123–25, below.

331. A city on the road to Ḥulwān, to the northeast of Baghdad. See Le Strange, *Lands*, 62–63.

The Caliphate of al-Muʿtamid ʿalā-Allāh

The Events of the Year 256 (cont'd)

(December 9, 869–November 28, 870)

In this year the oath of allegiance was rendered to Aḥmad b. Abī Jaʿfar, who was known as Ibn Fityān. He was given the regnal title al-Muʿtamid ʿalā-Allāh. The ceremony took place on Tuesday, the 16th of Rajab (June 19, 870).

In the same year news was despatched to Mūsā b. Bughā, who was then in Khāniqīn, about the death of Muḥammad b. al-Wāthiq and also that the oath of allegiance had been given to al-Muʿtamid as Caliph. Mūsā arrived in Sāmarrā on the 20th of Rajab (June 23, 870).

On the 2nd of Shaʿbān (July 5, 870) ʿUbaydallāh b. Yaḥyā b. Khāqān was appointed vizier.[332]

In the same year ʿAlī b. Zayd al-Ṭālibī[333] appeared in al-Kūfah. Al-Shāh b. Mikāl was sent with a large army to fight him, and ʿAlī and his troops met and routed him, killing a great many of his troops. Al-Shāh, however, managed to escape.

---

332. See Sourdel, *Vizirat*, I, 305–9. The text has ʿAbdallāh; the correct name is found in Manuscript C.

333. A descendant of al-Ḥasan b. ʿAlī b. Abī Ṭālib, he is first reported raising a rebellion in al-Kūfah in Rajab 255 (June 869); Ṭabarī III, 1709. Ibn al-Athīr, *Kāmil*, VII, 238–39, mentions another ʿAlid revolt that occurred at this time, this one in Upper Egypt, which caused the governor, Ibn Ṭulūn, to send a force to quell it.

Again in this same year, Muḥammad b. Wāṣil b. Ibrāhīm al-Tamīmī,[334] an inhabitant of Fārs, together with a Kurd called Aḥmad b. al-Layth, who was from the same region, attacked al-Ḥārith b. Sīmā al-Sharābī, the governor of Fārs. In the ensuing battle al-Ḥārith was killed, and this allowed Muḥammad b. Wāṣil to conquer Fārs.

[1840] Mufliḥ was sent into battle against Musāwir the Khārijite in this year as well.[335] Kanjūr was also despatched to fight ʿAlī b. Zayd al-Ṭālibī in al-Kūfah.[336]

The army of al-Ḥasan b. Zayd al-Ṭālibī conquered al-Rayy in the month of Ramaḍān (August 2 to 31, 870) of this year.

On the 11th of Shawwāl of this year (September 11, 870), Mūsā b. Bughā departed from Sāmarrā for al-Rayy with al-Muʿtamid publicly bidding him farewell.

In this year a battle occurred between Amājūr and one of the sons of ʿĪsā b. al-Shaykh[337] at the gate of Damascus. I heard a report from someone attending Amājūr that, on the day the skirmish took place, he had prepared an expeditionary force for himself and departed from the city of Damascus. At the same moment the son of ʿĪsā b. al-Shaykh and one of his commanders called Abū al-Ṣahbāʾ were with their own forces in the vicinity of Damascus. They received intelligence of Amājūr's departure with a small contingent of troops. Spoiling for a fight, they advanced toward Amājūr, who was unaware of their approach until they were upon him. The two sides engaged in fierce hand-to-hand combat and Abū al-Ṣahbāʾ was killed. The rest of his troops and those of Ibn ʿĪsā were put to flight. I heard it

---

334. For these developments, see Bosworth, "Ṭāhirids," 112–13, where the name is given as Muḥammad b. Wāṣil al-Ḥanẓalī.

335. The battle, according to Ibn al-Athīr, *Kāmil*, VII, 240, occurred in the Khāniqīn district. Mufliḥ, facing greater numbers of the enemy, nevertheless managed to slay many of the Khārijite forces.

336. Kanjūr succeeded in driving the ʿAlid from al-Kūfah and pursued him as far as Junbulā, where he defeated the rebel and captured many of his men, in Dhū al-Ḥijjah 256 (October 30–November 28, 870). See Ibn al-Athīr, *Kāmil*, VII, 239–40, where the account of Kanjūr is complete. Ṭabarī mentions the circumstances of his death later under events of 259/872–73, p. 150, below.

337. Ibn al-Athīr's account, *Kāmil*, VII, 238, is clearer than Ṭabarī's, although differing slightly in some details. ʿĪsā b. al-Shaykh had been appointed over Damascus; he appropriated a sum of 700,000 dinars, which had been sent from Egypt en route to Baghdad and then claimed to have distributed it to his troops. The Caliph al-Muʿtamid sent Amājūr to Damascus as governor with a thousand troops. As Amājūr approached the city, he encountered the greater force of Manṣūr, ʿĪsā's son who was defeated and killed. ʿĪsā himself escaped toward Armenia, and Amājūr took control of Damascus.

mentioned that on that day the forces of Ibn ʿĪsā and Abū al-Ṣahbāʾ combined were about twenty thousand men, whereas Amājūr had only some two to four hundred men.

On Wednesday, the 13th of Dhū al-Ḥijjah (November 11, 870), Abū Aḥmad (al-Muwaffaq), the son of al-Mutawakkil, set out from Mecca for Sāmarrā.

In the same year Abū Naṣr Ismāʿīl b. ʿAbdallāh al-Marwazī, the [1841] judge Muḥammad b. ʿUbaydallāh al-Kurayzī and al-Ḥusayn the eunuch, otherwise known as ʿAraq al-Mawt,[338] were sent to ʿĪsā b. al-Shaykh in order to offer him the governorship of Armenia,[339] on condition that he leave Syria, he being given a pledge of safe-conduct to do so. ʿĪsā accepted and set out from Syria for Armenia.[340]

Leading the pilgrimage in this year was Muḥammad b. Aḥmad b. ʿĪsā b. Abī Jaʿfar al-Manṣūr.[341]

---

338. "[Smelling of the] sweat of death" is an approximation to the meaning of the man's name.

339. See *EI*,[2] s.v. "Armīniya."

340. The details in the paragraphs here are not recounted by Ibn al-Athīr. See n. 335, above.

341. Great-grandson of the Caliph al-Manṣūr; he was known as Kaʿb al-Baqar. This appears to have been the first pilgrimage he led. His father had performed the same office in 252/865.

The Events of the Year 257

(November 29, 870–November 18, 871)

Among the significant events of this year was the arrival in Fārs of Ya'qūb b. al-Layth. In Sha'bān of this year (June 24–July 22, 871) al-Mu'tamid sent to him a delegation comprising Ṭughtā and Ismā'īl b. Isḥāq and Abū Sa'īd al-Anṣārī. Abū Aḥmad b. al-Mutawakkil also despatched to him confirmation of the governorship of Balkh and Ṭukhāristān including adjacent areas in Kirmān, Sijistān, Sind, and elsewhere, together with the stipulation of the annual amount of his revenue. Ya'qūb accepted these arrangements and departed.

In Rabī' II (February 26–March 26, 871) of this year, one of Ya'qūb's messengers arrived [in Sāmarrā] with idols he had reportedly seized from Kābul.

On the 12th of Ṣafar (January 9, 871) al-Mu'tamid conferred upon his brother Abū Aḥmad[342] the overall control of al-Kūfah, the Mecca

342. Known by the honorific title of al-Muwaffaq; he was unlike many of the 'Abbāsid family in that he seems to have embarked upon a military career from an early age. He retained close links with the Turkish commander Mūsā b. Bughā, with whose help he rebuilt the army's strength in order to conduct the campaign aginst the Zanj. He was appointed commander-in-chief of the army in Ṣafar 257 (December 29, 870–January 26, 871). See Popovic, *Révolte,* 104; Sourdel, *Vizirat,* I, 307–25.

Road, the Ḥaramayn,[343] and the Yemen. Later, on the 7th of Ramaḍān (July 29, 871), Baghdad, the Sawād, Wāsiṭ, the districts of the Tigris, al-Baṣrah, al-Ahwāz, and Fārs were added to the others. The Caliph ordered that the governor of Baghdad take administrative charge of
[1842] Abū Aḥmad's districts. He also conferred upon Yārjūkh control of al-Baṣrah, the Tigris districts, al-Yamāmah and al-Baḥrayn in place of Saʿīd b. Ṣāliḥ. Yārjūkh then appointed Manṣūr b. Jaʿfar b. Dīnār as administrator of al-Baṣrah and the Tigris districts and other areas adjacent to al-Ahwāz.

Also in the same year, Bughrāj was commissioned to press Saʿīd (b. Ṣāliḥ) al-Ḥājib to proceed to the Tigris and station himself opposite the army camp of the Zanj leader.[344] Bughrāj did so and Saʿīd carried out this task in the month of Rajab (May 25–June 23, 871) of this year. It was reported that when Saʿīd reached the Nahr Maʿqil he found the forces of the Zanj leader there at a canal called the Murghāb,[345] one of the tributaries of the Nahr Maʿqil, Saʿīd engaged the Zanj in battle and routed them; he also managed to free women who had been held prisoner among them, as well as seizing booty. During the encounter Saʿīd received some wounds, one of them in the mouth. Afterward he departed for a spot known as the army camp of Abū Jaʿfar al-Manṣūr[346] and remained there one night. Next he moved on and camped at a place called Haṭmah[347] in the Euphrates valley. He remained there for some days, inspecting his troops and preparing them for a further encounter with the Zanj leader. During his sojourn in Haṭmah, word reached Saʿīd that an army of the Zanj leader was in the Euphrates area. So with a contingent of his own troops, he headed for the Zanj and succeeded in routing them. Among the defeated was ʿImrān, who was married to the grandmother of Ankalāy, son of the Zanj leader. This ʿImrān sought a pledge of safe-conduct from Bughrāj, after which the sides dispersed.

---

343. That is, the two holy cities of Mecca and Medina. See *EI*,[2] s.v. "al-Ḥaramayn."

344. See Popovic, *Révolte*, 97.

345. Yāqūt, *Muʿjam*, IV, 499.

346. Named after the former ʿAbbāsid Caliph.

347. Manuscript C has Hamṭah; Ibn al-Athīr, *Kāmil*, VII, 242, calls it Haṭṭah and places it on the eastern side of the Tigris. The location cannot be identified, and, as this instance illustrates, many of the locations (and their correct names) that appear in connection with the Zanj uprising in the vast southern Iraqi swamplands were unfamiliar, even to a contemporary writer like Ṭabarī.

Muḥammad b. al-Ḥasan said: "Once I saw a woman from among the inhabitants of the Euphrates valley who discovered one of the Zanj concealed in some dense underbrush. She seized him and [1843] brought him without resistance to Saʿīd's camp." Later Saʿīd set out again to fight the abominable one. He crossed over to the western side of the Tigris and engaged him in several skirmishes over a period of days. Saʿīd then returned to his camp in Haṭmah and from there pursued the struggle against the abominable one throughout the remainder of Rajab and most of Saʿīd (from early June through mid-July 871).

In the same year Ibrāhīm b. Muḥammad b. al-Mudabbir[348] escaped from prison where he had been detained by the abominable one. The reason for this was that he had reportedly been confined to one room in the residence of Yaḥyā b. Muḥammad al-Baḥrānī. As al-Baḥrānī felt cramped in these quarters, Ibrāhīm was moved to an apartment in his palace and locked up there. Two men who lived in an adjacent building to that in which Ibrāhīm was held were put in charge of him. Ibrāhīm went to considerable lengths to excite the mens' cupidity. They ran a tunnel from their own quarters to the place where Ibrāhīm was confined, and both he and his nephew called Abū Ghālib made their escape along with a man from the Banū Hāshim who had been imprisoned with them.

During the course of the year the abominable one's forces fought against those of Saʿīd, who himself was killed along with many of his followers.

An Account of the Battle [between Saʿīd al-Ḥājib and the Zanj]

It was reported that the abominable one sent orders to Yaḥyā b. Muḥammad al-Baḥrānī, who at the time was stationed on the Nahr Maʿqil with a large army, for him to proceed by night with a thousand of his troops toward Saʿīd's army. The force was to be commanded by Sulaymān b. Jāmiʿ and Abū al-Layth al-Iṣbahānī. They were instructed to attack Saʿīd at the break of dawn. Sulaymān and Abū al-Layth set out for Saʿīd's army to execute their orders and happened to encounter him quite unprepared. In the ensuing battle a large

348. See n. 328, above; Ibn al-Athīr, *Kāmil*, VII, 242.

number of Saʿīd's troops were slain, the Zanj on that occasion burn-
[1844] ing Saʿīd's camp to the ground and thereby gravely weakening his position.

Owing to the night attacks the Zanj launched against them, Saʿīd's camp was thrown into a state of confusion. A complicating factor was the withholding of the soldiers' allotments, which had been assigned[349] to them from the revenue of al-Ahwāz. Manṣūr b. Jaʿfar al-Khayyāṭ, who was then in charge of military affairs in al-Ahwāz as well as having a hand in matters of taxes, had delayed the payment of the soldiers' allotments. When the position of Saʿīd b. Ṣāliḥ had deteriorated to such an extent, he was ordered to depart for the court in [Sāmarrā][350] and surrender both the army and his administrative duties to Manṣūr b. Jaʿfar. Saʿīd eventually carried out these instructions, although he had been unable to move following the night attacks of the Zanj and their burning his camp, until he was relieved of his duties.

In this same year there occurred a battle between Manṣūr b. Jaʿfar al-Khayyāṭ and the Zanj leader, during which many of Manṣūr's troops were slain.

An Account of the Battle [between Manṣūr b. Jaʿfar and the Zanj]

It was reported that when Saʿīd al-Ḥājib had been removed from his post in al-Baṣrah, Bughrāj remained behind to protect its inhabitants. Manṣūr began to organize the supply ships, having them escorted by barge as far as al-Baṣrah. As a result, the Zanj were low on provisions. Then Manṣūr mustered his troops and added to the barges he had the Jannābī[351] barges and other boats. He headed in the direction of the Zanj leader's army camp, scaled the walls of a castle located beside the Tigris, and burned it to the ground and everything around it. Approaching from the same side he entered the Zanj encampment. The Zanj lay in ambush for them and attacked and killed

349. *Subbibat lahum*. See Ṭabarī, *Glossarium*, CCLXXXIV, and n. 57 above.

350. The text reads *Bāb al-Sulṭān*, headquarters of the central authorities.

351. The reading is uncertain; the word in manuscript B is unpointed, while C reads al-Ḥan(n)āniyyāt. *Jannābī* barges would have been made in the city of Jannāba, located on the coast of the province of Fārs. See Ṭabarī, *Glossarium*, CLXXI; Le Strange, *Lands*, 259.

a large number of [Manṣūr's] troops while the rest sought escape in the waters of the Tigris where many more were drowned. On that occasion about five hundred heads were reportedly borne away to the camp of Yaḥyā b. Muḥammad al-Baḥrānī on the Nahr Maʿqil, where he ordered them publicly displayed. [1845]

In the same year, at a place called Birkat Zalzal, a strangler from Baghdad was apprehended. He had murdered a number of women and buried them in the house where he was living. He was brought to al-Muʿtamid, and I learned that he had ordered the prisoner whipped. He was given two thousand lashes and four hundred strokes with a bastinado, yet he continued to live. Only when the executioners beat his testicles with two wooden flogging posts (*ʿuqābayn*)[352] did he finally expire. His body was then returned to Baghdad, where it was strung up in the public view; the corpse was later burned.[353]

In this year Shāhīn b. Bisṭām was killed and Ibrāhīm b. Sīmā put to flight.[354]

The Death of Shāhīn b. Bisṭām and the Flight of Ibrāhīm b. Sīmā

Al-Baḥrānī had reportedly written to the abominable one advising the despatch of an army to accupy al-Ahwāz and arousing his interest in such a plan. He suggested the operation commence with the destruction of the Arbuk bridge (*qanṭarah*)[355] to prevent the [enemy's] cavalry[356] from reaching his army. The abominable one sent ʿAlī b. Abān to destroy the bridge. ʿAlī was met by Ibrāhīm b. Sīmā, who was returning from Fārs where he had been with al-Ḥārith b. Sīmā[357] in a tract of desert known as the Dast Arbuk, which was situated between al-Ahwāz and the aforementioned bridge.

---

352. Lane, *Lexicon*, s.v. *ʿ-q-b. Al-ʿuqābān* are two pieces of wood stuck in the ground, between which a man is extended to be flogged.

353. This tale seems curously out of place amid the narrative of events of greater import to the state; it was one that evidently caught Ṭabarī's personal interest.

354. See Popovic, *Révolte*, 96–98; Ibn al-Athīr, *Kāmil*, VII, 243–44.

355. This was the only bridge crossing the Dujayl. See Yāqūt, *Muʿjam*, I, 185.

356. *Al-Khayl.* A feminine singular noun with the collective meaning "horses" and in a metonymous sense "mounted troops." See Lane, *Lexicon*, s.v. *kh-y-l*; and *EI*,² s.v. "Khayl." The verb in the sentence should be emended to *taṣil*.

357. The governor of Fārs, as mentioned p. 116, above.

When ʿAlī b. Abān reached the bridge he and his troops established a camp hidden from view. However, when Ibrāhīm's cavalry had crossed this desert tract they were able to attack ʿAlī from several sides and as a result a great number of the Zanj were slain. ʿAlī himself was forced to flee. Ibrāhīm's cavalry pursued him as far as
[1846] al-Fandam[358] but a foot wound prevented ʿAlī from proceeding farther toward al-Ahwāz. Therefore he backtracked and headed for Jubbā.[359]

Saʿīd b. Yaksīn was removed from his post and Ibrāhīm b. Sīmā was appointed [to combat the Zanj].[360] His secretary was Shāhīn. The two men set out at the same time, Ibrāhīm b. Sīmā taking the Euphrates Road and heading for the mouth of the Nahr Jubbā.[361] ʿAlī b. Abān was at this moment in al-Khayzurāniyyah.[362] For his part, Shāhīn b. Bisṭām set out along the Nahr Mūsā road, judging that he would meet up with Ibrāhīm at a spot they had previously agreed upon. They had also made prior arrangements to attack ʿAlī b. Abān, and Shāhīn arrived at the spot first. Now an inhabitant of the Nahr Mūsā district came to ʿAlī b. Abān and informed him of Shāhīn's approach. ʿAlī advanced toward Shāhīn, and the two sides met in the afternoon at the Abū al-ʿAbbās canal, situated between the Nahr Mūsā and the Nahr Jubbā. Battle broke out between the two sides. At first Shāhīn's troops held fast and fought fiercely. But then, recovering, the Zanj dealt their opponents a crushing blow, causing them to turn heel and flee. In fact the first to fall mortally wounded that day were Shāhīn himself and a cousin of his named Ḥayyān; this was because he had been in the vanguard of the troops. A great many of his men were slain as well.

Another informant came to ʿAlī b. Abān and told him of Ibrāhīm b. Sīmā's arrival. This was after ʿAlī's battle with Shāhīn was over. Without delay ʿAlī departed for the Nahr Jubbā, where Ibrāhīm b. Sīmā's army was camped. As yet Ibrāhīm had heard no word of Shāhīn's fate. At the time of the last evening prayer, ʿAlī drew in

358. Yāqūt, *Muʿjam*, IV, 278, places this in [the district] of al-Ahwāz and adds, "But I don't know what it is."

359. A town lying on a canal of the same name, east of the Dujayl and below al-Ahwāz in an area occupied by many villages. See Le Strange, *Lands*, 243.

360. Ibrāhīm was appointed to replace Saʿīd as military governor of al-Ahwāz.

361. The text of Ibn al-Athīr, *Kāmil*, VII, 243, has incorrectly, Nahr Jayy.

362. A town on the eastern side of the Tigris above Fam al-Ṣilḥ, in the district of Wāsiṭ. See Le Strange, "Ibn Serapion's Description," 301.

close upon Ibrāhīm's position and then attacked ferociously, slaying his troops in droves. Thus in the brief span of time between the afternoon and evening prayers, Shāhīn had been killed and Ibrāhīm routed.

Muḥammad b. al-Ḥasan said that he had once heard ʿAlī b. Abān talking of these events. He said, "That day, as it happened, I had [1847] come down with one of the bouts of fever to which I was subject. When my troops had achieved their victory over Shāhīn, they dispersed so that there were only about fifty left with me when I set out for Ibrāhīm b. Sīmā's army camp. When I reached it, I got close enough to hear the commotion of the soldiers and even some of their conversations. When the place fell quiet, I went onto the attack."

ʿAlī b. Abān left Jubbā when Shāhīn had been killed and Ibrāhīm b. Sīmā routed, after a despatch arrived for him from the abominable one with orders to proceed to al-Baṣrah and wage war against its inhabitants.

In this year the troops of the abominable one entered al-Baṣrah.

The Events that Led up to [the] Entry of al-Baṣrah [by the Zanj] and What Transpired Thereafter[363]

It was reported that, when Saʿīd b. Ṣāliḥ (al-Ḥājib) left al-Baṣrah, the central authorities handed over his duties to Manṣūr b. Jaʿfar al-Khayyāṭ. The events concerning Manṣūr and the troops of the abominable one we have dealt with already: They told of Manṣūr's enfeebled position, his inability to engage the abominable one in battle, contenting himself with providing protection for the supply ships[364] sufficient to relieve the inhabitants of al-Baṣrah of the harm caused when the flow of these supplies was interrupted. Word of this reached the abominable one, who was then frustrated by the news that the Baṣrans had been relieved. This caused him to send ʿAlī b. Abān to the districts of Jubbā, where he established camp in al-Khayzurāniyyah. This distracted Manṣūr b. Jaʿfar from the protection of the supply boats to al-Baṣrah, so once again the Baṣrans [1848] experienced straitened circumstances.

The abominable one's troops harassed the inhabitants of al-Baṣ-

363. See Popovic, *Révolte*, 98–104; Ibn al-Athīr, *Kāmil*, VII, 244–46.
364. *Al-Qayrawānāt*. See n. 211, above.

rah day and night with attacks. Then, in the month of Shawwāl (August 22–September 19, 871) of this year, the abominable one determined to rally his forces together for a concerted assault on the Baṣrans and a serious [attempt to] destroy it. The decision was taken because he was aware of their weakness, their disunity, and the damaging effects upon them of the blockade and the destruction of surrounding villages. Moreover, the abominable one had consulted the astrological charts and discovered that there would be a lunar eclipse on Tuesday evening, the 14th of the month (September 4, 871).

Muḥammad b. al-Ḥasan b. Sahl reported that he had heard the abominable one say, "I earnestly prayed to God for help against the people of al-Baṣrah and humbly beseeched Him to hasten its destruction. A voice addressed me saying that al-Baṣrah was but a loaf of bread, which one could nibble around the edges; when half the loaf had been devoured, al-Baṣrah would be destroyed. I took this to mean that devouring half a loaf indicated the eclipse of the moon, which was expected at this time, so it was entirely plausible that the fate of al-Baṣrah would occur soon afterward."

Muḥammad continued: "The abominable one continued speaking in this vein to such an extent that he overwhelmed his followers with the story, repeating it among them ad nauseam. Then he deputized Muḥammad b. Yazīd al-Dārimī, one of his adherents in al-Baḥrayn, to go among the Arab tribesmen, many of whom were successfully won over to the Zanj cause. They camped at a place called al-Qandal, and the abominable one sent Sulaymān b. Mūsā al-Shaʿrānī to join them, and then ordered the whole force to head for al-Baṣrah and attack it. He forwarded instructions to Sulaymān b. Mūsā to drill the tribesmen in the execution of such an operation.

[1849] When the lunar eclipse occurred, the Zanj leader sent ʿAlī b. Abān with a detachment of Arab tribesmen, ordering him to approach al-Baṣrah by way of the territory of the Banū Saʿd. Likewise Yaḥyā b. Muḥammad al-Baḥrānī, who was then blockading the Baṣrans, was instructed to approach the city via the Nahr ʿAdī with the remainder of the tribesmen who were attached to him."

Muḥammad b. al-Ḥasan said that Shibl (b. Sālim) had observed that the first attack on the Baṣrans was led by ʿAlī b. Abān. This was at the time when Bughrāj was present in the city with a detachment of soldiers. For two days the battle raged between the two sides, the people in general supporting Bughrāj. Yaḥyā (b. Muḥammad al-Baḥrānī) approached with his troops by way of Qaṣr Anas, making their way to the bridge. ʿAlī b. Abān al-Muhallabī entered the city at the time of the Friday congregational prayers on the 17th of Shawwāl (September 7, 871). Killing and burning continued through the day and into the evening and throughout all of Saturday as well. Yaḥyā approached al-Baṣrah early on Sunday morning. Bughrāj and Burayh with a force of troops blocked his way and drove him back. Yaḥyā returned and held his ground for the rest of the day. On Monday morning he (Yaḥyā) made a further attempt, but, when he finally secured entry into the city, the defenders had scattered, Burayh had fled, and Bughrāj had withdrawn with his troops, leaving no opposition. Ibrāhīm b. Yaḥyā al-Muhallabī met Yaḥyā and sought a promise of protection from him on behalf of the inhabitants and this was granted.

Ibrāhīm b. Yaḥyā's town crier proclaimed the protection to anyone who sought it; he had only to present himself at Ibrāhīm's palace. The inhabitants of al-Baṣrah responded without exception, thronging the city squares. When he saw[365] the great gathering, he seized the opportunity to blockade every street, roadway, and alley, thus preventing anyone from escaping. Behaving in this treacherous manner, he then gave the order for his troops to kill, and, with rare exceptions, everyone present was slain. The perpetrator of this act departed the same day to stay in Qaṣr ʿĪsā b. Jaʿfar in al-Khuraybah. [1850]

Muḥammad continued: Al-Faḍl b. ʿAdī al-Dārimī recounted to me the following: "At the time the traitor[366] was warring against the people of al-Baṣrah, I was in the district, staying among the Banū Saʿd." Al-Faḍl continued, saying that someone had arrived one night and mentioned that he had seen some passing cavalry heading for Qaṣr ʿĪsā in al-Khuraybah. [Al-Faḍl said], "My companions said to me, 'Go and gather some information for us about this troop.' I did so, and, when I came upon a part of the Banū Tamīm and the Banū Asad, I inquired what they were doing. They claimed to be supporters of the ʿAlawite and attached to ʿAlī b. Abān, who was supposed

365. The subject of the verb here is unclear. Grammatical requirements point to Ibrāhīm b. Yaḥyā as the perpetrator of the ensuing massacre, but it was certainly the work of Yaḥyā b. Muḥammad al-Baḥrānī. See p. 131, below, for another account.

366. Ṭabarī uses the word *khāʾin* for the Zanj leader, a change from the monotonous *khabīth*, "abominable one."

to reach al-Baṣrah the following morning, his destination being the quarter of the Banū Saʿd. Yaḥyā b. Muḥammad was also with another contingent, heading for the quarter of the Āl al-Muhallab. They said to me, 'Tell your companions from the Banū Saʿd, "If you wish to protect your women and children, then make haste to evacuate them before the army surrounds you."' "

Al-Faḍl said, "I returned to my companions and gave them the news from the Arab tribesmen." Having made their preparations, they sent someone to Burayh to inform him, too, of the situation. He came to them at dawn with the remaining chattels and a contingent of soldiers. They then marched out until they eventually reached a trench called Banū Ḥimmān. Some Banū Tamīm and fighters of the Saʿdiyyah met up with them, but it was not long before ʿAlī b. Abān overtook them with a contingent of Zanj and Arab tribesmen on horseback. Burayh became alarmed before even encountering this crowd and so he returned to his residence [in al-Baṣrah]. This was as good as admitting defeat. The Banū Tamīm who had gathered now dispersed and ʿAlī was able to approach the city unopposed, and he made his way to the quarter of al-Mirbad.[367] Burayh sent word to the Banū Tamīm requesting assistance, and a group of them responded.
[1851] Fighting broke out in al-Mirbad in front of Burayh's palace. Thereupon Burayh fled, and his supporters scattered. The Zanj burned his palace to the ground, having plundered all its contents. The killing continued, the Baṣrans' position having been gravely weakened, while that of the Zanj grew stronger. The sides battled on until the end of the day, when ʿAlī reached the congregational mosque and ordered it burned down. Fatḥ, the servant of Abū Shīth, together with a group of Baṣrans, took ʿAlī by surprise, and he had to retreat with his men, some of the Zanj being killed. ʿAlī thereupon turned back and established his army camp at a place called the graveyard of the Banū Shaybān.

People sought for someone in authority with whom they could join in battle, but none was found. When they looked for Burayh, they discovered that he had fled. On Saturday the Baṣrans realized that ʿAlī b. Abān had not returned, but early on Sunday morning he

367. Located at the western gate of al-Baṣrah, it was the quarter where caravans halted and hence was one of the busiest in the city. See Le Strange, *Lands*, 45; *EI*,[2] s.v. "al-Baṣrah."

did so, without encountering any opposition, and took al-Baṣrah in triumph.

Muḥammad b. al-Ḥasan related as follows from Muḥammad b. Simʿān: "At the time the Zanj entered al-Baṣrah, I was living in the city. I used to attend the assembly held by Ibrāhīm b. Muḥammad b. Ismāʿīl, who was known as Burayh. On Friday, the 10th of Shawwāl 257 (August 31, 871), I was there, and Shihāb b. al-ʿAlāʾ al-ʿAnbarī was present as well. I heard Shihāb telling Ibrāhīm that the traitor had sent money and supplies into the desert in order to raise a force from among the Arab tribesmen; that he had in fact managed to muster a large toop of horsemen, and with them and his own Zanj infantry he intended to infiltrate al-Baṣrah. At the time al-Baṣrah was defended by only some fifty cavalry of the government forces under Bughrāj. Burayh told Shihāb that the Arab tribesmen would not venture to act with hostility toward him [because] he was obeyed and respected by the Arabs." [1852]

Ibn Simʿān continued: "I left Burayh's assembly and came across the secretary, Aḥmad b. Ayyūb, whom I overheard talking about Hārūn b. ʿAbd al-Raḥīm al-Shīʿī, who at the time was in charge of the postal service (*barīd*) in al-Baṣrah. Hārūn confirmed that the traitor, on the 3rd of Shawwāl (August 24, 871), had performed the congregational prayer[368] with nine persons, while al-Baṣrah's leading commanders and its resident governor remained in total ignorance about what the traitor was up to, as I have described."

The blockade had driven the populace to hunger, and disease was on the increase. Conflict erupted in the city between the two factions of the Bilāliyyah and the Saʿdiyyah. Then on Friday morning, the 16th of Shawwāl (September 6, 871) of this year, the traitor's cavalry attacked al-Baṣrah on three fronts, the Banū Saʿd district, al-Mirbad, and al-Khuraybah. ʿAlī b. Abān led the army, which was despatched against al-Mirbad. He had divided his troops into two contingents: One was in the charge of Rafīq, the servant of Yaḥyā b. ʿAbd al-Raḥmān b. Khāqān, who was ordered to march into the Banū Saʿd district, and the other, with whom he himself remained,

368. The expression is *jammaʿa fī tisʿa anfus*. See Lane, *Lexicon*, s.v. *j-m-ʿ*. Although the date was actually a Saturday, the meaning seems to be that ʿAlī b. Muḥammad had the temerity to pray with nine persons (with nine of his companions or with only nine other persons?) in the congregational mosque in al-Baṣrah prior to the final assault and under the noses of the authorities.

set out for al-Mirbad. Yaḥyā b. Muḥammad al-Azraq al-Baḥrānī led the cavalry, which was sent to al-Khuraybah, having assembled his troops together on one front. Those Baṣrans of little circumstance who could, despite being exhausted by hunger and the blockade, went out to face each of these divisions. The cavalry accompanying Bughrāj split up into two groups, one of which made for the district of al-Mirbad and the other for al-Khuraybah. Those [of ʿAlī's forces] who reached the Banū Saʿd district engaged in battle a contingent of the Saʿdiyyah fighters, along with Fatḥ, the slave of Abū Shīth and
[1853] his companions, but a few Baṣrans were no match for the assembled forces of the abominable one, whose troops attacked on horse and on foot.

Ibn Simʿān said: "On that day I was present in the congregational mosque when flames engulfed three areas, Zahrān, al-Mirbad, and Banū Ḥimmān, at the same time, as if they had been set by arsonists at an agreed moment. That was at the beginning of the day, on Friday. The calamity worsened, and Baṣrans were convinced that they were doomed. Those in the main mosque strove to reach their homes as swiftly as possible. I was hastening toward my own house, which was on the Mirbad Road. On the way, fleeing Baṣrans passed me retreating to the great mosque. Al-Qāsim b. Jaʿfar b. Sulaymān al-Hāshimī brought up their rear, seated upon a donkey and girt with a sword. He cried out to the crowd, 'Woe upon you! Will you surrender your city and your families? This is your enemy who has just entered your city!' But none paid heed to him or listened to his plea, and he went upon his way. Then the Mirbad Road cleared of people, and between those in flight and the Zanj there was empty space as far as the eye could see."

Muḥammad[369] said, "When I saw what was happening, I entered my house and locked the door. From the upper floor of the house I looked down and saw the cavalry of the Arab tribesmen and the Zanj foot soldiers led by a man riding a chestnut horse and carrying a spear bearing a yellow lappet.[370] Sometime later, after I had been taken to the traitor's city, I inquired about the man's identity. ʿAlī b. Abān claimed that he had been the one I had seen with the yellow streamer."

---

369. That is, Muḥammad b. Simʿān.

370. *ʿAdhabah*. Lane, *Lexicon*, s.v. *ʿ-dh-b*, describes this as a strip of linen or the like that is bound to the head of a spear.

The [Zanj] troops entered the city and disappeared down the Mirbad Road, proceeding to the ʿUthmān Gate. By then it was late in the day. Then they left. The ignorant young clods of the city imagined that they were off to attend the Friday prayer, but what had really [1854] frightened them off was possible attack from bands of the Bilāliyyah and Saʿdiyyah who might attack them from the square,[371] for they feared ambushes there. So they left.

Those [Zanj] who were in the quarters of Zahrān and Banū Ḥiṣn also departed after they had burned, pillaged, and overwhelmed the city, for they knew no one could stop them. They let Saturday and Sunday go by. Then they came again on Monday, and found no one defending the city. The population[372] was collected before the palace of Ibrāhīm b. Yaḥyā al-Muhallabī and promised their security.

Muḥammad b. Simʿān recounted the following from al-Ḥasan b. ʿUthmān al-Muhallabī, who was nicknamed Mundaliqah[373] and was one of Yaḥyā b. Muḥammad's companions. That morning Yaḥyā had ordered him to go to the graveyard of the Banū Yashkur and bring back as many ovens[374] as he could fetch. "I did so," said al-Ḥasan, "and brought back some twenty ovens carried on porters' heads. I took them to the palace of Ibrāhīm b. Yaḥyā, and people thought they were for the purpose of preparing food for them, as they suffered from hunger resulting from the harsh blockade and the strain of events. A crowd developed in front of Ibrāhīm b. Yaḥyā's palace, people coming and going and increasing in number through the night until sunrise."

Ibn Simʿān continued. "At this time I had moved residence from the Mirbad Road to the palace belonging to my mother's grandfather Hishām, who was called al-Dāff. It was located in the district of the Banū Tamīm; [I did this] because the Banū Tamīm were rumored among the populace to have accepted the traitor's peace. I was there [1855] when some informants brought news of the battle in front of the palace of Ibrāhīm b. Yaḥyā. They said that Yaḥyā b. Muḥammad al-Baḥrānī had ordered the Zanj to surround the crowd. He allowed any of the Muhallabī family to enter Ibrāhīm b. Yaḥya's palace. A small

---

371. *Al-Murabbaʿah.* The reading is uncertain, though some location seems indicated by the context. Manuscript B has *al-muʿarabah* and C *al-murīʿah.*

372. *Al-nās.* The word is typically ambiguous and could also mean the Baṣran troops.

373. The reading is conjectural; manuscript B is unpointed, while C reads *s-da-l-ʿ-h.*

374. See n. 226, above.

number did so, and the gates were then shut. Finally, the Zanj were given the word to massacre the rest of the crowd, which they proceeded to do, to the very last person."

Muḥammad b. ʿAbdallāh, known as Abū al-Layth al-Iṣbahānī, was the one who had given the signal[375] to the Zanj, which they recognized as the order to commence the slaughter. The sword did the rest.

Al-Ḥasan b. ʿUthmān said, "I could hear their uproar, crying out 'There is no God but Allāh' as they were put to the sword. Their voices rang out with the cry of 'There is no God but Allāh' so loudly that they could be heard far away, in al-Ṭafāwah." After the crowd had been massacred, as we have described, the Zanj proceeded to slay anyone [else] they encountered. That day ʿAlī b. Abān burned down the congregational mosque; he also burned the harbor from the cable (*ḥabl*)[376] to the bridge, the fire destroying all before it, including people, animals, goods, and merchandise. Throughout the morning and afternoon the Zanj harassed anyone they found, driving everybody to Yaḥyā b. Muḥammad (al-Baḥrānī), who was then residing in Sayḥān; anyone with some money was tortured to extract it and then killed, but anyone who was poor was killed straightaway.

Shibl reportedly said that Yaḥyā entered al-Baṣrah early on Tuesday, following the massacre of the crowd in front of Ibrāhīm b. Yaḥyā's palace. An offer of safety and security was publicly proclaimed,
[1856] to try to lure people into the open, but no one appeared. The news reached the abominable one, and he removed ʿAlī b. Abān from al-Baṣrah, assigning Yaḥyā b. Muḥammad to the city on his own, sanctioning and approving the massacre, and expressing his affection for him. The abominable one judged ʿAlī b. Abān al-Muhallabī's performance lacking in regard to his restraint from seizing booty in the Banū Saʿd district. ʿAlī b. Abān had deputed a party of the Banū Saʿd to go to the abominable one, but, as they gained no benefit from him, they departed for ʿAbbādān.

Yaḥyā b. Muḥammad remained in al-Baṣrah. The abominable one sent him a despatch ordering the public announcement of Shibl as his deputy in al-Baṣrah in order to calm the fears of the populace and so that those in hiding would begin to reemerge and those who were

375. The signal was a verbal one, which, in the text, reads *kīlū*, an imperative meaning "measure!" or "weigh!"

376. See Ṭabarī, *Glossarium*, CLXXIX.

known to be wealthy. When these reappeared, they were to be forced to reveal the money they had buried and hidden. Yaḥyā carried out this order. Not a day passed when a group of affluent persons was not stripped of their possessions and then put to death. Others of no evident substance were summarily put to death; none who appeared before Yaḥyā survived and many fled as best they could. Finally the abominable one withdrew his army from al-Baṣrah.

Muḥammad b. al-Ḥasan said, "When the traitor had completed the destruction of al-Baṣrah and word had reached him of the enormities perpetrated by his troops, I heard him comment that he had invoked Allāh's [judgment] upon the populace of al-Baṣrah the day his troops entered the city. He said: 'I prayed earnestly and prostrated myself, praying all the while, and behold I was given a vision of al-Baṣrah. I could see the city and my troops fighting there. I had the vision of a man standing in thin air between earth and the sky in the image of Jaʿfar b. Maʿlūf,[377] who was formerly put in charge of the registry of land taxes in Sāmarrā. He was standing with his left hand lowered and his right hand raised, about to overturn al-Baṣrah [1857] and its inhabitants. I knew then that the angels alone had been charged with the destruction of the city, and not my troops, for had they been responsible for that, the destruction would not have reached the vast proportions people speak about. The angels brought victory and supported me in my battle and kept my troops from being fainthearted.'"

Muḥammad b. al-Ḥasan continued: "It was following the destruction of al-Baṣrah that the abominable one claimed his descent from Yaḥyā b. Zayd b. ʿAlī,[378] because a large number of ʿAlawites who had been in al-Baṣrah joined his ranks. Among them were ʿAlī b. Aḥmad b. ʿĪsā b. Zayd and ʿAbdallāh b. ʿAlī,[379] together with their womenfolk and families. When they joined him, he abandoned his

---

377. He was involved in the torture and execution of the secretary Najāḥ b. Salamah in 245/857. See Ṭabarī, III, 1442, 1444, 1446, and n. 255, above.

378. Zayd b. ʿAlī, a descendant of the fourth Caliph, ʿAlī b. Abī Ṭālib, had raised a revolt in al-Kūfah against the Umayyad dynasty in 122/740, in which he was killed. His son, Yaḥyā, who participated in the rebellion, escaped to Khurāsān. The Zanj leader here is professing to be the great-grandson of this Yaḥyā. Although by this time his line was extinct, there were descendants from Yaḥyā's half-brothers, whose mother had been a slave. See Popovic, *Révolte*, 101, and annexes 1 and 2; *EI*,[1] s.v. "Zaid b. ʿAlī."

379. That is, ʿAbdallāh was the son of ʿAlī b. Aḥmad b. ʿĪsā b. Zayd. When they joined the Zanj, the Zanj leader ʿAlī b. Muḥammad switched his claim of descent

claim to be descended from Aḥmad b. ʿĪsā, alleging instead to belong to the line of Yaḥyā b. Zayd.

Muḥammad b. al-Ḥasan continued: "When a group of Nawfaliyyūn were with him, I heard al-Qāsim b. al-Ḥasan al-Nawfalī say that they had heard that he was a descendant of Aḥmad b. ʿĪsā b. Zayd, but the abominable one replied, 'I am not a descendant of ʿĪsā, but of Yaḥyā b. Zayd.' He lied about that; it is generally accepted about Yaḥyā that he had no offspring but a daughter who died in infancy."[380]

In the same year the central government despatched Muḥammad[381] al-Muwallad to al-Baṣrah in order to fight the Zanj leader. He left Sāmarrā on Friday, the 1st of Dhū al-Qaʿdah (September 20, 871).

An Account of al-Muwallad's Expedition

Muḥammad al-Muwallad reached the area and was quartered in al-Ubullah.[382] Burayh arrived and established himself in al-Baṣrah. A large number of Baṣrans who had previously fled the city gathered
[1858] around Burayh. When Yaḥyā (b. Muḥammad) withdrew from the city, he set up camp on the Nahr al-Ghūthā.

Muḥammad b. al-Ḥasan, reporting from Shibl, said that, when Muḥammad al-Muwallad arrived, the abominable one sent Yaḥyā instructions to proceed to the Nahr Awwā. He arrived there with his army and set about engaging al-Muwallad in battle for ten days. Al-Muwallad had selected a place of residence and settled himself in but had devoted less attention to pursuing hostilities. The abominable one ordered Yaḥyā to launch a night attack against him and sent him barges with Abū al-Layth al-Iṣbahānī. Yaḥyā launched the night attack and al-Muwallad ventured forth with his troops. The two sides fought until morning and well into the next afternoon. Then he turned and withdrew while the Zanj entered his camp and

---

from Aḥmad b. ʿĪsā b. Zayd to that of Yaḥyā b. Zayd. Ṭabarī is, in fact, saying that the claim was fabricated. Thus the Zanj leader's reason for altering his claim would have been to make it more difficult for opponents and skeptics to challenge its truth, especially if descent from Yaḥyā meant from one of his several half-brothers.

380. This is probably a reference to Yaḥyā's daughter by a woman of the Azd tribe, whom he married in al-Kūfah. See *EI*,[1] s.v. "Zaid b. ʿAlī."

381. Ibn al-Athīr, *Kāmil*, VII, 246, refers to him as Aḥmad al-Muwallad.

382. See Popovic, *Révolte*, 103 n. 2, on the nature of Muḥammad's forces.

plundered it. Yaḥyā sent word of this to the abominable one, who sent further instructions that Yaḥyā should pursue al-Muwallad. Yaḥyā chased after al-Muwallad as far as al-Ḥawānīt[383] before making his way back. He then passed by al-Jāmidah,[384] attacked its inhabitants, and plundered all the neighboring villages, spilling as much blood as he could in the course of the operation. Next he set up his army camp in al-Jālah and remained there a while before returning to the Nahr Maʿqil.

In the same year Muḥammad al-Muwallad captured Saʿīd b. Aḥmad b. Saʿīd b. Salm al-Bāhilī, who, with the aid of his Bāhilite troops, had gained control over the swamp region and made the land routes very insecure.

In this year as well Muḥammad b. Wāṣil violated his allegiance to the central authorities by conquering the province of Fārs.

Leading the pilgimage this year was al-Faḍl b. Isḥāq b. al-Ḥasan b. Ismāʿīl b. al-ʿAbbās b. Muḥammad b. ʿAlī b. ʿAbdallāh b. al-ʿAbbās.

In this year Basīl,[385] one of the ruling household, who was known as al-Ṣaqlabī because his mother was a Ṣaqlabī,[386] attacked and [1859] killed Michael, the son of Tawfīl, the king of Byzantium. Michael had ruled alone for twenty-four years, and after him the Ṣaqlabī became ruler of Byzantium.

383. The name means "toll booths," and the place lay on the eastern bank of the Tigris, just north of the great swamp region. See Le Strange, "Ibn Serapion's Description," 33, 46.

384. A large village in the Wāsiṭ district. See Le Strange, "Ibn Serapion's Description," 274. Ibn al-Athīr, *Kāmil*, VII, 137, notes that Yaḥyā pursued al-Muwallad to al-Jāmidah; he does not mention al-Ḥawānīt.

385. Basil I, founder of the Macedonian dynasty, ruled from 867 to 886. He had his co-emperor, Michael III, murdered in his bed, enabling himself to become sole ruler of the Byzantine empire. See Ostrogorsky, *History of the Byzantine State*, 233ff.

386. See *EI*,[1] s.v "Ṣaḳāliba," a term meaning "Slav," widely applied to peoples of various origins who lived in territory lying between Constantinople and the lands of the Bulgars.

The Events of the Year 258

(November 18, 871–November 6, 872)

Among the important events of this year was the arrival of Saʿīd b. Aḥmad b. Saʿīd b. Salm al-Bāhilī before the central authorities, who ordered that he be punished with seven hundred lashes. This was in the month of Rabīʿ II (February 15–March 14, 872). Saʿīd died, and his body was placed on public display.[387]

In the same year also one of the religious judges of the Zanj leader, who had represented him in ʿAbbādān, was beheaded. Fourteen other Zanj, who had been captured in the district of al-Baṣrah, were beheaded at the Public Gate in Sāmarrā.

Mufliḥ fought with some Arab tribesmen in Takrīt.[388] It was reported that they were sympathetic to Musāwir the Khārijite.

Masrūr al-Balkhī engaged in battle the Kurds of the Yaʿqūbiyyah, routing them and inflicting casualties among them.

---

387. Saʿīd and the activities of the Bāhilah in the marshland areas have already been mentioned, p. 135, above. The capture and death of the Bāhilah chief, Saʿīd, caused the tribe to go over to the cause of the Zanj. See *EI*,[2] s.v. "Bāhila."

388. At this time Takrīt, located 30 miles north of Sāmarrā on the west bank of the Tigris, was regarded by the early Arab geographers as situated on the frontier between the province of Iraq and the Jazīrah but within the former. See Le Strange, *Lands*, 25, 57.

Muḥammad b. Wāṣil submitted obediently to the central authorities and delivered the taxes (*kharāj*) and the revenue of the estates in Fārs to Muḥammad b. al-Ḥusayn b. al-Fayyāḍ.

The Caliph al-Muʿtamid put his brother Abū Aḥmad in charge of the districts of Diyār Muḍar,[389] Qinnasrīn,[390] and al-ʿAwāṣim.[391] This occurred on Monday, the 20th of Rabīʿ I (February 4, 872). On [1860] Thursday, at the commencement of the new moon of Rabīʿ II (around February 29, 872), the Caliph in assembly bestowed robes of honor upon both his brother and Mufliḥ. The two of them set out for al-Baṣrah, riding in a public procession, with al-Muʿtamid accompanying Abū Aḥmad as far as Bazkuwār,[392] whence he returned to Sāmarrā.

Manṣūr b. Jaʿfar b. Dīnār al-Khayyāṭ was killed in the course of this year.[393]

An Account of [Manṣūr b. Jaʿfar's] Death

It was reported that, following the carnage wrought by his troops in al-Baṣrah, the abominable one ordered ʿAlī b. Abān al-Muhallabī to march toward Jubbā to wage war against Manṣūr b. Jaʿfar, who at the time was in Al-Ahwāz. ʿAlī camped opposite ʿAlī's army, which was then stationed in al-Khayzurāniyyah, Manṣūr employing at this moment small contingents of infantry. The abominable one then sent twelve barges to ʿAlī b. Abān, manned with the toughest of his troops, and placed in their charge Abū al-Layth al-Iṣbahānī.[394] He ordered Abū al-Layth to obey ʿAlī's commands, but this he failed to do to the extent of imposing his own views upon ʿAlī. As Manṣūr was approaching with his own barges to make one of his regular at-

389. Lying along the banks of the Euphrates, one of the three districts constituting the province of the Jazīrah; it was named after the tribe of Muḍar. See Le Strange, *Lands*, 86.

390. The ancient Chalcis in northern Syria.

391. See Le Strange, *Lands*, 101–2; *EI*,[2] s.v. "al-ʿAwāṣim." This was part of the frontier zone between Byzantium and the ʿAbbāsid domains in the north and northeast of Syria. Abū Aḥmad's responsibilities in these districts were nominal; his real task was to conduct the campaign against the Zanj, as the remainder of the paragraph makes clear.

392. A town on the Tigris near al-Qādisiyyah, variously referred to as Barkuwāra, Balkuwāra (see Le Strange, *Lands*, 52), or Barkuwān, as in manuscript C.

393. Ibn al-Athīr, *Kāmil*, VII, 251–52.

394. Abū al-Layth appears to have been the chief, if not the only, commander, or "admiral," of the Zanj flotilla.

tacks on the enemy, Abū al-Layth suddenly set out to meet him without first having consulted ʿAlī about this. Manṣūr seized Abū al-Layth's barges and killed a large number of both whites and Zanj who were aboard them. Abū al-Layth himself managed to escape and found his way back to the abominable one. ʿAlī b. Abān turned back as well with all his forces and remained in camp for a whole month. Then with his infantry troops he set out again to fight Manṣūr. After establishing his new camp, he sent out scouts to gather information concerning Manṣūr and his soldiers.

[1861] Now Manṣūr had a prefect stationed at Karnabā.[395] ʿAlī b. Abān launched a night attack against this commander, killing him along with most of those based there. ʿAlī looted the camp, took some horses, and burned the place to the ground. He returned during the course of the same night, and arrived at the mouth of the Nahr Jubbā. News of this reached Manṣūr, who ventured forth, finally approaching [ʿAlī's base] in al-Khayzurāniyyah. ʿAlī went out to challenge him with a small band of troops, and the battle between them lasted that day from mid-morning until noon. Manṣūr was forced to flee, and his own troops scattered, abandoning him. A party of Zanj caught up with Manṣūr and tracked him as far as the canal owned by ʿUmar b. Mihrān. Manṣūr repeatedly turned to attack his pursuers until at last his spears were all broken and his supply of arrows depleted, leaving him completely defenseless. He then made his way to the edge of the canal, intending to cross over. He shouted encouragement to his horse and it leaped, but failed to reach the other bank, and he plunged into the water.

Shibl said that the reason why the horse was unable to make the crossing successfully was because one of the Zanj had seen Manṣūr head for the canal bank, intending to cross over. Hurriedly throwing himself into the water, he swam across ahead of Manṣūr. When Manṣūr's horse jumped, the black confronted it, causing the horse to shy away, tumbling both itself and its rider into the water. Manṣūr's head bobbed to the surface, and a slave from among the blacks of Muṣliḥ's lieutenants called Abrūn struck him a mortal blow and then commenced to rob him. A large number of those with Manṣūr were killed, including his brother Khalaf b. Jaʿfar. Yārjūkh then placed [a

395. The reading is uncertain.

Turk named] Aṣghajūn[396] in charge of Manṣūr's administrative duties.

On Tuesday, the 18th of Jumādā I (April 1, 872), Mufliḥ was killed by an untipped arrow, which struck him in the temple. He died the following morning; his body was borne to Sāmarrā, and he was buried there. [1862]

An Account of [Mufliḥ's] Death[397]

I have already recounted how Abū Aḥmad [al-Muwaffaq] b. al-Mutawakkil departed from Sāmarrā and headed for al-Baṣrah to do battle with the cursed one.[398] I myself witnessed[399] in Baghdad the army with which Abū Aḥmad and Mufliḥ had set out. This was after the news had reached Abū Aḥmad and al-Muʿtamid concerning the atrocities endured by Muslims in al-Baṣrah and adjacent territories. The army passed by the Bāb al-Ṭāq,[400] the quarter where I was then staying, and I happened to hear a group of the elders of Baghdad saying that they had seen many armies of the caliphs but none that appeared larger and better equipped or prepared than this one. A large enthusiastic crowd of Baghdad's citizenry accompanied the army on its way through the city.

Muḥammad b. al-Ḥasan recounted that Yaḥyā b. Muḥammad al-Baḥrānī was camped on the Nahr Maʿqil before Abū Aḥmad's arrival in the locality of the abominable one. Yaḥyā sought permission of the Zanj leader to march on to the Nahr al-ʿAbbās, but this was strongly rejected out of fear that the central authorities' forces would arrive while his own troops were scattered in various places. Yaḥyā persisted, however, until he secured permission, and he departed, followed by the greater part of the abominable one's forces.

---

396. Thus in manuscript B; C, however, gives such alternative readings as Aṣfahūr and Asfajūr.

397. See Ibn al-Athīr, *Kāmil*, VII, 252–53.

398. This is the fourth epithet (*al-laʿīn*) Ṭabarī employs for the Zanj leader, the others being "abominable one," "traitor," and "enemy of God."

399. A rare personal comment by Ṭabarī on an event at which he himself was present.

400. This was the great arched gate at the eastern end of the Main Bridge in Baghdad, which opened directly onto the major market street of the eastern quarter of the city. See Le Strange, *Baghdad*, 178; Lassner, *Topography*, 173–76.

ʿAlī b. Abān was stationed in Jubbā with a large number of the Zanj. Al-Baṣrah had already been plundered by his troops and they were busy moving back and forth transporting the goods they had seized
[1863] from it. And so, at that time there were not many troops available to man the abominable one's own camp. His situation remained thus when Abū Aḥmad arrived with Mufliḥ and his army, a formidable and mighty force such as had never before been sent against the abominable one.

When this war machine reached the Nahr Maʿqil, those of the Zanj leader's troops who were stationed there fled, terrified, to join him. The abominable one was alarmed by this development, and he summoned two of his army chiefs who had been present at the Nahr Maʿqil and asked them why they had abandoned their position. They told him of the might of the approaching army they had seen, its equipment, and its high state of preparedness. There was no way their own forces were sufficient to stop it. The abominable one inquired whether they knew the identity of the army commander. They did not; although efforts had been made to discover who he was, they had failed, owing to the lack of a trustworthy informant. So the abominable one despatched scouts in skiffs to attempt to glean this intelligence. His messengers returned with information concerning the imposing might of the army, but none had been able to find out who the commander-in-chief or the other leaders were. This lack of information only served to increase his apprehension and dismay. So [the Zanj leader] sent urgent word to ʿAlī b. Abān informing him of the approaching danger and ordering him to bring to him such troops as he had available. The government's army arrived and established camp in front of the Zanj position. On the day of the battle, which was a Wednesday, the abominable one ventured forth on foot, making the rounds of his army to examine carefully the state of affairs on his own side, as well as those confronting him.

[1864] That day a light rain had fallen. The ground was wet, making it slippery underfoot. The Zanj leader had made an early morning reconnaissance and after his return he called for ink and paper to despatch a message to ʿAlī b. Abān. He informed him of what he had observed of the government forces and ordered him to send whatever number of infantry he could spare.

While [the Zanj leader] was thus engaged, someone called Abū Dulaf, who was one of the commanders of the blacks, came to him and said, "The enemy has advanced and the Zanj have fled from them; they had no leader among them to check their flight until they reached the fourth *ḥabl*."[401] The Zanj leader berated him loudly, saying, "Get out of my sight, you liar! You don't know what you're talking about. You have only been alarmed by the numbers of troops you have seen."

Abū Dulaf left him, and the abominable one then turned to his secretary, who had ordered Jaʿfar b. Ibrāhīm al-Sajjān[402] to summon the Zanj to move into the battlefield. Al-Sajjān informed the Zanj leader that he had despatched them and that his troops had seized two skiffs. Al-Sajjān was next commanded to get the infantry ready. It was only a short while after this that Mufliḥ was struck by an arrow from a concealed archer. Thereafter defeat was unavoidable, as the Zanj overwhelmed their enemy and engulfed them in a bloodbath. The Zanj brought to the abominable one heads of the enemy, holding them by their teeth, and tossed them at his feet; that day the heads of the enemy filled every corner. The Zanj even began to apportion the flesh of their victims among themselves and to exchange it as gifts. A prisoner from Farāghinah was brought before the traitor, who asked him who the commander of the army was, and he told him of the whereabouts of Abū Aḥmad and Mufliḥ. The Zanj leader was alarmed at the mention of Abū Aḥmad's name. Whenever he became alarmed by something, he would deny its truth. He said, [1865] "There is no leader in the army other than Mufliḥ, for I have heard mention of none save him. If the one this prisoner mentioned were in the army, he would be of such importance that Mufliḥ would only be his subordinate and adjutant to his associates."

When Abū Aḥmad's troops attacked the abominable one's camp, the noncombatants were filled with such fear that they fled from their dwellings and sought refuge by the Nahr Abī al-Khaṣīb. At this time there were no bridges spanning the water, and as a consequence

401. See Ṭabarī, *Glossarium*, CLXXIX, where the suggested meaning is one attested in Lane, *Lexicon*, as "'the station of the horses collected for a race before they are let go,' which was probably marked by an extended rope and was for that reason thus called." More likely, however, *ḥabl* means here a measure of distance, indicated by some marker. Le Strange, *Baghdad*, 326 n. 1, notes that al-Khaṭīb al-Baghdādī used the term *ḥabl* for a length equivalent to the side of a *jarīb*. See also Hinz, *Islamische Masse*, 62.

402. As his name suggests, he was a jailer.

a great number of women and children drowned in the attempt to cross it.

The abominable one had not long to wait after the battle before ʿAlī b. Abān arrived with a number of his troops, although by then there was little need of them. Shortly after Mufliḥ's death, Abū Aḥmad withdrew to al-Ubullah to reassemble his shattered forces and renew his preparations for war. Finally, he set out for Nahr Abī al-Asad and set up his camp there.

Muḥammad b. al-Ḥasan reported that the abominable one did not know how Mufliḥ had been killed.[403] But, when he heard that he had been hit by a stray arrow that no one claimed, he boasted that he had himself shot it. Muḥammad continued: "I heard him say that an arrow had fallen near him and his servant Wah[404] picked it up and brought it to him. He then shot it and killed Mufliḥ. I know that he lied about that, because I was present and witnessed the whole thing; he did not get off his horse until the battle was over and the news arrived of the enemy's defeat and the heads were brought."

In this year an epidemic struck the population of the Tigris districts, and many people died in Madīnat al-Salām, Sāmarrā, Wāsiṭ, and elsewhere.

In this year as well Khuraskhāris[405] was killed, along with a number of his troops in Byzantine territory.

[1866] Yaḥyā b. Muḥammad al-Baḥrānī, the close associate of the Zanj leader, was captured in this year and killed.

An Account of [Yaḥyā b. Muḥammad's] Capture and Death[406]

Muḥammad b. Simʿān the secretary reportedly said that when Yaḥyā b. Muḥammad reached the Nahr al-ʿAbbās he encountered at the mouth of the canal three hundred seventy horsemen from the forces of Aṣghajūn, who was in those days the financial administrator of al-Ahwāz; the horsemen were recruited from the same area. Upon seeing them, Yaḥyā underestimated their number and imagined

403. See Popovic, *Révolte*, 105 and n. 3.
404. Thus in Manuscript B; C is unpointed and could be read *bah/nah*, etc.
405. The reading is uncertain.
406. See Ibn al-Athīr, *Kāmil*, VII, 254.

that he had nothing to fear, given the size of his own force. So, without anything to protect them from danger, his troops attacked, and Aṣghajūn's soldiers rained arrows down upon them, injuring many. Yaḥyā then despatched one hundred twenty of his own horsemen across the canal, together with a large number of foot soldiers. Aṣghajūn's troops withdrew, allowing al-Baḥrānī's force to enter the canal. This was at a time of low water and the transport boats were stranded in the mud. The men on the boats saw the approaching Zanj and decided to abandon them, whereupon they were seized and an immense amount of valuable goods were plundered from them. The Zanj then headed for the marsh area known as the Baṭīḥah al-Ṣaḥnāh, carrying their spoils, but they left the well-traveled road, owing to the mutual envy that existed between al-Baḥrānī and ʿAlī b. Abān al-Muhallabī. Yaḥyā's companions advised him not to take the road frequented by ʿAlī's army. Yaḥyā accepted their advice, and [1867]
they set out for and finally entered the marshland, showing him the road we have just mentioned. There Yaḥyā granted leave to the cavalry and ordered Abū al-Layth al-Iṣbahānī to march them to the encampment of the Zanj commander.

The abominable one had sent word to Yaḥyā alerting him of the approaching army that he had encountered and urging him to be on his guard on his return lest he also run into the enemy. Al-Baḥrānī sent out some scouting parties to the Tigris and they left just as Abī Aḥmad's army was setting off from al-Ubullah for the Nahr Abī al-Asad.

The reason for the departure of the government's forces to the Nahr Abū al-Asad was that Rāfiʿ b. Bisṭām and others from the neighborhood of Nahr al-ʿAbbās and the Baṭīḥah al-Ṣaḥnāh had communicated with Abū Aḥmad informing him of al-Baḥrānī and the size of his forces and, moreover, that he was planning to leave Nahr al-ʿAbbās for the Tigris. They thus advised Abū Aḥmad to advance to the Nahr Abū al-Asad and establish his army camp there in order to interrupt the flow of supplies to al-Baḥrānī and preventing anyone coming to or going from his camp. Yaḥyā's scouts returned with the news of Abū Aḥmad's army, causing him increasingly to fear an encounter. He therefore turned back along the road he had come from, both he and his troops experiencing great hardship. They succumbed to a sickness owing to their constant exposure in the swamp and many of their number fell ill. As they neared the

Nahr al-ʿAbbās, Yaḥyā b. Muḥammad placed Sulaymān b. Jāmiʿ in charge of the vanguard of the Zanj who were engaged in towing their boats out of the Nahr al-ʿAbbās. The government forces, however, had barges and skiffs provided by Aṣghajūn guarding the mouth of the canal, along with contingents of cavalry and infantry. This situation caused considerable concern to Yaḥyā and his soldiers. The Zanj then abandoned their boats and took themselves off to the west
[1868] of the Nahr al-ʿAbbās making for the al-Zaydān road and the encampment of the abominable one.

Yaḥyā was totally in the dark about what had happened to this group [of Zanj]. No news reached him in the central sector of his army, which had just reached the Qūraj al-ʿAbbās Bridge (*qanṭarah*), at a narrow spot where the water flowed very swiftly in the channel. From there he could oversee his Zanj troops as they towed their boats, some of which sank while others were rescued.

Muḥammad b. Simʿān reported that while he was standing there by the bridge, Yaḥyā came up to him and was clearly astonished by the violent force of the water and the great difficulty experienced by his men in towing their boats. He said, "What do you imagine would happen if the enemy attacked us now; what situation could be worse the ours?" He was interrupted by the arrival of Ṭāshtimur al-Turkī with the army that Abū Aḥmad had despatched upon his return from al-Ubullah to the Nahr Abī al-Asad. Great consternation broke out among Yaḥyā's troops.

Muḥammad (b. Simān) continued: "I jumped up to take a look and saw red flags appear on the western side of the Nahr al-ʿAbbās were Yaḥyā was located. The Zanj spotted them and, throwing themselves into the canal, they crossed over to the eastern side. Yaḥyā's location became deserted, and only a few dozen men remained with him. At that Yaḥyā took up his shield and sword and wrapped a cloth around his waist. He met the approaching enemy with his small band and Ṭāshtimur's troops showered arrows upon them, swiftly causing many wounds. Al-Baḥrānī himself was wounded in three places, both his arms and his left leg. When his companions saw him injured, they scattered. However, as he was not recognized and no one made to finish him off, he retraced his way to one of the
[1869] boats and crossed over [as well] to the eastern side of the canal. The time was about midmorning."

The wounds that Yaḥyā had sustained sapped his strength. His

condition caused the Zanj's fear to increase and their resolve to weaken. They abandoned the battle, their only concern now being to save their own skins. The government troops plundered the boats situated on the western bank of the canal. When they had finished, they boarded one of the boats with fire-throwing machines and crossed over to the opposite bank where they proceeded to burn the craft the Zanj had abandoned there. The Zanj themselves had scattered, leaving Yaḥyā on his own. For the remainder of the day, those who could do so slipped away, leaving many dead and captured behind them, finally escaping under the protective cover of darkness. Seeing the total collapse of his forces, Yaḥyā boarded a galley that one of the white fighters was in charge of. He brought with him a practitioner of the medical arts called Abū Jaysh ʿAbbād, because of the injuries he was suffering from. His only desire was to make good his escape to the camp of the abominable one. As they approached the mouth of the canal, the sailors in the galley saw ahead of them barges and gallies [of the government forces] blockading the canal. They feared to approach too near, certain as they were to be apprehended. They then crossed over to the western bank and put Yaḥyā and those with him on shore at a small plantation. Yaḥyā made some distance on foot moving with difficulty until, too exhausted to go further, he dropped and spent the night where he was. The next morning the physician ʿAbbād, who was still with him, set out on foot carefully on the lookout for anyone. When he came across some of the government's troops, he signaled to them, told them where Yaḥyā was hiding, and then showed them the way, so that he fell into their hands. Some claim, however, that it had been another group of [1870]
people who, in passing by Yaḥyā, saw him and gave his position away so that he was captured. The news of Yaḥyā's fate reached the abominable one, leader of the Zanj, which greatly increased his unease and heightened his sense of sorrow at the loss.

Yaḥyā b. Muḥammad al-Azraq al-Baḥrānī was taken to Abū Aḥmad who transported him to al-Muʿtamid in Sāmarrā. A platform was ordered constructed at al-Ḥayr by the racecourse; Yaḥyā was then elevated before the crowd so they could witness him being publicly flogged. It is reported that he entered Sāmarrā on Wednesday, the 9th of Rajab (May 21, 872), seated upon a camel. Al-Muʿtamid held an assembly on the following morning, which was Thursday, and Yaḥyā was given two hundred strokes of a whip end in the Caliph's presence. Next his hands and legs were severed from opposite sides.[407] Then he was beaten severely with swords, drawn and quartered, and finally his body was burned.

Muḥammad b. al-Ḥasan related that, when Yaḥyā al-Baḥrānī was executed and the news of this reached the leader of the Zanj, he said, "Yaḥyā's death was deeply distressing to me and my anxiety was intense, when a voice addressed me saying that his death was a blessing for me, as he was a greedy person." Sometime later he approached a group of people I was standing with and said that an example of Yaḥyā's cupidity was the following story: "Once we had acquired a great deal of booty from one of the towns we took, and there came into his possession two necklaces of which the larger and more precious he concealed from me, showing me only the less valuable one, requesting that I give it to him as a gift. This I did. But I was then informed of the one he had hidden, and, summoning him, I said, 'Give me the necklace that you have concealed.' However, he produced only the one I had already presented to him, denying that he had taken any other. But, when I began to describe the necklace that had been reported to me, watching him, he became pale and speechless. He left and later brought me the second necklace and beseeched me to give it to him as a gift also. I did so and ordered him
[1871] to seek God's forgiveness for his deed."

Muḥammad b. al-Ḥasan — Muḥammad b. Simʿān reported that one day the Zanj leader said to him that he had been offered prophethood but that he had refused. Ibn Simʿān asked why and received the reply that prophethood involved burdens[408] he feared he had not the strength to bear.

In this same year Abū Aḥmad b. al-Mutawakkil withdrew from his position in the neighborhood of the Zanj leader and made for Wāsiṭ.

An Account of [Abū Aḥmad's] Withdrawal to Wāsiṭ[409]

After Abū Aḥmad had gone to the Nahr Abū al-Asad and camped there, illness and disease spread among his soldiers and others ac-

407. A punishment prescribed in Qur'ān 5:33 (al-Mā'idah).

408. Popovic, *Révolte*, 107, reads this word as *ʿabā*, "robe" (of prophethood), rather than *aʿbāʾan*, a plural in the accusative, as in the text; the emendation does not seem justified. See Halm, *Traditionen*, 215.

409. See Ibn al-Athīr, *Kāmil*, VII, 255–56.

companying him. A number died, but he could not move until those who survived had managed to recover. Abū Aḥmad then set out to return to Bādhāward,[410] where he camped. He ordered the renewal of the army's equipment and the distribution to the troops of their allotments. He also refurbished the barges, galleys, and ferries and placed them under the command of men from among his freedmen.[411]

Setting out in pursuit of the abominable one's army, Abū Aḥmad ordered a group of his commanders to make for certain spots that he listed, including the Nahr Abī al-Khaṣīb and other places. Other commanders he ordered to stay with him to fight at the spot he himself would select. When the battle resumed between the two sides, most of his forces moved toward the Nahr Abī al-Khaṣīb, while Abū Aḥmad remained with only a handful of his troops. He held his position for fear that the Zanj might be tempted to attack him and other groups of his forces exposed to them while they were in the salt flats of Nahr Mankā. The Zanj observed the dispersal of Abū [1872]
Aḥmad's troops and found out his [precarious] position, so they concentrated on it. Battle flared up furiously with many dead and injured on both sides. Abū Aḥmad's troops burned many of the fortified places and dwellings of the Zanj and rescued a large number of female [captives]. The Zanj then directed all their efforts toward the place where Abū Aḥmad was stationed. (Abū Aḥmad) al-Muwaffaq appeared on a barge and plunged into the middle of the battle, urging on his troops, until there arrived a crowd of Zanj whom he knew he could not combat, given the small number of his own followers. Realizing that the better part of valor would be to disengage from battle, he commanded his own troops to retreat to their boats in deliberate and orderly fashion. Abū Aḥmad then reboarded his barge after ensuring that most of his men were safely aboard their boats. A detachment remained behind, and they sought refuge in the heavy thickets and narrow waterways. They were completely cut off from their comrades. The Zanj ambushed them and picked them off one by one. These men defended themselves and in the hand-to-hand combat many Zanj met their fate. Nevertheless, some one hundred ten heads of Abū Aḥmad's soldiers were sent to the leader of the Zanj, which only served to increase his arrogance.

---

410. Located between al-Baṣrah and Wāsiṭ. See Yaḥyā, *Muʿjam*, I, 462.

411. The phrase is *min mawālihi wa-ghilmānihi*.

Abū Aḥmad finally managed to make it back with his army to al-Bādhāward, where he stayed, mustering his troops for another round against the Zanj. A fire broke out at one end of the camp during a period of violent wind storms and the camp burned down. Then, in Shaʿbān of this year (June 12–July 10, 872), Abū Aḥmad made the return journey to Wāsiṭ and, after his arrival, the bulk of his troops dispersed.

On the 10th of Shaʿbān (June 21, 872) a dreadful, thunderous
[1873] earthquake[412] occurred in al-Ṣaymarah.[413] Then the following morning, which was Sunday, an even greater crash than the first was heard, and as a result most of the city was destroyed. Everywhere walls of buildings collapsed, and, according to what was said, some twenty thousand persons were killed.

A man known as Abū Faqʿas was roundly beaten at the Public Gate in Sāmarrā, one thousand twenty strokes being administered. The charge against him was abusing the pious ancestors (*salaf*). He died on Thursday, the 7th of Ramaḍān (July 15, 872).

On Friday, the 8th of Ramaḍān (July 16, 872), Yārjūkh died. Abū ʿĪsā b. al-Mutawakkil recited the funerary prayers for him, with Jaʿfar b. al-Muʿtamid present.

In this year as well there occurred a battle between Mūsā b. Bughā and the troops of al-Ḥasan b. Zayd, who were routed.

Masrūr al-Balkhī returned to Sāmarrā after his campaign against the Khārijite Musāwir. He brought back Khārijite prisoners and left Juʿlān behind as deputy of his army in al-Ḥadīthah.[414] Later Masrūr himself set out for the district of al-Bawāzīj,[415] where he encountered Musāwir again. In the ensuing battle a number of Musāwir's troops were captured. Before the end of Dhū al-Ḥijjah (October 8 to November 6, 872) Masrūr set out on the return journey.

412. The word is *haddah*, which Lane, *Lexicon*, s.v. *h-d-d*, states is a violent sound occasioned by a falling wall or part of a mountain; an earthquake certainly seems to have been the cause of the destruction.

413. The chief town in the district of Mihrajānqudhaq, on the frontier of Iraq. See Le Strange, *Lands*, 201–2.

414. This is Ḥadīthat al-Nūrah (Ḥadīthah of the Chalk Pit), which is on the Tigris and must be distinguished from the city al-Ḥadīthah on the Euphrates. See Le Strange, *Lands*, 64. Ibn al-Athīr, *Kāmil*, VII, 257, calls the location Ḥadīthat al-Mawṣil, which would refer to the same place, that is, Ḥadīthah in the district of al-Mawṣil.

415. The town of Bawāzīj lay on the bank of the Lower Zab river, east of Sinn on the Tigris. See Le Strange, *Lands*, 91.

In the same year a malady overcame people in Baghdad. It was called *quffāʿ*.[416]

In this year most of the Ḥājj pilgrims returned from al-Qarʿāʾ[417] out of a fear of thirst. But those who went on to Mecca arrived safely. The leader of the pilgrimage this year was al-Faḍl b. Isḥāq b. al-Ḥasan.[418]

---

416. A person described as *aqfaʿ* is one whose toes are misshapen. See A. de Biberstein Kazimirski, *Dictionnaire arabe-français*, s.v. *q-f-ʿ*.

417. Literally, "bare," so named, according to Yaḥyā, *Muʿjam*, IV, 325, because of its lack of vegetation. It was a stage on the route from al-Kūfah to Mecca.

418. This was the second year in succession that he had led the pilgrimage. See p. 135, above.

The Events of the Year 259[419]

(November 7, 872–October 26, 873)

Among the events of this year was the return of Abū Aḥmad b. al-Mutawakkil from Wāsiṭ to Sāmarrā. He arrived on Friday, the 26th of Rabīʿ I (January 30, 873). He appointed Muḥammad al-Muwallad to be responsible for Wāsiṭ and for pursuing the war against the abominable one in the area.[420]

The death of Kanjūr[421] occurred in this year.

An Account of [Kanjūr's] Death

At the time he was governor of al-Kūfah, Kanjūr left it without official sanction for Sāmarrā. He refused an order to return to al-Kūfah and so, according to what has been reported, money was transported

---

419. Popovic, *Révolte*, 109, notes the disproportionate amount of detail that Ṭabarī provides on the Zanj revolt. The years 255–58/868–72 cover more than twice the space given to the succeeding period, 259–65/873–79. In this latter period, Ṭabarī highlights only the important developments in the revolt.

420. See Popovic, *Révolte*, 108ff.

421. See n. 336, above.

to him to be distributed among his troops for their allotments. This failed to mollify Kanjūr, and he continued as far as ʿUkbarāʾ[422] in the month of Rabīʿ I (January 5–February 3, 873). In response, a number of army commanders were sent from Sāmarrā to deal with him, among them Sātikīn, Takīn, ʿAbd al-Raḥmān b. Mufliḥ, Mūsā b. Utāmish, and others. They butchered him and sent his head to Sāmarrā. This was on the 29th of Rabīʿ I (February 2, 873). Some forty thousand dinars were seized from him at the same time. Kanjūr's Christian secretary was forced to surrender more money. Then in the following month, Rabīʿ II (February 4 to March 4, 873), this secretary was punished by being given one thousand lashes at the Public Gate [in Sāmarrā], from which he died.

In this year Sharkab al-Jammāl conquered Marv and its adjacent territories and plundered them.

Yaʿqūb b. al-Layth returned from Balkh in this year and resided in [1875]
Quhistān.[423] He appointed financial prefects over Herāt, Būshanj, and Bādhghīs, and then he departed for Sijistān.[424]

In this year as well ʿAbdallāh al-Sijzī[425] abandoned Yaʿqūb ibn al-Layth, breaking his bond of loyalty to him, and blockaded Naysābūr.[426] Then Muḥammad b. Ṭāhir sent messengers and legists to sort out matters, and they went back and forth between them [conducting negotiations], and finally ʿAbdallāh was appointed governor of al-Ṭabasayn and Quhistān.[427]

---

422. A town lying on the east bank of the Tigris, about halfway between Baghdad and Sāmarrā. See Le Strange, *Lands*, 50, 51; Le Strange, "Ibn Serapion's Description," 33, 38–39.

423. The province of Quhistān was generally regarded by Arab geographers as a dependency of Khurāsān. See Le Strange, *Lands*, 352ff. The movements of Yaʿqūb b. al-Layth mentioned in this paragraph reflect the expansion of his power in the eastern provinces of the ʿAbbāsid domains. See Bosworth, "Ṭāhirids," 115ff.

424. The province situated on the southern border of Khurāsān; it was also called Sīstān. Le Strange, *Lands*, 334–51, 431.

425. That is, a native of the province of Sijistān. See also Ibn al-Athīr, *Kāmil*, VII, 261–62.

426. One of the four major cities of the province of Khurāsān, the others being Marv, Herāt, and Balkh. See Le Strange, *Lands*, 382–88.

427. There were two places in Quhistān called Ṭabas; Ṭabas al-Tamr and Ṭabas al-ʿUnnāb, which are often referred to in the dual form Ṭabasayn. This province of Quhistān, which means "mountain land," is not to be confused with the Persian equivalent of the district known in Arabic as al-Jibāl. See Le Strange, *Lands*, 186, 359.

On the 6th of Rajab (May 8, 873) of this year (ʿAlī b. Abān) al-Muhallabī and Yaḥyā b. Khalaf al-Nahrabaṭṭī overran Sūq al-Ahwāz and killed a great many inhabitants, including the chief of security.

An Account of [the] Battle [at Sūq al-Ahwāz] and How the Army Commander[428] of the Central Authorities Was Killed

The burning of Abū Aḥmad's military camp in al-Bādhāward was reported to have been kept from the leader of the Zanj. He discovered what had happened only three days later, when two men from ʿAbbādān visited him and gave him the news.

At this the Zanj leader returned to plundering, as supplies of food were cut off from him. He sent off ʿAlī b. Abān al-Muhallabī with most of the army accompanied by Sulaymān b. Jāmiʿ, who had taken charge of the forces formerly under Yaḥyā b. Muḥammad al-Baḥrānī and Sulaymān b. Mūsā al-Shaʿrānī. Sulaymān was also placed in charge of the cavalry while the rest of the troops were with ʿAlī b. Abān al-Muhallabī.

At the time the governor of al-Ahwāz was someone called Aṣghajūn; stationed there with him were Nayzak and a number of other
[1876] commanders. ʿAlī b. Abān approached al-Ahwāz with his Zanj forces, and when Aṣghajūn was alerted to this he advanced toward ʿAlī with his own troops, the two sides meeting in the desert wastes of Dastimārān. That day fate was against Aṣghajūn, who was drowned, while Nayzak and many of his troops were slain. Al-Ḥasan b. Harthamah al-Shār and al-Ḥasan b. Jaʿfar Zāwashār were both taken prisoner the same day.

Muḥammad b. al-Ḥasan — al-Ḥasan b. (al-Harthamah) al-Shār said, "That day we left al-Ahwāz with Aṣghajūn to meet the Zanj, but our troops were unable to stand their ground, and they fled; Nayzak was killed, and Aṣghajūn went missing. When I became aware of this, I dismounted from my own crop-tailed horse.[429] By leading another horse I had with me into the river and seizing hold of its tail, I planned to make good my escape. But my servant beat me to it, making his escape and leaving me behind. I then tried to join Mūsā

428. *Ṣāḥib al-ḥarb.*
429. *Faras mahdhūf.* See Lane, *Lexicon,* s.v. *h-dh-f.*

b. Ja'far so the two us could get away together, but he had boarded a rivercraft and departed without waiting for me. I caught sight of another boat, which I managed to board, but a crowd gathered round demanding to be taken on board as well, and, with so many clinging to the craft, they caused it to capsize. I scrambled onto the overturned hull and the crowd departed just as the Zanj arrived. They began shooting arrows at me and, as I felt my end was near, I cried out to them, 'Stop shooting and toss me something that I can grab myself and reach you.' So they extended a spear, which I grabbed with my hand, and they pulled me out. As for al-Ḥasan b. Ja'far, his brother put him on a horse and set him up to act as a messenger between him and the commander of the army. But, in the wake of [1877] defeat and in his haste to find safety, his horse stumbled, and he was captured."

'Alī b. Abān relayed the news of the battle to the abominable one and sent him many enemy heads and banners as well. Al-Ḥasan b. al-Shār, al-Ḥasan b. Ja'far, and Aḥmad b. Rūḥ, along with other captives, were ordered imprisoned. Meanwhile 'Alī b. Abān entered al-Ahwāz and systematically pillaged it, forcing the central authorities to assign Mūsā b. Bughā to the task of waging war against the abominable one.

Mūsā b. Bughā left Sāmarrā for this purpose on the 17th of Dhū al-Qa'dah (September 14, 873). Al-Mu'tamid accompanied him in public procession as far as the city walls and there bestowed robes of honor upon him.

This same year 'Abd al-Raḥmān b. Mufliḥ arrived in al-Ahwāz, Isḥāq b. Kundāj[430] in al-Baṣrah, and Ibrāhīm b. Sīmā in Bādhāward, all acting on authority of Mūsā b. Bughā in preparation for waging war aginst the Zanj leader.

An Account of How [Mūsā b. Bughā's Commanders] Fared against the Zanj[431]

Following Ibn Mufliḥ's arrival in al-Ahwāz, he reportedly encamped for ten days at the Arbuk Bridge and then set out against ('Alī b. Abān) al-Muhallabī. Ibn Mufliḥ was defeated in the encounter by al-

430. Ibn al-Athīr, *Kāmil*, VII, 260, calls him Isḥāq b. Kandajīq.
431. See Ibn al-Athīr, *Kāmil*, VII, 259–60.

Muhallabī and forced to withdraw to regroup his forces. Ibn Mufliḥ returned to do battle again. In the violent fighting the Zanj were dealt a devastating blow in numbers killed and taken captive. ʿAlī b. Abān was routed, yet managed to escape with some followers to Bayān. The abominable one tried to induce them to return to battle but, owing to the fear that gripped their hearts, they could not. When he saw the situation as it was, he allowed them to enter his camp;
[1878] they did so and settled for a time in his city.

ʿAbd al-Raḥmān (b. Mufliḥ) arrived in Ḥiṣn al-Mahdī[432] to establish his army there. The abominable one sent ʿAlī b. Abān to fight him but, as ʿAlī was unable to overcome Ibn Mufliḥ, he headed for a place called al-Dakar. At this time Ibrāhīm b. Sīmā was in al-Bādhāward, and in one engagement he defeated ʿAlī, who, when he returned to the attack, was beaten again. During the night ʿAlī left and, accompanied by some guides who led him through the dense thickets and copses, he reached Nahr Yaḥyā. ʿAbd al-Raḥmān received news of ʿAlī's [movements] and despatched Ṭāshtimur against him with a contingent of *mawlās*. However, owing to the inaccessibility of ʿAlī's position and the impenetrable barrier of reeds and grasses, Ṭāshtimur failed to reach him. So he forced them out by setting fire to the vegetation. A number of Zanj were captured, and Ṭāshtimur brought them and [news of] the victory to ʿAbd al-Raḥmān b. Mufliḥ while ʿAlī b. Abān made his way to Nasūkhā[433] and set up camp there with the remainder of his forces. News of ʿAlī's move reached ʿAbd al-Raḥmān b. Mufliḥ, and he immediately shifted his own camp to al-ʿAmūd.

Meanwhile, ʿAlī b. Abān had gone toward Nahr al-Sidrah,[434] where he wrote to the abominable one seeking his reinforcements and barges. Thirteen barges were sent containing several contingents of Zanj troops. With these ʿAlī set out to meet ʿAbd al-Raḥmān b. Mufliḥ, who had also made his way toward an encounter. However, no fighting occurred and the two armies stood arrayed against each other for the whole day. After nightfall, ʿAlī hand-
[1879] picked a number of his troops, in whose courage and fortitude he had

---

432. A fortress situated at the head of the estuary of the Dujayl. See Le Strange, *Lands*, 238, 243; Le Strange, "Ibn Serapion's Description," 313.

433. The reading is conjectural.

434. The broad reach of the Dujayl below al-Ahwāz was known as Nahr al-Sidrah, the Lotus canal. See Yāqūt, *Muʿjam*, II, 258.

complete trust. Leaving the rest of his army behind in order to conceal his real intentions, ʿAlī set out with these select few accompanied by Sulaymān b. Mūsā al-Shaʿrānī. Taking up a position in the rear of ʿAbd al-Raḥmān, ʿAlī launched a surprise night attack on the camp and inflicted serious losses on him and his troops, forcing ʿAbd al-Raḥmān to retreat and abandon four of his own fleet of barges; ʿAlī recovered these and departed. ʿAbd al-Raḥmān proceeded as far as al-Dūlāb,[435] where he reestablished his camp. Placing Ṭāshtimur in command of some of his infantry troops, he sent them into another campaign against ʿAlī b. Abān. Ṭāshtimur and ʿAlī met each other in the environs of Bayān Āzar.[436] In the fighting ʿAlī was forced to flee to Nahr al-Sidrah. When Ṭāshtimur sent word of ʿAlī's defeat to ʿAbd al-Raḥmān, he set out with his army to reach al-ʿAmūd, where he set up camp and prepared his troops for battle. The barges, over which Ṭāshtimur was given command, were put in order and with them he ventured forth to the mouth of Nahr al-Sidrah, where he engaged ʿAlī b. Abān in a major battle. ʿAlī was again routed, losing ten of his barges and being forced to return in defeat to the abominable one. ʿAbd al-Raḥmān immediately set up his army camp in Bayān, from which both he and Ibrāhīm b. Sīmā advanced and attacked by turns the abominable one's position, stirring great fear among those in his camp.

Isḥāq b. Kundāj, who at the time was stationed in al-Baṣrah, had cut off the flow of supplies to the army of the abominable one. On the day that he feared that ʿAbd al-Raḥmān and Ibrāhīm b. Sīmā would come out against him, the abominable one would gather together his forces until the battle was over and then send a detach- [1880] ment of them to the outskirts of al-Baṣrah, where Isḥāq b. Kundāj would attack them. For over ten months they remained deadlocked in this fashion, until Mūsā b. Bughā was replaced by Masrūr al-Balkhī as the one in charge of conducting the campaign against the abominable one. News of this change reached the abominable one.

In this same year al-Ḥasan b. Zayd conquered Qūmis,[437] and his troops occupied the city.

---

435. Yāqūt, *Muʿjam*, II, 622, where it is written as al-Dawlab.

436. Emended from the text: Bayāb Āzar. The critical apparatus suggests Bayān is a possible reading in Manuscript B, which is supported also in C. The reading Bayān would also seem to be supported by its mention a few lines later, though in both B and C it is unpointed.

437. This small province stretched along the foot of the chain of the Alburz moun-

In this year as well a battle occurred between Muḥammad b. al-Faḍl b. Sinān al-Qazwīnī and Wahsūdhān b. Justān al-Daylamī,[438] who was routed by Muḥammad.

Mūsā b. Bughā appointed al-Ṣalābī[439] this year as governor of al-Rayy, at the time when Kayghalagh attacked Takīn[440] and killed him. Al-Ṣalābī went to take up his post.

The Byzantine emperor[441] conquered Sumaysāṭ[442] in this year and also attacked Malaṭyah[443] and besieged its inhabitants, who fought back and succeeded in driving him off. Aḥmad b. Muḥammad al-Qābūs killed Naṣr al-Iqrīṭashī, the supreme commander.[444]

This year, too, a group of Zanj prisoners was sent to Sāmarrā from al-Ahwāz. The Sāmarrān mob attacked and killed many of them and stripped their bodies.

Yaʿqūb b. al-Layth entered Naysābūr this year.

[1881]

An Account of [Yaʿqūb b. al-Layth's Entry into Naysābūr][445]

Yaʿqūb b. al-Layth had reportedly gone to Herāt and then headed for Naysābūr. As he approached the city, intending to enter it, Muḥammad b. Ṭāhir sent word to him requesting that Yaʿqūb receive him, but he refused to comply. So Muḥammad had some of his kinsmen intercede on his behalf with Yaʿqūb, after which, in the evening of the 4th of Shawwāl (August 3, 873), Yaʿqūb entered the city and encamped in one of the suburbs called Dāʾūdābādh. Muḥammad b. Ṭāhir rode out to meet Yaʿqūb in his pavilion, where he was closely

tains. The capital town was al-Damghān, which the Arabs often called (Madīnat) Qūmis. See Le Strange, *Lands*, 364–65.

438. One of the chiefs of the Daylamites who, in 250/864, had sworn allegiance to the ʿAlid al-Ḥasan b. Zayd in a collaborative campaign against the Ṭāhirid Sulaymān b. ʿAbdallāh. See Ṭabarī, III, 1527–28.

439. Unidentified.

440. The reading is uncertain, and therefore it is not clear that this is the same person as the army commander mentioned on p. 151, above, who was despatched with others to deal with Kanjūr. There is no evidence that the latter Takīn held the governorship of al-Rayy, which is what the context suggests.

441. See n. 385, above.

442. A town on the Euphrates in the district of Diyār Muḍar, which bordered on the province of the Jazīrah. Le Strange, *Lands*, 87.

443. Called by the Greeks Melitene; it was an important fortress on the frontier between Muslim and Byzantine territory. See Le Strange, *Lands*, 120.

444. *Biṭrīq al-Baṭāriqah*, commander of ten thousand men.

445. See also Ibn al-Athīr, *Kāmil*, VII, 261–62.

questioned. Yaʿqūb then began to upbraid and rebuke Muḥammad for neglecting his duties, after which he appointed ʿUzayz b. al-Sarī as his agent and replaced Muḥammad b. Ṭāhir with him as governor of Naysābūr. Muḥammad b. Ṭāhir and his kinsmen were imprisoned, and, when news of this reached the central authorities, they despatched Ḥātim b. Zayrak b. Salām to Yaʿqūb at once. One the 20th of Dhū al-Qaʿdah (September 17, 873) the central authorities received Yaʿqūb's communications. According to report, Jaʿfar b. al-Muʿtamid and Abū Aḥmad b. al-Mutawakkil held an audience in the main hall of the Jawsaq palace, attended by the army commanders. Permission was granted Yaʿqūb's messengers to address them, and they related details that had come to Yaʿqūb's attention concerning the state of affairs among the population of Khurāsān, where Khārijites and brigands had overrun the place, gravely weakening Muḥammad b. Ṭāhir's position. This had caused people to correspond with Yaʿqūb, imploring him to come to their assistance, to which request he responded. When Yaʿqūb was still ten *farsakh*s[446] from Naysābūr, people from the city met him and surrendered it, allowing him to enter.

Abū Aḥmad (b. al-Mutawakkil) and ʿUbaydallāh b. Yaḥyā then spoke to the messengers, saying that the Commander of the Faithful [1882] could not condone what Yaʿqūb had done. He was therefore ordering Yaʿqūb to return to the duties in his own province. As he had no justification for doing what he had done without orders, he must return [to his province]. If he returned, he would be behaving as a governor should; if not, then he would be treated as a rebel. Yaʿqūb's messengers were sent back. [Before they left] they were each presented with a three-piece robe of honor.[447] They had brought with them a head stuck upon a lance with a message on it, which read: "This is the head of God's enemy ʿAbd al-Raḥmān the Khārijite, who for thirty years falsely professed himself caliph in Herāt. He was slain by Yaʿqūb b. al-Layth."

Leading the pilgrimage this year was Ibrāhīm b. Muḥammad b. Ismāʿīl b. Jaʿfar b. Sulaymān b. ʿAlī b. ʿAbdallāh b. ʿAbbās, who was known as Burayh.[448]

---

446. About 60 km.

447. *Khilʿah fīha thalāthah athwāb*. See n. 257, above.

448. Ibn al-Athīr, *Kāmil*, VII, 272, identifies him as governor (*al-ʿāmil*) and *amīr* of Mecca.

The Events of the Year 260

(October 27, 873–October 15, 874)

Among the events taking place this year was the death of Muḥammad b. Hārūn b. al-Muʿammar,[449] who was slain by one of the Kurds of Musāwir the Khārijite. Discovered aboard a boat heading for Sāmarrā, Muḥammad was killed, and his severed head sent to Musāwir. In Jumādā II (March 24, 874 – April 21, 874) [the tribe of] Rabīʿah sought to avenge Muḥammad's death, and so Masrūr al-Balkhī and a number of the other commanders were ordered to go after Musāwir.

[1883] In this year as well the leader of the Zanj killed ʿAlī b. Zayd al-ʿAlawī,[450] the master of al-Kūfah.

Yaʿqūb b. al-Layth in this same year fought and routed al-Ḥasan b. Zayd al-Ṭālibī and then entered Ṭabaristān.

An Account of [the] Battle [in Ṭabaristān][451]

Well-informed sources related to me that in the struggle for dominance of Sijistān between Yaʿqūb and ʿAbdallāh al-Sijzī, Yaʿqūb got

449. Ibn al-Athīr, *Kāmil*, VII, 273, calls him Ibn al-Maʿmar.

450. His full name was ʿAlī b. Zayd b. al-Ḥusayn b. ʿĪsā b. Zayd b. ʿAlī b. al-Ḥusayn b. ʿAlī b. Abī Ṭālib. See Popovic, *Révolte*, 110, for details.

451. See Ibn al-Athīr, *Kāmil*, VII, 268–69.

the upper hand, while ʿAbdallāh managed to escape from him and join Muḥammad b. Ṭāhir in Naysābūr. When Yaʿqūb reached Naysābūr, ʿAbdallāh fled and joined up with al-Ḥasan b. Zayd,[452] following which Yaʿqūb set out in pursuit of him, after what went on between him and Muḥammad b. Ṭāhir, as I have already mentioned before.

On his way into Ṭabaristān he passed Asfarā'īm[453] and its territories. A man lived there whom I used to know, called Badīl al-Kashshī. He was a collector of prophetic traditions and [was known for] practicing supererogatory works and commanding the good. He had been well received by the common people of this district. When Yaʿqūb stayed there he sent word to Badīl, informing him that they were alike in their performance of supererogatory works. Yaʿqūb continued to treat him with courtesy until Badīl ventured to come to visit him. Once in his power, however, Yaʿqūb placed Badīl in fetters and took him along to Ṭabarīstān, where, as he approached Sāriyah,[454] he was met by al-Ḥasan b. Zayd.

I was also told that Yaʿqūb sent word to al-Ḥasan b. Zayd, requesting that he deliver ʿAbdallāh al-Sijzī to him, after which he would depart, as he had come to Ṭabaristān only for the sake of ʿAbdallāh, not to pick a fight with al-Ḥasan. However, al-Ḥasan b. Zayd refused [1884]
to hand over ʿAbdallāh. Yaʿqūb then informed al-Ḥasan of his intention to attack. The two armies met with neither side at first gaining the upper hand, though al-Ḥasan was finally forced to flee and head for al-Shirriz[455] and the country of Daylam. Yaʿqūb occupied Sāriyah and then proceeded toward Āmul,[456] collecting from its inhabitants a year's taxes. From Āmul he left for al-Shirriz in pursuit of al-Ḥasan b. Zayd. Upon reaching the mountains of Ṭabaristān, he encountered a period of uninterrupted rainfall which, according to my reports, lasted for some forty days. Only with extreme difficulty was he able to advance. As I was told, he had managed to ascend a moun-

452. Ṭabarī reported his last whereabouts in Qūmis, which he captured in 259. See p. 155, above. Ibn al-Athīr, *Kāmil*, VII, 268, reports that at this time he was in Ṭabaristān, where ʿAbdallāh joined him.

453. Also written as Asfarayn, for which, see Le Strange, *Lands*, 393. It was a prosperous city in Khurāsān, located in a large plain of the same name.

454. At this time Sāriyah, rather than Āmul, was the seat of the Ṭāhirid governor in Ṭabaristān. See Le Strange, *Lands*, 370.

455. The reading is uncertain.

456. Le Strange, *Lands*, 370, 381.

tain, but the descent was possible only by his being borne upon the shoulders of his men, as most of the pack animals had perished. Thereafter he resumed his pursuit of al-Ḥasan b. Zayd to al-Shirriz.

Someone from that district informed me that Yaʿqūb finally reached the road he had sought to join and there he paused with his troops. He advanced in front of them, carefully inspecting the way before finally rejoining his troops and ordering them to turn back. He said to his men, "If there is no other road than this, then there is no way of overtaking al-Ḥasan b. Zayd." The same person who had mentioned this to me also informed me that the women of this district said to their men, "Let him come, for, if Yaʿqūb ventures upon this road, we will take care of him for you. We will be responsible for seizing and imprisoning him for you."

When Yaʿqūb returned from the border area of Ṭabaristān, he reviewed his troops and discovered, as I was told, that he had lost forty thousand men along with the greater part of his horses, camels, and baggage, which were also lost.

It is said that he wrote to the central authorities about his expedition against al-Ḥasan b. Zayd and of his departure from Jurjān to
[1885] Ṭamīs,[457] which he conquered. He then noted his passage to Sāriyah where al-Ḥasan b. Zayd had destroyed the bridges and removed the ferries, thus preventing any advance along that road. Al-Ḥasan b. Zayd was camped before the gate of Sāriyah, naturally protected by the surrounding great river valleys. Khurshād b. Jīlaw, the chief of Daylam, had come to al-Ḥasan's aid, providing a powerful force composed of troops gathered from Ṭabaristān, Daylam, Khurāsān, Qumm, al-Jabal, al-Shām, and al-Jazīrah. Yaʿqūb said, "I routed al-Ḥasan and slew a greater number of the enemy than I've ever seen before, capturing as well seventy of the Ṭālibiyyīn." That took place in Rajab (April 22–May 21, 874). Al-Ḥasan b. Zayd returned to al-Shirriz, taking the Daylamites with him.

In this year in many of the Islamic lands prices shot up. According to one report, those who were living in Mecca for religous reasons

457. Le Strange, *Lands*, 375, notes that Ṭamīs (or Ṭamīsah) lay on the eastern frontier of Ṭabaristān, three marches distant from Sāriyah; it stood "on the great causeway across the marches which had been built to carry the high road by King Anūshirwan the Just." See also Yāqūt, *Muʿjam*, III, 503–4. This description helps clarify Ḥasan b. Zayd's moves to prevent passage along the road.

abandoned it for Medina and other places because price rises were particularly severe [in Mecca]. The financial administrator, [Ibrāhīm b. Muḥammad] Burayh, who had been living in Mecca, also left the city. In Baghdad, too, prices rose, a *kurr*[458] of barley reaching one hundred twenty dinars, while wheat[459] reached one hundred fifty dinars a *kurr*. The situation remained this way for several months.[460]

Arab tribesmen this year killed Manjūr the governor of Ḥimṣ. Baktimur (b. Tashtimur) was made governor in his place.

Yaʿqūb b. al-Layth left Ṭabaristān this year for the district of al-Rayy. According to a report I received, the reason for this was the fact that, after Yaʿqūb's defeat of al-Ḥasan b. Zayd, ʿAbdallāh al-Sijzī had sought protection from Yaʿqūb with al-Ṣalābī, offering him the choice of either delivering ʿAbdallāh al-Sijzī to him, enabling him to return and leave al-Ṣalābī's jurisdiction, or else engaging in battle. According to what I was told, al-Ṣalābī chose to hand over ʿAbdallāh. [1886]
This done, Yaʿqūb killed ʿAbdallāh and then departed al-Ṣalābī's territory.

In this year al-ʿAlāʾ b. Aḥmad al-Azdī was slain.

An Account of [al-Azdī's] Death

It was reported that al-ʿAlāʾ b. Aḥmad suffered a stroke and became gravely incapacitated as a result. The central authorities sent to Abū al-Rudaynī ʿUmar b. ʿAlī b. Murr, confirming him in the governorship of Adharbayjān, a position held by al-ʿAlāʾ b. Aḥmad. Abū al-Rudaynī set out to take possession of the province from al-ʿAlāʾ. In Ramaḍān (June 20–July 19, 874) al-ʿAlāʾ, borne upon a litter, went forth to confront in battle Abū al-Rudaynī, who was accompanined by a crowd of Khārijites and others. Al-ʿAlāʾ was killed. It is also reported that al-Rudaynī sent a number of his men to seize al-ʿAlāʾ's possessions, which he had left behind; goods valued at two million

---

458. A measure of wheat, etc., consisting of six assloads. See Lane, *Lexicon*, s.v. *k-r-r*. See also Hinz, *Islamische Masse*, 64.

459. Ibn al-Athīr, *Kāmil*, VII, 272, mentions only the price of wheat, which rose to one hundred twenty dinars.

460. Ibn al-Athīr, *Kāmil*, VII, 273, adds in a separate note that price increases were also severe in Ifrīqiyah, the Maghrib, al-Andalus, and other places, which resulted in many deaths from epidemics and plague.

seven hundred thousand dirhams were removed from his fortress.

In this year the Byzantines captured Luʾluʾah[461] from the Muslims.

Leading the pilgrimage this year was Ibrāhīm b. Muḥammad b. Ismāʿīl b. Jaʿfar b. Sulaymān b. ʿAlī, known as Burayh.

---

461. See Yāqūt, *Muʿjam*, IV, 371, who identifies Luʾluʾah as a fortress near Tarsus. At this time it seemed to change hands regularly; Ṭabarī notes at the end of the year 263 (877) that the fortress was (again?) surrendered by the Muslims to their enemies.

The Events of the Year 261

(October 16, 874–October 5, 875)

Among the events occurring this year was the departure of al-Ḥasan b. Zayd from the land of Daylam for Ṭabaristān. He destroyed Shālūs[462] by fire [in revenge] for the assistance its people had given to Yaʿqūb. He also converted their estates into fiefs for the Daylamites.

Also this year the central authorities ordered ʿUbaydallāh b. ʿAbdallāh b. Ṭāhir to round up the pilgrims present in Baghdad from [1887]
Khurāsān, al-Rayy, Ṭabaristān, and Jurjān. This he did in Ṣafar (November 15 – December 13, 874) and read to them a declaration in which they were informed by the central authorities that Yaʿqūb b. al-Layth had not been commissioned as governor of Khurāsān. They were, furthermore, ordered to disavow him, because the Caliph disapproved his entry into Khurāsān and his capture of Muḥammad b. Ṭāhir.

ʿAbdallāh b. al-Wāthiq died this year in the army camp of Yaʿqūb al-Ṣaffār.

---

462. A city two days march west of Āmul, with a large stone castle and adjoining congregational mosque. See Le Strange, *Lands*, 373.

In this year as well, during the month of Jumādā II (February 11–March 12, 875), Musāwir the Khārijite killed Yaḥyā b. Ḥafṣ, who administered the Khurāsān Road, in Karkh Juddān.[463] Masrūr al-Balkhī went out in pursuit of Musāwir, and he was followed by Abū Aḥmad b. al-Mutawakkil. Musāwir withdrew and was not overtaken by his pursuers.

In Jumādā I (February 1–March 1, 876) of this year Abū Hāshim Dāʾūd b. Sulaymān al-Jaʿfarī was slain.

A battle took place in Rāmhurmuz this year between Muḥammad b. Wāṣil and ʿAbd al-Raḥmān b. Mufliḥ, who was with Ṭāshtimur. Ibn Wāṣil killed Ṭāshtimur and captured Ibn Mufliḥ.

An Account of [the] Battle [of Rāmhurmuz][464]

According to reports I have received, the cause was because Ibn Wāṣil had killed al-Ḥārith b. Sīmā, the agent of the central government in Fārs, which had now fallen to Ibn Wāṣil. Fārs, along with al-Ahwāz, al-Baṣrah, al-Baḥrayn, and al-Yamāmah, was now assigned
[1888] to Mūsā b. Bughā, in addition to the east, which he already controlled. Mūsā b. Bughā despatched ʿAbd al-Raḥmān b. Mufliḥ to al-Ahwāz to govern it and Fārs, giving him the assistance of Ṭāshtimur. Ibn Wāṣil got word of Mūsā's decision and also that Ibn Mufliḥ was headed for Fārs in pursuit of him, having previously been stationed in al-Ahwāz, where he had conducted a campaign against the Khārijite in al-Baṣrah.

Ibn Wāṣil marched toward Ibn Mufliḥ, and the two sides met in Rāmhurmuz, where Abū Dāʾūd al-Ṣaʿlūk[465] joined forces with Ibn Wāṣil as support against Ibn Mufliḥ. In his triumph Ibn Wāṣil captured Ibn Mufliḥ, while destroying his army and slaying Ṭāshtimur. Ibn Mufliḥ remained captive until he was killed, although the central authorities had sent to Ibn Wāṣil Ismāʿīl b. Isḥāq [the judge][466] to negotiate his release, but without securing any response from Ibn Wāṣil. Once Ibn Wāṣil was rid of Ibn Mufliḥ, he openly declared his intention of making for Wāsiṭ to fight Mūsā b. Bughā. He progressed

463. Located close to the border between Iraq and Iran. See Yāqūt, *Muʿjam*, IV, 449.
464. See Ibn al-Athīr, *Kāmil*, VII, 275.
465. See n. 48, above.
466. He had been a member of the delegation sent by al-Muʿtamid to Yaʿqūb b. al-Layth in Fārs. See p. 119, above.

as far as al-Ahwāz, where Ibrāhīm b. Sīmā was stationed with a large force. Mūsā b. Bughā, realizing the seriousness of matters, with the rising wave of rebels in the eastern districts and with resources insufficient to check them, requested to be relieved of his duties over these provinces. This was granted, and his territories were added to those of Abū Aḥmad b. al-Mutawakkil, who was made governor over them all. Mūsā b. Bughā meanwhile retired from Wāsiṭ to the central authorities [in Sāmarrā], along with his administrative prefects from the eastern districts.

In this year Abū al-Sāj[467] was made governor of al-Ahwāz and given responsibility for the conduct of the campaign against the Zanj leader. Abū al-Sāj made for al-Ahwāz after ʿAbd al-Raḥmān b. Mufliḥ had left for Fārs.

In this year as well a battle occurred between ʿAbd al-Raḥmān [who was related by marriage to Abū al-Sāj] and ʿAlī b. Abān in the [1889]
district of al-Dūlāb. ʿAbd al-Raḥmān was slain, and Abū al-Sāj departed for ʿAskar Mukram. The Zanj occupied al-Ahwāz and put some of its inhabitants to the sword, taking others captive and plundering and burning the houses. Thereafter Abū al-Sāj was removed from his duties in al-Ahwāz and his responsibilities for fighting the Zanj, being replaced as governor by Ibrāhīm b. Sīmā. He remained in charge, leaving al-Ahwāz only at the time when Mūsā b. Bughā was relieved of control of the eastern districts.

During this year Muḥammad b. Aws al-Balkhī was made governor of the Khurāsān Road.

When Abū Aḥmad took over control of the eastern provinces he appointed Masrūr al-Balkhī governor of al-Ahwāz, al-Baṣrah, the Tigris districts, al-Yamāmah, and al-Baḥrayn in Shaʿbān (May 11 – June 8, 875) of this year. He was also given the task of campaigning against the leader of the Zanj.

In Ramaḍān (June 9 – July 8, 875) Naṣr b. Aḥmad b. Asad al-Sāmānī[468] was appointed governor of the land beyond the river of Balkh[469]; he received a letter of appointment to this post.

---

467. His full name was Abū al-Sāj Diwdad b. Diwdast. He had previously held a post in al-Kūfah, with responsibility for repairing the Meccan road in 252 (866–67). See Ṭabarī, III, 1682–85; Ibn al-Athīr, *Kāmil*, VII, 276; *EI*,[1] s.v. "Sādjites."

468. Ibn al-Athīr, *Kāmil*, VII, 279–82, provides more details on these developments; see also R. N. Frye, "The Sāmānids."

469. This was the territory known as *Mā warāʾ al-nahr*, "what was beyond the

In Shawwāl (July 9–August 6, 875) Yaʿqūb b. al-Layth marched toward Fārs. Ibn Wāṣil was still encamped in al-Ahwāz, and from there he set out for Fārs; in Dhū al-Qaʿdah (August 7–September 5, 875) he clashed with Yaʿqūb b. al-Layth, who routed him and destroyed his army. Yaʿqūb sent off men to Khurramah to strip clean Ibn Wāṣil's fortress,[470] the contents of which reportedly reached a value of forty million dirhams. He also took prisoner Mirdās, Ibn Wāṣil's maternal uncle.

[1890] During the year the troops of Yaʿqūb b. al-Layth assaulted the inhabitants of Zamm[471] Mūsā b. Mihrān al-Kurdī for the assistance they had rendered to Muḥammad b. Wāṣil. The troops killed them, forcing Mūsā b. Mihrān to flee.

On the 12th of Shawwāl (July 20, 875) of this year al-Muʿtamid held an assembly in the Public Audience Hall (*dār al-ʿāmmah*), at which he appointed his son Jaʿfar his heir, giving him the honorific title al-Mufawwaḍ ilā-Allāh. He also made him governor of the western regions, attaching Mūsā b. Bughā to him as governor of Ifrīqiyah, Egypt, Syria, al-Jazīrah, Mosul, Armenia, the Khurāsān Road, Mihrajānqadhaq, and Ḥulwān. Al-Muʿtamid also appointed his brother Abū Aḥmad[472] heir after Jaʿfar, making him governor of the eastern regions. Masrūr al-Balkhī was attached to him as governor of Baghdad, the Sawād, al-Kūfah, the Mecca Road, Medina, the Yemen, Kaskar, the Tigris districts, al-Ahwāz, Fārs, Iṣfahān, Qumm, al-Karaj, al-Dīnawar, al-Rayy, Zanjān, Qazwīn, Khurāsān, Ṭabaristān, Jurjān, Kirmān, Sijistān, and Sind. Al-Muʿtamid also bestowed upon each of his heirs two standards, one black, the other white. He stipulated that, in the event of his death, if Jaʿfar could not fulfill the duties of the caliphate,[473] it would pass first to Abū Aḥmad and then to Jaʿfar. On these terms the oath of allegiance was rendered by the people, and copies of the succession decree were dis-

---

river," the river understood as the Oxus, the frontier between the Persian-speaking region of Khurāsān and Turkish Transoxania. See Le Strange, *Lands*, 433ff.

470. See Le Strange, *Lands*, 278. This was located some 80 km. from Shīrāz, on the road to Kirmān; see also Iṣṭakhrī, *Kitāb al-masālik wa-al-mamālik*, 102.

471. Known also as Zamm al-Bazanjān. See Ṭabarī, *Index*; also Iṣṭakhrī, *Masālik*, 145.

472. Ibn al-Athīr, *Kāmil*, VII, 278, notes that at this ceremony Abū Aḥmad received his honorific title, al-Nāṣir li-Dīn Allāh al-Muwaffaq.

473. That is, because Jaʿfar would not have reached the age of maturity, when he could assume these responsibilities.

seminated. One such copy was despatched with al-Ḥasan b. Muḥammad b. Abī al-Shawārib to affix to the Kaʿbah [in Mecca]. In Shawwāl (July 9–August 6, 875) Jaʿfar al-Mufawwaḍ made Mūsā b. Bughā his deputy over the western regions and sent Muḥammad al-Muwallad to him with an agreement to this effect.

Muḥammad b. Zaydawayh deserted Yaʿqūb b. al-Layth this year, [1891] withdrawing thousands of his troops from Yaʿqūb's army and going over to Abū al-Sāj, who welcomed him. Muḥammad stayed with him in al-Ahwāz and received a robe of honor from Sāmarrā. Ibn Zaydawayh then requested of the central authorities that al-Ḥusayn b. Ṭāhir b. ʿAbdallāh be sent with him to Khurāsān.

On the 7th of Dhū al-Ḥijjah (September 12, 875) Masrūr al-Balkhī set out from Sāmarrā as Abū Aḥmad's vanguard. According to report, robes of honor were bestowed upon him and thirty-four of his commanders. The two heirs publicly escorted him, and al-Muwaffaq followed him from Sāmarrā on the 21st of Dhū al-Ḥijjah (September 26, 875).

Leading the pilgrimage this year was al-Faḍl b. Isḥāq b. al-Ḥasan b. Ismāʿīl b. al-ʿAbbās b. Muḥammad b. ʿAlī b. ʿAbdallāh b. ʿAbbās.

Al-Ḥasan b. Muḥammad b. Abī al-Shawārib died this year after he had performed the pilgrimage.

The Events of the Year 262

(October 6, 875–September 23, 876)

Among the events taking place this year were the arrival of Yaʿqūb b. al-Layth in Rāmhurmuz in the month of al-Muḥarram (October 6–November 4, 875) and the despatch of Ismāʿīl b. Isḥāq and Bughrāj to him by the central authorities.[474] The central authorities also released from prison Yaʿqūb b. al-Layth's supporters. At the time of the dispute between Yaʿqūb and Muḥammad b. Ṭāhir, the authorities had imprisoned Yaʿqūb's servant Waṣīf and other supporters who had stood by him. They were released from prison following Ya-
[1892] qūb's arrival in Rāmhurmuz on the 5th of Rabīʿ I (November 9, 875).

Thereafter Ismāʿīl b. Isḥāq left Yaʿqūb for Sāmarrā bearing a message from him. Meanwhile, Abū Aḥmad (al-Muwaffaq) held an audience in Baghdad, to which he summoned a group of merchants, informing them that the Commander of the Faithful had appointed Yaʿqūb b. al-Layth governor of Khurāsān, Ṭabaristān, Jurjān, al-Rayy, and Fārs and head of security in Madīnat al-Salām. One of Yaʿ-

474. Ibn al-Athīr, *Kāmil*, VII, 290, commences his account of this year by stating that Yaʿqūb journeyed from Fārs to al-Ahwāz in the month of al-Muḥarram; Rāmhurmuz was only a three-day march east of al-Ahwāz.

qūb's companions, Dirham b. Naṣr, was present at the audience. Al-Muʿtamid had sent this Dirham from Sāmarrā to Yaʿqūb [with a message] granting the latter what he had requested.[475] Dirham went to Yaʿqūb accompanied by ʿUmar b. Sīmā and Muḥammad b. Tarkashah.

Messengers of Ibn Zaydawayh arrived in Baghdad during the month of Rabīʿ I (December 14, 875 – January 12, 876) this year to deliver a communication from him. A robe of honor was bestowed upon him by Abū Aḥmad (al-Muwaffaq).

Later this same year those who had been sent by Yaʿqūb b. al-Layth returned to the Caliph and informed him that Yaʿqūb was not satisfied with merely corresponding with the Caliph, but he rather preferred to come in person to the caliphal palace. Yaʿqūb left ʿAskar Mukram,[476] while Abū al-Sāj went to meet him, and was received honorably and given presents. After the messengers had returned with Yaʿqūb's reply, al-Muʿtamid, on Saturday the 3rd of Jumādā II (March 15, 876), assembled his troops in al-Qāʾim, in Sāmarrā, leaving his son Jaʿfar in charge of Sāmarrā with the assistance of Muḥammad al-Muwallad. Departing from the city on Tuesday the 6th of Jumādā II (March 18, 876), al-Muʿtamid reached Baghdad on Wednesday the 14th of the month (March 26, 876). He passed straight through the metropolis, however, and proceeded to al-Zaʿ-
farāniyyah, where he set up camp. From al-Zaʿfarāniyyah he sent [1893]
ahead his brother Abū Aḥmad as vanguard, while Yaʿqūb proceeded with his army from ʿAskar Mukram, arriving within a *farsakh*'s[477] distance of Wāsiṭ. There he encountered flooded terrain created by Masrūr al-Balkhī, who had breached the dike on the Tigris in order to hinder Yaʿqūb's passage. Yaʿqūb remained there and managed to repair the breach, which allowed him to cross over the Tigris on the 24th of Jumādā II (March 23, 876) and advance toward Bādhibīn.[478] The next stage was the arrival of Muḥammad b. Kathīr, on behalf of Yaʿqūb, opposite the camp of Masrūr al-Balkhī, who then proceeded with his army to al-Nuʿmāniyyah.[479]

---

475. That is, the governorships to which he had been appointed.

476. An important town on the Masruqān canal, which irrigated some of the richest land in Khūzistān. See Le Strange, *Lands*, 236.

477. About 6 km.

478. Located east of Wāsiṭ, on the road to al-Ahwāz, Le Strange, *Lands*, 82, vocalizes the name Bādhbīn.

479. The halfway stage between Baghdad and Wāsiṭ. See Yāqūt, *Muʿjam*, IV, 796.

Meanwhile, Yaʿqūb had reached Wāsiṭ and entered it on the 24th of Jumādā II (March 23, 876). On Thursday, the last day of the month (March 29, 876), al-Muʿtamid left al-Zaʿfarāniyyah and advanced as far as Sīb Banī Kūmā,[480] where he was joined by Masrūr al-Balkhī who had traveled along the western bank of the Tigris before crossing over to the side where the Caliph's forces were located. Al-Muʿtamid remained in Sīb Banī Kūmā for a few days in order that his various troops and regiments could assemble together. For his part, Yaʿqūb advanced by stages from Wāsiṭ to Dayr al-ʿĀqūl[481] and from there toward the government forces. Al-Muʿtamid remained camped in Sīb, along with ʿUbaydallāh b. Yaḥyā, while he sent his brother Abū Aḥmad to engage Yaʿqūb in battle. Abū Aḥmad stationed Mūsā b. Bughā on his right flank and Masrūr al-Balkhī on his left, while he himself, with his elite cavalry and the pick of his infantry, held the center. The two sides met on Sunday, at the beginning of Rajab (April 1, 876), at a place called Iḍṭarbad,[482] which was
[1894] between Sīb Banī Kūmā and Dayr al-ʿĀqūl. Yaʿqūb's right wing attacked Abū Aḥmad's left flank, driving it back in disorder. A large number were slain, including some of the government's commanders, like Ibrāhīm b. Sīmā al-Turkī, Ṭabāghū al-Turkī, Muḥammad Ṭughtā al-Turkī, and one known as al-Mubaraqaʿ al-Maghribī, among others. Then those [on the left flank] who had been driven back regrouped, while the rest of Abū Aḥmad's forces stood their ground and launched a counterattack against Yaʿqūb's forces. They stood their ground and engaged the foe with courage and determination. Many of Yaʿqūb's valiant warriors were killed, among them al-Ḥasan al-Dirhamī and Muḥammad b. Kathīr, who had been in charge of Yaʿqūb's vanguard, and one known as Lubbādah. Yaʿqūb himself was struck by three arrows in his neck and hands. According to what was said, the two sides continued fighting until the time the afternoon prayer had passed. Later, al-Dayrānī and Muḥammad b. Aws reached Abū Aḥmad, completing the assembly of all of Abū

480. Situated on the east bank of the Tigris between Dayr al-ʿĀqūl and al-Madā'in, this small town was called Sīb of the Banū Kūmā to distinguish it from the Sīb farther south. See Le Strange, *Lands*, 36, 41; Le Strange, "Ibn Serapion's Description," 41.

481. This was a monastery located on the east bank of the Tigris, south of al-Madā'in. See Le Strange, *Lands*, 35; Le Strange, "Ibn Serapion's Description," 41; Yāqūt, *Muʿjam*, II, 676.

482. The word is unvocalized in Manuscripts B and C.

Aḥmad's troops. It had become apparent that many on Yaʿqūb's side had developed an aversion to fighting with him when they saw the Caliph appear on the battlefield, and [the assembled government troops] now attacked Yaʿqūb and those who still stood firmly by him. Yaʿqūb's regular troops were routed, leaving him to stand fast with the elite of his forces until they managed to withdraw from the field of battle.

More than ten thousand pack animals and mules were reportedly captured from Yaʿqūb's army along with a great many containers of musk and such an amount of dinars and dirhams that it wore out its bearers.

Muḥammad b. Ṭāhir b. ʿAbdallāh, who had been shackled in irons, was set free by the one who was in charge of guarding him. He was then presented to the Caliph, who bestowed upon him a robe of honor to accord with his rank. A statement was read out in public, in which it was said: [1895]

> The accursed renegade called Yaʿqūb b. al-Layth had always professed loyalty [to the central authorities] until he committed such foul acts as marching upon the governor of Khurāsān and overthrowing him; acting as leader of the public prayers there and committing other misdeeds; marching repeatedly into Fārs and seizing its revenues; advancing upon the seat of the Commander of the Faithful, on the pretext of requesting powers of which the Commander of the Faithful had already given him more than he deserved, in an attempt to appease him and avoid [direct contact] by taking a better way. Yaʿqūb had been given authority over Khurāsān, al-Rayy, Fārs, Qazwīn, Zanjān, and the security forces in Madīnat al-Salām. He was ordered to be humble in his correspondence. He had been granted valuable estates as fiefs; but that had only made him more unjust and oppressive. The Caliph then ordered him to turn back [from his march on Baghdad], but he refused. When the accursed one was on the road between Madīnat al-Salām and Wāsiṭ, flying flags, some of which bore the sign of the cross, the Commander of the Faithful set out to repel him.
>
> The Commander of the Faithful despatched his brother Abū Aḥmad al-Muwaffaq bi-Allāh, the Muslims' future

> ruler, in the center of his army, with Abū ʿImrān Mūsā b. Bughā on the right flank and Ibrāhīm b. Sīmā on its outer wing. Abū Hāshim Masrūr al-Balkhī occupied the left flank and al-Dayrānī its outer wing. Yaʿqūb and his supporters rushed into battle, and he fought until he was severely wounded and Abū ʿAbdallāh Muḥammad b. Ṭāhir was safely rescued from the enemy's hands. Yaʿqūb's forces retreated in full flight, broken and plundered, while the accursed one was forced to surrender all his accumulated fortune.

This statement was dated Tuesday, the 11th of Rajab (April 10, 876).

Al-Muʿtamid then returned to his army camp and wrote to Ibn
[1896] Wāṣil, granting him the governorship of Fārs. Ibn Wāṣil had already gone there to gather together some forces. Al-Muʿtamid returned to al-Madāʾin, while Abū Aḥmad, along with Masrūr and Sātikīn and a number of the commanders, proceeded to confiscate the property of Abū al-Sāj in the form of estates and buildings, which were then granted to Masrūr al-Balkhī as fiefs. On Monday, the 16th of Rajab (April 15, 876) Muḥammad b. Ṭāhir b. ʿAbdallāh came to Baghdad, his post having been restored, and a robe of honor was bestowed upon him in al-Ruṣāfah. He settled in the palace of ʿAbdallāh b. Ṭāhir; he removed no one and appointed no one, but was ordered to receive five hundred thousand dirhams.

The day of the battle between the central authorities and [Yaʿqūb] al-Ṣaffār was Palm Sunday (*yawm al-Shaʿānīn*).

Muḥammad b. ʿAlī b. Fayd al-Ṭāʾī praised Abū Aḥmad in a poem in which the business with al-Ṣaffār was alluded to.

The raven crowed—would that I could end his crowing—
 and my heart inclined to remembrance of beloved ones.
The raven proclaimed their departure,
 and my eyes responded to the departure of their saddles with a flood of tears.
They vanished, gentle ladies, like painted dolls,
 gentle friends;[483] like doe-eyed creatures, slender-waisted, full-bosomed.

483. *Atrāb*. For this expression, see Qurʾān 38:52, 56:37.

These fair ladies of yours made me adore them by their
locks, figures, and brows.
The Muslims' heir apparent has many honorable [1897]
qualities, the light from which has shone out in many offices
And ranks the summit of which cannot be scaled.
How noble are these peaks and ranks!
Al-Ṣaffār had arrived with impressive battle machines but
suffered a terrible calamity,
Fate having dealt him a swift end
in obedient execution of providence.
The accursed devil, Iblīs, had seduced him with his plot
and lured him with a false promise
Until, when they became allies and al-Ṣaffār imagined
he was mighty among armies and regiments,
Fortunate troops advanced toward him, and
they met, pushing forward with victorious banner,
In a huge, clamoring army in which heroes were seen
bearing shields, spears, and arrows.
The Imām appeared with triumphant flag
for Muḥammad—God's keen-honed sword.
The Muslims' heir apparent is Blessed
of God,[484] swifter than a shooting star,
Appearing among the people as a full shining moon, [1898]
rejoicing in light, among the stars.
When they met with Mashrāfī swords and spears, piercing and
thrusting in combat hand to hand,
The dust swirled round, above it a cloud
scattering a rain [of arrows].
He routed the multitude with the decisiveness of a piercing opinion,
separating comrades one from another.
God's blessing upon he who is with him, who is blessed (*muwaffaq*)
and joyous,
steadfast and persistent in battle.
O horsemen of the Arabs, [there is] no other the likes of whom
can be found, who is equal to disasters
That might come from evil times or from facing
an army that is treacherous, treasonous, and violent.

---

484. The regnal name of Muʿtamid's brother Abū Aḥmad, al-Muwaffaq ʿalā-Allāh means "Blessed of God."

In this year the Zanj leader despatched his forces to the territory of the salt flats and Dastumīsān.[485]

An Account of [the Zanj Attack on the Salt Flats][486]

The cause for this reportedly was that, when al-Muʿtamid removed Mūsā b. Bughā from his responsibilities for the eastern provinces and their adjoining districts, he included them instead with his brother Abū Aḥmad's duties. Abū Aḥmad himself added the Tigris districts to the duties of Masrūr al-Balkhī. Thus, as the districts of the Tigris had been left without any government protection except for al-Madā'in and regions lying to the north,[487] Yaʿqūb b. al-Layth
[1899] commenced his advance toward Abū Aḥmad and reached Wāsiṭ. Just prior to this Masrūr had sent Juʿlān al-Turkī to al-Bādhāward in place of Mūsā b. Utāmish. Now opposing Mūsā b. Utāmish on the Zanj side was Sulaymān b. Jāmiʿ. Before Ibn Utāmish was removed from al-Bādhāward, Sulaymān had already inflicted some damage on his army. Following his removal and replacement by Juʿlān, despatched a Baḥraynī called Thaʿlab b. Ḥafṣ to attack Juʿlān. Thaʿlab succeeded in inflicting casualties on both his cavalry and men. For his part the Zanj leader sent Aḥmad b. Mahdī, a man from Jubbā,[488] in command of galleys with marksmen on board and with orders to proceed to Nahr al-Mar'ah.[489] According to report, this man, al-Jubbā'ī, commenced plundering the villages in the neighborhood of al-Madhār, laying them waste before returning to Nahr al-Mar'ah, where he stationed himself. He communicated with the Zanj leader informing him that the salt flats were void of government troops, owing to the removal of Masrūr and his troops when Yaʿqūb b. Layth arrived in Wāsiṭ. The Zanj leader then ordered Sulaymān b. Jāmiʿ and a number of his commanders to march to al-Ḥawānīt. He also gave orders to one of the Bāhilīs, ʿUmayr b. ʿAmmār,[490] who knew

485. The word is vocalized thus in the Leiden edition, though it is also written Dast Maysān.

486. See Popovic, *Révolte*, 112–15; Ibn al-Athīr, *Kāmil*, VII, 290–92.

487. That is, between al-Madā'in and Baghdad.

488. A town on the estuary of the Dujayl below al-Ahwāz. See Le Strange, *Lands*, 243.

489. This canal was the northernmost of nine lying to the west of the Tigris estuary. See Le Strange, "Ibn Serapion's Description," 303, 305; Yāqūt, *Muʿjam*, IV, 844.

490. On the Bāhilah tribe, see Popovic, *Révolte*, 112 n. 3.

well the roads and byways through the salt flats to accompany al-Jubbā'ī and establish camp in al-Ḥawānīt.[491]

Muḥammad b. al-Ḥasan reported that Muḥammad b. ʿUthmān al-ʿAbbādānī said that, following the Zanj leader's decision to despatch his armies to the salt flats and Dastumīsān, he commanded Sulaymān b. Jāmiʿ to set up camp in al-Muṭṭawwiʿah and Sulaymān b. Mūsā was to establish his quarters at the head of Nahr al-Yahūdī;[492] these orders were carried out. They each remained in their camps until receiving word to advance: Sulaymān b. Mūsā proceeded to the village of al-Qādisiyyah and Sulaymān b. Jāmiʿ to al-Ḥawānīt, while al-Jubbā'ī was stationed with his galleys in front of this latter Sulaymān's army. Meanwhile, Abbā al-Turkī[493] sailed along the Tigris with thirty barges heading for the camp of the Zanj leader. Passing the village, which had made peace with the abominable one, he destroyed and burned it. The abominable one[494] contacted Sulaymān b. Mūsā by despatch to prevent his returning and Sulaymān blocked Abbā al-Turkī's way by engaging him in battle for a whole month until he managed to reach the region of the salt flats. [1900]

Muḥammad b. ʿUthmān reported that Jabbāsh the eunuch (*al-khādim*) claimed it was not Abbā al-Turkī who had ventured along the Tigris at this time but rather Nuṣayr Abū Ḥamzah.

When Sulaymān b. Jāmiʿ reportedly set out for al-Ḥawānīt, he reached a place called Nahr al-ʿAtīq, while al-Jubbā'ī, who had gone along the al-Mādiyān Road,[495] encountered Rumays, whom he engaged in battle and defeated. Al-Jubbā'ī captured twenty-four galleys and some thirty-odd larger craft (*ṣalghah*). Rumays escaped and [1901] took refuge in the woods. A group of the Jūkhāniyyīn[496] came upon

---

491. The word means "booths." Al-Ḥawānīt was situated on the eastern bank of the Tigris. Near there barriers, supervised by government officials, were moored across the river. See Le Strange, "Ibn Serapion's Description," 46.

492. One of the canals of al-Baṣrah on its western side; it lay between Nahr al-Ubullah and Nahr Abī al-Khaṣīb. See Le Strange, "Ibn Serapion's Description," 304, 306.

493. The copyists of Manuscripts B and C wrote his name with *tashdīd*, thus Abbā. Popovic *Révolte*, 112 n. 4, misreads this name as Abū al-Turkī and incorrectly identifies the patronymic as belonging to Masrūr al-Balkhī, whose *kunyah* was Abū Hāshim. The context of the passage on p. 178, below, makes this identification impossible. Ibn al-Athīr, *Kāmil*, VII, 293, calls him Ibn al-Turkī.

494. Ibn al-Athīr, *Kāmil*, VII, 293, who follows Ṭabarī closely here, lapses for the first time into calling ʿAlī b. Muḥammad "the abominable one" (*al-khabīth*).

495. The reading is conjectural.

496. See Ṭabarī, *Glossarium*, CLXXIV.

him and carried him off, but he manged to escape again. In their flight, Rumays's troops ran straight into Sulaymān (b. Jāmiʿ), who was just then emerging from Nahr al-ʿAtīq. In the ensuing battle, Rumays's forces were decimated while Rumays himself made his way to a place called Barr Musāwir. A number of the Bilāliyyah were reported to have joined up with Sulaymān with some one hundred fifty galleys. He interrogated them concerning what lay before him. They replied that neither government authority nor agents were present in the region between him and Wāsiṭ. Placing complete trust in this intelligence, Sulaymān was thrown off his guard and as he reached a spot called al-Jazīrah, he was met by one Abū Muʿādh al-Qurashī, who fought and routed Sulaymān, killing a number of his troops and capturing one of the Zanj commanders, Riyāḥ al-Qandalī. Sulaymān returned to his base camp, where two of the Bilāliyyah came and told him that there was no one in Wāsiṭ to defend it other than Abū Muʿādh with the five barges with which he had previously met him. So Sulaymān made his preparations, gathered his forces together, and sent word to the abominable one with some of the Bilāliyyah who had sought his protection, keeping a small select group to remain behind with him with ten galleys. However, the two who had informed him of the situation in Wāsiṭ he kept under close guard as he set out for Nahr Abān. Abū Muʿādh blocked his way and this sparked off fighting between the two sides. A strong
[1902] wind blew up, causing Abū Muʿādh's barges to flounder and giving Sulaymān and his men the chance to overpower him. Abū Muʿādh, nevertheless, managed to make good his escape while Sulaymān proceeded toward the Nahr Abān, where he swiftly burned and plundered [villages], taking women and children into captivity. News of this reached some of Abū Aḥmad's agents who were staying on one of his estates on the Nahr Sindād. They set out against Sulaymān with a detachment of troops, and in the battle that followed a large number of the Zanj were slain. Sulaymān and Aḥmad b. Mahdī and their followers fled back to their camp.

Muḥammad b. al-Ḥasan — Muḥammad b. ʿUthmān said that when Sulaymān b. Jāmiʿ had installed himself in al-Ḥawānit and set up a temporary camp on the Nahr Yaʿqūb b. al-Naḍr, he sent out someone to collect intelligence on Wāsiṭ and the disposition of government forces there. This was after the departure of Masrūr and his troops, owing to the arrival of Yaʿqūb (b. al-Layth). The spy returned to Sulaymān and reported Yaʿqūb's advance toward the government forces. Masrūr, before vacating Wāsiṭ for al-Sīb, had sent a man called Waṣīf al-Raḥḥāl with barges against Sulaymān. He fought and killed him, also seizing seven of the boats and killing the prisoners, dumping the dead in al-Ḥawānīt in order to instill fear in the hearts of government supporters who might happen by.[497]

After Sulaymān had received news of Masrūr's departure from Wāsiṭ, he summoned his deputy, ʿUmayr b. ʿAmmār, and one of the Bāhilī chiefs named Aḥmad b. Sharīk. He consulted them concerning withdrawal from the position, which could be reached by horses and boats, searching carefully instead for a spot joining a road that could be used as an escape route should he wish to make for the camp of the abominable one. The two men advised him to head for ʿAqr Māwar and entrench himself in Ṭahīthā[498] and its dense thickets. [1903]

The departure of Sulaymān b. Jāniʿ greatly annoyed the Bāhilites since, having become involved with him, they feared the retribution of the central authorities against them. Sulaymān set out with his troops to Ṭahītha via Nahr al-Barūr, having despatched al-Jubbāʾī to Nahr al-ʿAtīq with galleys. He ordered al-Jubbāʾī to make haste in bringing him intelligence on the strength of the government's forces in men and barges. He left behind a detachment of blacks to sent on any of his troops who had lagged behind. He headed for ʿAqr Māwar, setting up camp in the village of Qaryat Marwān, located on an island on the eastern side of Nahr Ṭahītha. There he gathered the Bāhilite chiefs and the men of al-Ṭufūf[499] and wrote to the abominable one, informing him of his movements. The abominable one replied, approving his plans and ordered him to transfer to him food supplies and animals that he had acquired. This was duly done. Meanwhile, Masrūr had proceeded to the spot of Sulaymān's previous camp. He found nothing there but that the enemy had already transferred their entire camp.

---

497. Popovic, *Révolte,* 113, takes this possibly to mean that the bodies were thrown into the Tigris at al-Ḥawānīt.

498. See Popovic, *Révolte,* 113 n. 1, where he states that the camp was located on the Ṭahītha canal. The reading Ṭahītha is uncertain. Ibn al-Athīr, *Kāmil,* VII, 293, writes it *ṭ-h-th-a* and reverses the relationship between it and ʿAqr Māwar; that is, Sulaymān was advised to entrench himself in the latter position.

499. *Ahl al-Ṭufūf.* The *Index* does not cite this as a place name, and it cannot be otherwise identified. It might also be loosely rendered "local inhabitants," that is, those living in cultivated areas along the canal banks. See Lane, *Lexicon,* s.v. *ṭ-f-f.*

Abbā al-Turkī descended toward the marshlands in pursuit of Sulaymān, who himself thought that [Abbā al-Turkī] had left the district altogether and gone away, heading in the direction of the abominable one's camp. He found no trace of Sulaymān. On his return, however, he discovered that Sulaymān had moved an army to al-Ḥa-
[1904] wānīt in order to surprise any stragglers who might become separated from Masrūr's army. Abbā al-Turkī avoided the road that he feared might lead him to Sulaymān's army and instead took another way, which finally brought him to Masrūr, whom he informed that he had no news of Sulaymān's [exact] whereabouts.[500]

Sulyamān's army set out for [the abominable one] with the required provisions. Sulaymān remained behind. He despatched al-Jubbā'ī with the barges to take care of the food and supply depots and arrange their transport. Al-Jubbā'ī, however, burned such food supplies as he found wherever he went. This greatly displeased Sulaymān, who forbade him from such action but al-Jubbā'ī paid no attention, justifying himself on the grounds that the supplies would benefit their enemies and that it was wrong to leave anything behind. At this Sulaymān wrote to the abominable one complaining about al-Jubbā'ī's behavior. The abominable one in turn instructed al-Jubbā'ī to obey Sulaymān and accept whatever he commanded.

News reached Sulaymān that Aghartimish and Khushaysh[501] were heading his way, leading cavalry and infantry troops with barges and galleys intending to engage him in battle. Sulaymān was much troubled by these developments and sent off al-Jubbā'ī to glean information about them. He commenced his preparations to meet them. Al-Jubbā'ī returned shortly thereafter in flight and informed Sulaymān that Aghartimish and Khushaysh had reached Bāb Ṭanj, which was only half a *farsakh*[502] from Sulaymān's forces. Sulaymān ordered al-Jubbā'ī to return and block their army's way, diverting it from advancing directly toward his camp until Sulaymān could join forces with him. When al-Jubbā'ī had departed to execute these or-
[1905] ders, Sulaymān ascended a rooftop, from which he observed the advancing army. Then, hastily descending, he crossed over Nahr Ṭahīthā and proceeded on foot, followed by a number of the command-

500. See n. 493, above.

501. The vocalization of the names of these two ʿAbbāsid officers is conjectural. Ibn al-Athīr, *Kāmil*, VII, 293, refers to the second as Ḥashīsh.

502. About 3 km.

ers of the blacks and their troops, finally arriving at Bāb Ṭanj. Aghartimish realized that he had arrived too late and left his troops to struggle back to his camp.

Sulaymān had ordered the deputy commander of his army not to allow any of the blacks to appear in view of any of Aghartimish's army, concealing themselves as best they could and letting the enemy penetrate along the waterway. Then, when they heard the sound of the drum roll, they should emerge and attack Aghartimish. Aghartimish approached with his army until there was no more than the Jārūrah Banī Marwān canal, which flowed from Ṭahīthā, between him and Sulaymān's force. Al-Jubbā'ī fled in the galleys and reached Ṭahīthā, and then leaving them there he retraced his way on foot to Sulaymān's army. This caused fear to deepen among Sulaymān's soldiers, and they scattered to the four winds.[503] A small group of men, however, among them one of the commanders of the blacks called Abū al-Nidā', took heart and attacked the enemy, preventing their entry into the camp, while Sulaymān pressed them from behind; then the Zanj beat their drums and throwing themselves into the water, crossed over the canal to join them. At this Aghartimish's troops were routed; the blacks who were in Ṭahītha fell upon them and put them to the sword. Khushaysh set out, riding upon a gray horse, intending to return to his soldiers, but he was met by blacks, who felled him with their swords and slew him. His head [1906] was taken to Sulaymān. Before being killed, as he was dragged away, he had said to them, "I am Khushaysh; you cannot kill me. Take me to your leader!" but they paid him no heed.

Aghartimish fled at the rear of his forces until he collapsed on the ground; he then proceeded on horseback, tracked by the Zanj until they reached their camp. The Zanj obtained their necessities from it, and seized Khushaysh's barges, while those who pursued the retreating army captured [more] barges that were with Aghartimish, containing much wealth. When news of this reached Aghartimish, he returned and managed to recover the boats from the Zanj.

Meanwhile, Sulaymān returned to his troops. He had succeeded in capturing booty and animals and sent word of the result of the battle to the Zanj commander, together with Khushaysh's head and

503. The phrase is *fa tafarraqū ayādiya sabā*; see H. Wehr, *A Dictionary of Modern Written Arabic*, s.v. *s-b-'*.

ring seal, and added the barges that he had seized to his own forces. When the abominable one received Sulaymān's communication and Khushaysh's head, he ordered the later circulated throughout the camp and then displayed for a day on a pole. The head was later sent to ʿAlī b. Abān, who at the time was in the districts of al-Ahwāz, and he was ordered to display it in public there as well. Sulaymān, al-Jubbāʾī, and a group of commanders of the blacks left for the district of al-Ḥawānīt, skirting its border. There they came across thirteen barges with Abū Tamīm, the brother of Abū ʿAwn, associate of Waṣīf al-Turkī. They attacked. Abū Tamīm was killed and thrown into the water. Eleven of his barges were confiscated.

Muḥammad b. al-Ḥasan said that this was the account of Muḥammad b. ʿUthmān al-ʿAbbādānī. As for Jabbāsh the eunuch, he claimed that Abū Tamīm had only eight barges. Two of these, which had arrived late on the scene, managed to slip away safely with all on
[1907] board. Sulaymān captured arms and spoils as well as most of the troops on the barges. Sulaymān returned to his camp and sent word to the abominable one of developments involving the slaying of Abū Tamīm and his companions and his confiscation of the barges in his camp.

In this year Ibn Zaydawayh took al-Ṭīb[504] by surprise and plundered it.

ʿAlī b. Muḥammad b. Abī al-Shawārib was appointed to the office of religious judge this year.[505]

Al-Ḥusayn b. Ṭāhir b. ʿAbdallāh b. Ṭāhir left Baghdad during the last days of [the month][506] for al-Jabal.

Al-Ṣalābī[507] died this year, and Kayghalagh was appointed governor of al-Rayy.

Ṣāliḥ b. ʿAlī b. Yaʿqūb b. (Abū al-Jaʿfar) al-Manṣūr died in Rabīʿ II (January 3–31, 876) of this year. Ismāʿīl b. Isḥāq was appointed re-

504. Le Strange, *Lands*, 64, 82. Yāqūt, *Muʿjam*, III, 566, says that in his day (the seven/thirteenth century) the inhabitants of this southeastern Iraqi town were Nabatean and still spoke a dialect of Aramaic.

505. That is, the brother of al-Ḥasan, who had been appointed chief religious judge in 252/866 and had died in 261/874–75. See p. 167 and n. 6 above; Sourdel, *Vizirat*, II, 654.

506. Ṭabarī does not mention the actual month, but Ibn al-Athīr, *Kāmil*, VII, 304, places this event in Ṣafar (November 5–December 3, 875).

507. Ibn al-Athīr, *Kāmil*, VII, 305, here confirms that he had been governor of al-Rayy.

ligious judge of the east side of Baghdad, thus holding the judgeship of both sides of the city.

Muḥammad b. ʿAttāb b. ʿAttāb was killed this year. He had been appointed governor of the two Sībs and had departed for the place, when he was killed by Arab tribesmen.

In the middle of Ramaḍān (June 12, 876) this year Mūsā b. Bughā arrived at al-Anbār on his way to al-Raqqah.

In this year al-Qaṭṭān, associate of Mufliḥ, was also slain. He was in charge of the administration of the taxes (*kharāj*) of Mosul. He was killed on the way back from it.

Kaftimur ʿAlī b. al-Ḥusayn b. Dāʾūd, secretary of Aḥmad b. Sahl [1908]
al-Luṭfī, was made leader of the Mecca Road in Ramaḍān (May 29–June 27, 876) of this year.

In Mecca the corn merchants (*al-ḥannāṭīn*)[508] and butchers fought each other on the day before *yawm al-Tarwiyah*,[509] so that people feared the pilgrimage would be canceled. Then the two sides made peace so that people could perform the pilgrimage rites. Seventeen persons had been killed.

Yaʿqūb b. al-Layth conquered Fārs this year, and Ibn Wāṣil fled from it.

A battle occurred this year between the Zanj and Aḥmad b. Laythawayh, in which many Zanj were killed. Abū Dāʾūd al-Ṣuʿlūk, who had been with the Zanj, was captured.

An Account of the Battle and Capture of al-Ṣuʿlūk[510]

Masrūr al-Balkhī reportedly sent Aḥmad b. Laythawayh to the region of the districts of al-Ahwāz. When he arrived in the region he settled at al-Sūs.[511] (Abū Layth) al-Ṣaffār had appointed Muḥammad b. ʿUbaydallāh b. Azārmard al-Kurdī governor of the districts of al-Ahwāz. Muḥammad b. ʿUbaydallāh corresponded with the Zanj leader,

---

508. The editor of the Leiden text has preferred this reading, though Manuscript B is unpointed and C has the possible reading *khayyāṭīn* "tailors," which is also the reading of Ibn al-Athīr, *Kāmil*, VII, 306.

509. This day, when pilgrims provided themselves with water for the afterlife, was the 8th of Dhū al-Ḥijjah (September 2, 876), the day before that of ʿArafāt. See *EI*,² s.v. "Ḥadjdj."

510. Popovic, *Révolte*, 114–15.

511. The ancient Sūsa, situated on the banks of the Karkhah river in Khūzistān. See Le Strange, *Lands*, 240.

holding forth the prospect that he was ready to go over to his side; indeed, he had been corresponding with him from the beginning of the Zanj leader's revolt. Muḥammad gave the impression that he would govern the districts of al-Ahwāz for him, although he would pretend to be loyal to (Abū Layth) al-Ṣaffār until he[512] had firm control of the district. The abominable one agreed to this, on condition
[1909] that his governor in the region be ʿAlī b. Abān and that Muḥammad b. ʿUbaydallāh be only his deputy, an offer that he accepted.

ʿAlī b. Abān despatched his brother al-Khalīl with a large number of blacks and others, while Muḥammad b. ʿUbaydallāh, together with Abū Dā'ūd al-Ṣuʿlūk, bolstered these forces, and they all made for al-Sūs. They did not, however, get that far, as Ibn Laythawayh and the troops of the central authorities accompanying him forced ʿAlī's troops to withdraw in full flight, losing a great many killed and others captured. Pushing forward, Aḥmad b. Laythawayh reached Junday Sābūr.[513]

Meanwhile, ʿAlī b. Abān left al-Ahwāz to lend Muḥammad b. ʿUbaydallāh assistance against Aḥmad b. Laythawayh. Muḥammad, with a troop of Kurds and a ragtag collection of others (*ṣaʿālīk*), met up with ʿAlī, and, as Muḥammad approached each side proceeded along opposite banks of the Masruqān canal.[514] Muḥammad sent one of his aides with three hundred horsemen to join ʿAlī b. Abān. Both men arrived finally at ʿAskar Mukram. Muḥammad went alone to ʿAlī b. Abān, the two men meeting [for awhile] to discuss matters. Upon returning to his camp, Muḥammad sent to ʿAlī al-Qāsim b. ʿAlī and one of the Kurdish chiefs named Ḥāzim and a shaykh called al-Ṭalāqānī from among the associates of [Abū Layth] al-Ṣaffār; they arrived and greeted ʿAlī. Muḥammad and ʿAlī remained amicable until ʿAlī reached the Fārs bridge (*qanṭarah*) and Muḥammad b. ʿUbaydallah entered Tustar. It reached Aḥmad b. Laythaway's attention that ʿAlī b. Abān and Muḥammad b. ʿUbaydallāh planned to assist each other in fighting him, and so he departed from
[1910] Junday Sābūr and made for al-Sūs.

Now ʿAlī reached the Fārs bridge on Friday. Muḥammad b. ʿUbay-

---

512. It is not clear whether the pronoun refers to Muḥammad or to the Zanj leader.

513. Written thus in the text but also found as Jundī Sābūr. See Le Strange, *Lands*, 238.

514. A canal that left the Dujayl river and rejoined it at a point near the city of ʿAskar Mukram. See Le Strange, *Lands*, 236–37.

dallāh had promised him to have the preacher make a sermon[515] that day and invoke blessings upon the leader of the Zanj and ʿAlī from the *minbar*[516] of the mosque in Tustar. ʿAlī remained [at the Fārs bridge], expecting such to happen, and he sent Bahbūdh b. ʿAbd al-Wahhāb to attend the Friday prayer and bring him news of it. When the prayer session commenced, the preacher rose and invoked blessings upon al-Muʿtamid, [Abu Layth] al-Ṣaffār, and Muḥammad b. ʿUbaydallāh. Bahbūdh returned to ʿAlī with this news. Immediately ʿAlī set out upon his horse and ordered his troops to leave for al-Ahwāz, sending them on in front of him with his nephew Muḥammad b. Ṣāliḥ, Muḥammad b. Yaḥyā al-Kirmānī his deputy, and his secretary. ʿAlī stayed behind until his troops had crossed over the bridge, and then he destroyed it so that he could not be followed by horses.

Muḥammad b. al-Ḥasan said: "I was among those of ʿAlī's troops who had been sent on ahead. The army traveled swiftly all that night, reaching ʿAskar Mukram by sunrise. ʿAskar Mukram had negotiated a peace with the abominable one, but now his soldiers broke the pact, attacking and pillaging the city. ʿAlī b. Abān arrived in the wake of what the troops had done, found out what they had done, but was unable to change it, and proceeded directly to al-Ahwāz. When word of ʿAlī's withdrawal reached Aḥmad b. Laythawayh, he retraced his way toward Tustar. There he clashed with Muḥammad b. ʿUbaydallāh and his followers. Muḥammad escaped, but the one called Abū Dāʾūd al-Ṣuʿluk fell into Aḥmad's hands, and he was transported to the court of the al-Muʿtamid. Aḥmad himself remained in Tustar."

Muḥammad b. al-Ḥasan—al-Faḍl b. ʿAdī al-Dārimī, one of the as- [1911]
sociates of the Zanj leader who had been attached to Muḥammad b. Abān, ʿAlī's brother, recounted as follows: After Aḥmad b. Laythawayh had settled himself in Tustar, ʿAlī b. Abān set out with his army toward him. He stopped at a village called Baranjān, and arranged for scouts to bring him information about Aḥmad. They re-

515. The sermon (*al-khuṭbah*) has a fixed place in the Friday service in the mosque. It was customary for the preacher to mention the name of the sovereign in the prayer on behalf of the faithful, thus indicating the preacher's political opinion or loyalty. See *EI*,[2] s.v. "Khuṭba."

516. The "pulpit" of a mosque, from which the Friday prayer is given. See *EI*,[2] s.v. "Masdjid."

turned to tell him that Ibn Laythawayh was already on his way, his forward cavalry having reached a village called al-Bāhiliyyīn. ʿAlī advanced toward Aḥmad, spreading good cheer among his troops, promising them victory, and recounting to them [the exploits] of the abominable one.

When ʿAlī reached al-Bāhiliyyīn, Ibn Laythawayh met him with his cavalry of around four hundred horsemen; they were quickly joined by reinforcements. As the government's cavalry forces were overwhelming in numbers, a group of Arab tribesmen who were on the side of ʿAlī b. Abān sought safe-conduct to join Ibn Laythawayh. The remainder of ʿAlī's cavalry was routed with only a small detachment of foot soldiers standing firm, most of them too having scattered. The fighting intensified between the two sides and ʿAlī b. Abān dismounted and joined the battle by himself on foot with one of his slave soldiers called Fatḥ, who was known as the slave of Abū al-Ḥadīd, joining him in the fray. Abu Naṣr Salhab and Badr al-Rūmī al-Shaʿrānī, who knew ʿAlī by sight, spotted him and shouted a warning to the troops. ʿAlī fled seeking the safety of the Masruqān canal. He threw himself into the water, followed by Fatḥ who threw himself into the water, followed by Fatḥ who threw himself in after ʿAlī, but he drowned. ʿAlī b. Abān reached Naṣr al-Rūmī, who pulled him out of the water and put him aboard a galley, ʿAlī having received a wound in the leg from an arrow. Utterly defeated, he escaped. A large number of Zanj solders and their brave ones had been slain.

[1912] In this year al-Faḍl b. Isḥāq b. al-Ḥasan b. al-ʿAbbās b. Muḥammad led the pilgrimage.[517]

517. The same person who led the pilgrimage in the previous year.

The Events of the Year 263

(September 24, 876–September 12, 877)

Among the events taking place this year was the victory of ʿUzayz b. al-Sarī, the associate of Yaʿqūb b. al-Layth, over Muḥammad b. Wāṣil, who was taken prisoner.

In this year as well there occurred a battle between Mūsā Dāljuwayh[518] and Arab tribesmen in the district of al-Anbār. They defeated and routed him. Abū Aḥmad sent his son Aḥmad with a group of his commanders to seek out the tribesmen responsible for Mūsā Dāljuwayh's defeat.

This year, too, [Abū Aḥmad] al-Dayrānī attacked [Muḥammad] b. Aws. He launched the assault during the night, dispersing his personnel and plundering his camp. Ibn Aws escaped and made his way to Wāsiṭ.

One of the Farāghinah appeared along the Mosul Road this year indulging in highway robbery. He was finally captured and killed.

Yaʿqūb b. al-Layth advanced from Fārs this year and, when he reached al-Nūbandajān,[519] Aḥmad b. Laythawayh departed from

518. The reading is uncertain.

519. A city in the district of Anburān, in Fārs province. See Le Strange, *Lands*, 262–65.

Tustar. Then Yaʿqūb this year headed for al-Ahwāz. Before his departure from Tustar, Aḥmad had engaged in a battle against the brother of ʿAlī b. Abān, who was defeated; many of his Zanj troops were taken.[520]

[1913] *An Account of [the] Battle [at ʿAskar Mukram]*[521]

Following Ibn Laythawayh's defeat of ʿAlī b. Abān with the Bāhiliyyīn in which he had been wounded, ʿAlī reportedly reached al-Ahwāz but, without remaining there, made his way to the camp[522] of his master, the Zanj leader. There he was treated for his wounds until he completely recovered.

ʿAlī then set out again for al-Ahwāz, despatching at the same time his brother al-Khalīl b. Abān and his nephew Abū Sahl Muḥammad b. Ṣāliḥ with a huge army against Ibn Laythawayh, who at the time was stationed in ʿAskar Mukram. The two men advanced with their forces and were met by Ibn Laythawayh, who was heading toward them about a *farsakh* from ʿAskar Mukram. The two sides drew upon each other and Ibn Laythawayh, who had prepared an ambush, fell back when fighting flared up. In their zeal to get him, the Zanj pursued him, passing by the ambush Ibn Laythawayh had set up. The ambushers emerged behind the Zanj, who were routed and scattered. Ibn Laythawayh then turned back to attack them and finished the job, while the Zanj returned to base in full flight. Ibn Laythawayh set off for Tustar, taking with him enemy heads. ʿAlī b. Abān sent off to the Masruqān canal against Aḥmad b. Laythawayh another army detachment led by Ankluwayh. Ibn Laythawayh despatched thirty of his best cavalry to engage Ankalwayh and, when al-Khalīl b. Abān heard of their mission, he laid an ambush for them. They reached his position and he attacked; not one of them escaped, slain to the last man. Their heads were taken to ʿAlī b. Abān in al-Ahwāz and he forwarded them to the abominable one.

Then (Yaʿqūb) al-Ṣaffār arrived in al-Ahwāz, while Ibn Laythawayh fled from it.

---

520. Ibn al-Athīr, *Kāmil*, VII, 307–8, adds the detail that Yaʿqūb b. al-Layth established himself in Junday Sābūr before setting off for al-Ahwāz. Ṭabari's account is disjointed, and he mentions this point farther on, at p. 187, below.

521. Popovic, *Révolte*, 115.

522. This would be a reference to ʿAlī b. Muḥammad's capital, al-Mukhtārah.

An Account of [Yaʿqūb] al-Ṣaffār's Activities This Year[523] [1914]

When Yaʿqūb b. al-Layth reached Junday Sābūr and established himself there, all who were in the service of the central authorities had reportedly moved out of this district. Yaʿqūb sent to al-Ahwāz on his behalf a man called al-Ḥiṣn b. al-ʿAnbar.[524] As he approached the city, ʿAlī b. Abān, the associate of the Zanj leader, left and set up camp at the Nahr al-Sidrah.[525] Ḥiṣn[526] entered al-Ahwāz and established his quarters there. His troops and those of ʿAlī b. Abān began to make forays against each other, and both sides suffered losses. This continued until ʿAlī b. Abān was prepared to set out for al-Ahwāz where he clashed with al-Ḥiṣn and his troops in a vicious encounter in which a large number of Yaʿqūb's troops were killed, cavalry horses captured, and a great deal of booty seized. Al-Ḥiṣn and his followers fled to ʿAskar Mukram, while ʿAlī remained in al-Ahwāz confiscating what was left in it. He then returned to the Nahr al-Sidrah and instructed Bahbūdh to attack a Kurdish associate of [Yaʿqūb] al-Ṣaffār stationed in Dawraq.[527] Bahbūdh did as he was ordered and slew a number of his men, taking the Kurd prisoner. However, he acted generously toward the man and released him. After this, ʿAlī was expecting Yaʿqūb to set out against him, but he did not; instead he sent as support to al-Ḥiṣn b. al-ʿAnbar his brother al-Faḍl b. al-ʿAnbar and ordered them to refrain from confronting the abominable one's troops in battle and to restrict themselves to al-Ahwāz. Yaʿqūb wrote to ʿAlī b. Abān seeking to conclude a truce with him so that he might leave his troops in al-Ahwāz. ʿAlī rejected this proposal, unless he could transfer food supplies from the city. (Yaʿqūb) al-Ṣaffār withdrew, allowing him to move the food supplies while ʿAlī in turn withdrew, so Yaʿqūb could remove the [1915] animal forage in al-Ahwāz. So ʿAlī had the food supplies moved and left the forage and the two sides, both ʿAlī's and Yaʿqūb's troops, refrained from interfering with each other.

In this year, the Khārijite Musāwir b. ʿAbd al-Ḥamīd died.[528]

---

523. See Popovic, *Révolte*, 115–17.
524. Ibn al-Athīr, *Kāmil*, VII, 308, calls him al-Khiḍr b. al-ʿAnbar.
525. Yāqūt, *Muʿjam*, II, 258.
526. Here without the article.
527. A town in Khūzistān. See Yāqūt, *Muʿjam*, II, 618–19.
528. Ibn al-Athīr, *Kāmil*, VII, 309, supplies a few more details.

On Friday, the 10th of Dhū al-Qaʿdah of this year (August 24, 877) ʿUbaydallāh b. Yaḥyā b. Khāqān died, having fallen from his horse in the main square in a collision with his eunuch, Rashīq. With blood flowing from his nose and ears, he died three hours after his fall. Abū Aḥmad b. al-Mutawwakil performed the obsequies and accompanied the funeral procession.

The following day he appointed al-Ḥasan b. Makhlad as vizier.[529] Then, on the 27th of Dhū al-Qaʿdah (August 11, 877), Mūsā b. Bughā arrived in Sāmarrā, and al-Ḥasan b. Makhlad fled to Baghdad. In his place Sulaymān b. Wahb was appointed vizier, on the 6th of Dhū al-Ḥijjah (August 20, 877). ʿUbaydallāh b. Sulaymān was appointed secretary of al-Mufawwaḍ and al-Muwaffaq, in addition to his role of secretary to Mūsā b. Bughā. The palace of ʿUbaydallāh b. Yaḥyā was presented to Kayghalagh.

In this year the brother of Sharkab drove al-Ḥusayn b. Ṭāhir out of Naysābūr and occupied it. He forced its inhabitants to surrender to him a third of their wealth. Al-Ḥusayn went to Marv, where the brother of the Khwārazm Shāh[530] appealed to Muḥammad b. Ṭāhir.

In this year the Slavs surrendered Lu'lu'ah to the tyrant.[531]

In this year al-Faḍl b. Isḥāq b. al-Ḥasan b. Ismāʿīl led the pilgrimage.[532]

---

529. On these developments, see Sourdel, *Vizirat*, I, 309ff.

530. See *EI*,² s.v. "Khʷārazm-Shāhs." Ibn al-Athīr, *Kāmil*, VII, 310, says it was the son, rather than the brother, who was in Marv.

531. See n. 461, above. "The tyrant" is Ṭabarī's epithet for the Byzantine emperor. Ibn al-Athīr, *Kāmil*, VII, 308–9, gives more detail, revealing that the fortress was surrendered voluntarily by its garrison because payment of their allotments and supplies were long overdue.

532. This is the same person who led the pilgrimmage in the two previous years; his full name is given on p. 167, above.

The Events of the Year 264

(SEPTEMBER 13, 877–SEPTEMBER 2, 878)

The events taking place this year included the despatch of an army by Yaʿqūb al-Ṣaffār to al-Ṣaymarah. Yaʿqūb marched at the head of the army toward al-Ṣaymarah. Ṣayghūn was arrested and brought to Yaʿqūb, and he died while being held his prisoner.[533]

On the 11th of al-Muḥarram (September 23, 877) Abū Aḥmad, together with Mūsā b. Bughā assembled the army in al-Qāʾim (in Sāmarrā), and it was escorted in public procession by al-Muʿtamid. Then the two men departed from Sāmarrā on the 2nd of Ṣafar (October 14, 877). After they had reached Baghdad, Mūsā b. Bughā died, and he was transported back to Sāmarrā for burial.

In the month of Rabīʿ I (November 11–December 10, 877) Qabīḥah, the mother of al-Muʿtazz, died.

In this year Ibn al-Dayrānī went to al-Dīnawar,[534] where Ibn ʿIyāḍ

533. Manuscript C adds that he died on the 11th of al-Muḥarram (September 23, 877), though the copyist may have confused it with the line immediately following, on the mustering of the army by Abū Aḥmad, which (by coincidence?) occurred on the same day.

534. A city in the province of Jibāl, between Ḥulwān and Hamadhān. See Le Strange, *Lands*, 188, 189.

and Dulaf b. ʿAbd al-ʿAzīz b. Abī Dulaf united against him, forcing him to flee, after which they seized his property and estates. Ibn al-Dayrānī returned to Ḥulwān in defeat.

In this year as well, the Byzantines captured ʿAbdallāh b. Rashīd b. Kāwus.[535]

An Account of [the] Capture [of ʿAbdallāh b. Rashīd]

The reason for this was that ʿAbdallāh had entered Byzantine territory with four thousand troops of the Syrian frontier districts (*thughūr*).[536] He ventured to Ḥiṣnayn and al-Maskanīn.[537] The Muslims seized booty and then set off on the return journey. They had
[1917] just left al-Badandūn[538] when they were surrounded by the army commanders (*biṭrīq*)[539] of Salūqīyah[540] — Qadhaydhīyah, Qurrah, Kawkab, and Kharshanah. The Muslims dismounted and hocked their animals, and in the fighting all of them were slain, save for five or six hundred who laid on the whips to their riding beasts and escaped. The Byzantines killed many and captured ʿAbdallāh b. Rashīd, who was struck down by numerous blows; he was taken to Luʾluʾah and then on to the tyrant,[541] along the post road.

Muḥammad al-Muwallad was made governor of Wāsiṭ this year. Sulaymān b. Jāmiʿ, who gathered the taxes of areas adjacent to Wāsiṭ on behalf of the Zanj leader, engaged Muḥammad in battle, defeated him and, after driving him from Wāsiṭ, occupied it.

An Account of [the] Battle [at Wāsiṭ][542]

Sulaymān b. Jāmiʿ had been sent by the leader of the Zanj to the districts of al-Ḥawānīt and the marshlands. Following his defeat of Ju-

535. Ibn al-Athīr, *Kāmil*, VII, 312.

536. See *EI*,² s.v. "al-ʿAwāṣim"; Le Strange, *Lands*, 128ff.

537. The force led by ʿAbdallāh took one of the most common routes through the Taurus mountains into Byzantine-controlled territory, the Darb al-Salāmah, or Safety Pass, which went through the famous Cilician Gates. See Le Strange, *Lands*, 134.

538. See Le Strange, *Lands*, 133, where he transliterates it Badhandūn. This was the place, near Tarsus, where the Caliph al-Maʾmūn died.

539. See Lane, *Lexicon*, s.v. *b-ṭ-r-q*; he equates the Byzantine term *biṭrīq* with *qāʾid* "commander" in Muslim military ranks.

540. The ancient Seleucia, southwest of Tarsus. See Le Strange, *Lands*, 133.

541. Ibn al-Athīr, *Kāmil*, VII, 312, uses the more polite expression "king of Rūm."

542. See Popovic, *Révolte*, 116ff. Ibn al-Athīr, *Kāmil*, VII, 312–15.

lān al-Turkī, the central authorities' tax collector, and his battle against Aghartimish, whose army he routed, and his killing Khushaysh, whose camp he plundered, Sulaymān wrote to the Zanj leader, seeking permission to come and renew his bond with him and put in order various of his own domestic affairs.

After he had sent the letter, Aḥmad b. Mahdī al-Jubbā'ī advised Sulaymān to attack the forces of [Takīn] al-Bukhārī, who at the time was staioned in Bardūdā.[543] Sulaymān agreed and set out for Bardūdā. He arrived at a spot called Akramahr, which was about five [1918] *farsakhs*[544] from Takīn's army camp.

When he reached the place, al-Jubbā'ī[545] said to Sulaymān that in his opinion Sulaymān should remain [in Akramahr] while he would proceed in the boats to attract the enemy toward him, causing them considerable trouble and effort on the way. He said, "By the time they reach you, they will be exhausted, and you can deal with them as you wish." Sulaymān followed this advice and mustered his cavalry and foot soldiers on the spot, while Aḥmad b. Mahdī set out early in the morning in the galleys. He reached Takīn's camp and fighting broke out for a while as Takīn prepared his own cavalry and infantry. Al-Jubbā'ī fell back from him and despatched a young man to inform Sulaymān that Takīn's troops were approaching him with their cavalry. The messenger found that Sulaymān had already begun to follow after al-Jubbā'ī when news was slow in reaching him. The messenger sent him back to his camp, while another messenger from al-Jubbā'ī arrived with the same information. After Sulaymān returned to his troops, he sent off Tha'lab b. Ḥafṣ al-Baḥrānī and one of the Zanj commanders called Manīnā with a detachment of Zanj. They were to set up an ambush in the countryside along the route that Takīn's cavalry would have to take, and Sulaymān ordered them to attack from the rear once they had passed by. When al-Jubbā'ī learned that Sulaymān had strengthened their position with his horsemen and ordered the setting up of an ambush, in a voice loud

543. See Le Strange, *Lands*, 41; Le Strange, "Ibn Serapion's Description," 271. The Bardūdā was a canal issuing from the Tigris and flowing into the great swampland (*al-baṭīḥah*). The reference here could be to the canal or to a place of the same name located on it.

544. About 30 km.

545. Throughout the passage describing these events, Ibn al-Athīr, *Kāmil*, VII, 313, refers to him as al-Ḥayātī.

enough to allow Takīn's troops to hear, he addressed his own troops saying, "You have deceived me! Destroyed me! I ordered you not to enter this canal,[546] but you insisted. Now you have put us in this position from which I can see no escape." When Takīn's troops heard al-Jubbāʾī's remarks, they eagerly renewed the pursuit, shouting
[1919] that they had "a bird[547] in a cage."

Al-Jubbāʾī hastened off, with Takīn's troops following and raining arrows down upon them. They passed by the spot where the ambush was set, approaching Sulaymān's camp where he himself was concealed behind a wall with his horsemen and soldiers. Sulaymān then advanced to meet the enemy army as the ambush emerged behind the cavalry and al-Jubbāʾī turned the fronts of his galleys around [to face] those [of the enemy] who were on the canal. Victory over the enemy was achieved on all fronts. The Zanj pursued them, killing and plundering, for a distance of some three *farsakh*s.[548] Then Sulaymān stopped and said to al-Jubbāʾī, "Let's turn back. We have won easily and are in good shape. Security is preferable to anything else." To which al-Jubbāʾī replied, "On the contrary! Our trick worked well on them and we have made their hearts faint. The best thing now is to take them again by surprise this very night. Perhaps we could drive them out of their camp and scatter them." Sulaymān put al-Jubbāʾī's advice into action and marched toward Takīn's camp, reaching it at sunset. He attacked, and Takīn and his followers responded as a ferocious battle developed. Then Sulaymān and his troops finally withdrew from the fighting. He halted to restore order to his troops and then despatched Shibl with a detachment of horsemen, together with some foot soldiers, into the countryside. He ordered al-Jubbāʾī to sail his galleys along the canal. Sulaymān set off with his cavalry and infantry, leading them himself, and he reached Takīn without obstacle. They, however, withdrew entirely, abandoning their camp. Sulaymān seized as booty all that could be found and then burned the camp. Upon returning to his own camp with all the booty that had been gathered, he found a letter awaiting him from the abominable one granting him permission to return home. Sulay-
[1920] mān left al-Jubbāʾī behind in charge. He took with him the banners found in Takīn's camp, the barges seized from Abū Tamīm, Khu-

546. Literally "entrance" or "mouth," here clearly meaning a canal.
547. Literally *bulbul*, a nightingale.
548. About 18 km.

shaysh, and Takīn as well and journeyed to the abominable one's base, arriving there in Jumādā I in the year 264 (January 9–February 7, 878).[549]

An Account of How the Abominable One Prepared His Zanj to Occupy Wāsiṭ[550] *(and Other Events of the Year 264)*[551]

Yaḥyā b. Khalaf[552] al-Jubbā'ī left for Māzrawān in the galleys and with the troops over which Sulaymān had given him charge. This was reportedly after Sulaymān b. Jāmi' had departed from his camp following the battle with Takīn and gone to the leader of the Zanj. Al-Jubbā'ī headed there in search of supplies, together with a group of blacks, but Ju'lān's troops challenged him and seized the boats accompanying him; they routed him and he returned in defeat to Ṭahītha. There he received letters from villagers[553] informing him that when Manjūr, a *mawlā* of the Commander of the Faithful, and Muḥammad b. 'Alī b. Ḥabīb al-Yashkūrī learned of Sulaymān b. Jāmi''s absence from Ṭahītha, they joined forces, assembled their soldiers and set upon the village, killing and burning, and then departed. Those who escaped from the village went to another called al-Ḥajjā- [1921] jiyyah and remained there.

Al-Jubbā'ī wrote to Sulaymān with the information contained in the villagers' communication and also mentioned his encounter with Ju'lān's troops. The Zanj leader bade Sulaymān to hasten back to Ṭahītha. He arrived there and gave it about that he intended to go into battle against Ju'lān and mustered his army in preparation. Al-Jubbā'ī was sent in advance of Sulaymān with the galleys containing horses and men and with orders to reach Māzrawān and station himself opposite Ju'lān's army. He was instructed to let the horses be exposed to graze where Ju'lān's troops could see them; but (al-Jubbā'ī) was not to attack them.

---

549. Ibn al-Athīr, *Kāmil*, VII, 314, says this event occurred in the year 263.

550. Popovic, *Révolte*, 118–22.

551. This subheading is not in the form usually employed by Ṭabarī.

552. Manuscripts B and C have this reading, albeit a corrupt one, for al-Jubbā'ī's name was Aḥmad b. Mahdī.

553. These may have been from the village of Marwān, which, as noted on p. 177, above, was near Ṭahīthā.

Sulaymān, for his part, rode out with his entire army, except for a handful that he left behind in his camp, and entered the region of the Ahwār.[554] He at last came upon two such stretches of open water called al-Rabbah and al-ʿAmraqah. Sulaymān then headed for Muḥammad b. ʿAlī b. Ḥabīb, who was at that time at a spot called Tallfakhkhār.[555] When he reached him, a major battle broke out. Many were slain and Sulaymān was able to seize a large number of horses and abundant booty. He killed a brother of Muḥammad b. ʿAlī, though Muḥammad himself escaped. Sulaymān set out on return journey and when he was in the open countryside between al-Bazzāq and the village,[556] horsemen of the Banū Shaybān appeared. Now Sulaymān had struck down one of the chiefs of the Banū Shaybān in Tallfakhkhār, killing him, taking one of his young sons prisoner, and confiscating the mare he was riding. News of this had reached the tribe, and so now they confronted Sulaymān in the open with four hundred horsemen. At the time Sulaymān had marched against Ibn Ḥabīb, he had sent for his deputy in al-Ṭaff,[557] ʿUmayr b. ʿAmmār, to act as guide owing to his knowledge of the roads. When Sulaymān
[1922] spotted the horsemen of the Banū Shaybān, he sent off all his troops leaving ʿUmayr b. ʿAmmār on his own. The Banū Shaybān fought and killed him, carrying off his head when they left. The abominable one was greatly distressed at the news of ʿUmayr's death. Sulaymān had transported to the abominable one all that had been acquired in the territory of Muḥammad b. ʿAlī b. Ḥabīb, this occurring at the end of Rajab (March 9–April 7, 878) of this year.

In Shaʿbān (April 8–May 6, 878) Sulaymān took a detachment of his troops to Qaryat Ḥassān,[558] where, at the time, one of the central authorities' commanders called Jaysh b. Ḥamartakīn was stationed. Sulaymān attacked the village, causing Jaysh to flee in fear and allowing Sulaymān to capture, plunder, and burn it. He took with him horses [as booty] and returned to his own camp.

Next, on the 10th of Shaʿbān (April 17, 878), Sulaymān left for the

---

554. Ibn Serapion describes a *hawr* (pl. *ahwār*) as a great sheet of clear water in which no reeds grow. See Le Strange, "Ibn Serapion's Description," 297–98; *EI*,[1] s.v. "Maisān."

555. The reading is uncertain.

556. The name of the place is not specified, but it may refer to the village of Marwān, as earlier in this passage.

557. A certain area in the district of al-Kūfah. See Yāqūt, *Muʿjam*, IV, 36.

558. A village between Dayr al-ʿĀqūl and Wāsiṭ. See Yāqūt, *Muʿjam*, II, 266.

region of al-Ḥawānīt[559] and sent al-Jubbā'ī upstream in the galleys toward Bar(r) Musāwir.[560] There he found a number of large boats, which Juʿlān had wanted to use to reach the Nahr Abān; they contained his horses, with which he used to go out hunting. Al-Jubbā'ī attacked the vessels, killed the crews, and seized the horses, of which there were twelve, and then returned to Ṭahīthā.

On the 26th of Shaʿbān (May 3, 878) Sulaymān attacked Tall Rumānā. The inhabitants evacuated the place, and Sulaymān gathered all he could in booty and returned to his camp. Next, on the 10th of Ramaḍān (May 16, 878), he went to al-Jazīrah, where Abbā[561] was at the time, while Juʿlān was in Māzrawān. Sulaymān had written to the abominable one, asking that he send him barges; he provided ten with a man from ʿAbbādān in charge called al-Ṣaqr b. al- [1923]
Ḥusayn. When al-Ṣaqr reached Sulaymān with the barges, he pretended to be planning to attack Juʿlān. The news that Sulaymān intended to advance on him soon reached Juʿlān's ears, and thus his main concern was to protect his own camp. But, as Sulaymān approached Abbā's location, he turned aside to Abbā and attacked him, thus taking him by surprise, when he was not expecting him. Sulaymān succeeded in achieving his goal and in acquiring six barges.

Muḥammad b. al-Ḥasan said—Jabbāsh the eunuch said that Sulaymān actually found eight barges in [Abbā's] camp, and two of them, which were on the shore, he burned. He seized horses, weapons, and other booty and returned to his own camp.

Sulaymān next made it known that he intended attacking Takīn al-Bukhārī. To this end he equipped some boats with [the assistance of] al-Jubbā'ī and Jaʿfar b. Aḥmad, a maternal uncle of Ankalay,[562] son of the accursed abominable one. But, when the boats neared Juʿlān's camp, Juʿlān pursued, attacked, and seized possession of them. Sulaymān then launched an assault on Juʿlān from the landward side and drove him to flight toward al-Ruṣāfah.[563] He recovered

559. See Le Strange, "Ibn Serapion's Description," 46.
560. The reading is very uncertain. See p. 176, above.
561. Popovic, *Révolte,* 117, queries whether this person might be one of Juʿlān's officers. It is possible, too, that he is same Abbā al-Turkī, who has already been reported as operating in this area. See p. 178, above.
562. Halm, *Traditionen,* 55, notes that Ankalay is a Persian name, which supports the view that the Zanj leader, ʿAlī b. Muḥammad, was of Persian origin.
563. A town lying on the east bank of the Tigris below Wāsiṭ. See Le Strange, *Lands,* 40; Yāqūt, *Muʿjam,* II, 782.

the boats, as well as twenty-seven horses, two foals of Juʿlān's, and three mules, to say nothing of considerable quantities of other booty and weapons. Once again Sulaymān returned to Ṭahītha.

Muḥammad (b. al-Ḥasan) said that Jabbāsh denied any mention of Takīn in this context; nor did he know anything concerning him from the evidence of [al-Ṣaqr b. al-Ḥusayn] al-ʿAbbādānī but claimed that Sulaymān's only objective was against Juʿlān.[564] In fact, Sulaymān's troops had no information of him until it was rumored that he and al-Jubbāʾī had both been killed, which caused great anxiety among his followers.[565] Then hard news emerged of developments in the fighting against Juʿlān. They calmed down and waited quietly until Sulaymān came to them. Sulaymān wrote to the abominable
[1924] one of his exploits and sent him banners and weapons.

In Dhū al-Qaʿdah (July 5 – August 3, 878) Sulaymān went to al-Ruṣāfah and attacked Maṭar b. Jāmiʿ, who was stationed there. He seized much booty, burned and plundered al-Ruṣāfah, and sent banners to the abominable one. On the 5th of Dhū al-Ḥijjah 264 (August 8, 878) Sulaymān arrived at the abominable one's city.[566] He stayed to celebrate the feast[567] and remain at home. Maṭar b. Jāmiʿ went and attacked the village of al-Ḥajjājiyyah, taking a number of its inhabitants captive. One of these was Sulaymān's religious judge called Saʿīd b. al-Sayyid al-ʿAdawī, who was captured and sent to Wāsiṭ along with Thaʿlab b. Ḥafṣ (al-Baḥrānī) and four commanders who were with him. They had gone to al-Ḥarjaliyyah, about two and a half *farsakh*s from Ṭahītha, when al-Jubbāʾī set out with horses and men to thwart Maṭar. Al-Jubbāʾī arrived in the district, however, after Maṭar had already committed his acts there, and so al-Jubbāʾī retired and sent the news to Sulaymān, who arrived on Tuesday, the 28th of Dhū al-Ḥijjah of this year (August 31, 878).

---

564. There appears to be some confusion or misunderstanding among the sources Ṭabarī is using here. There is a parallel, however, between Sulaymān's two campaigns against Abbā and Juʿlān, each of which was preceded by the spread of "disinformation" on his real intention. Jabbāsh seems not to have known about the first attack against Abbā, when Sulaymān had pretended to be campaigning against Juʿlān.

565. Apparently Sulaymān had left his main army and was using only the boats and the troops on them in his forays against Abbā and al-Jubbāʾī.

566. That is, al-Mukhtārah.

567. That is, the feast of the sacrifice, the major celebration of the pilgrimage. See *EI*,[2] s.vv. "Ḥadjdj," "ʿĪd al-Aḍḥāʾ."

Juʿlān was removed from his post, and Aḥmad b. Laythawayh arrived and stationed himself in al-Shadīdiyyah.[568]

Sulaymān ventured to the Nahr Abān where he discovered one of Ibn Laythawayh's commanders called Ṭurnāj,[569] whom he attacked and killed.

Muḥammad (b. al-Ḥasan) — Jabbāsh said that the one killed at that place was Bīnak; and, as for Ṭurnāj, he was slain in Māzrawān.

Next Sulaymān reached al-Ruṣāfah, where the army of Maṭar b. Jāmiʿ was then located. Sulaymān attacked and plundered his camp, capturing from it seven barges, two of which he burned. That was in [1925]
the month of Rabīʿ II (December 11, 877–January 8, 878) of the year 264.[570]

Muḥammad — Jabbāsh said that six barges were seized and that this conflict was at al-Shadīdiyyah.

Following this, Sulaymān ventured forth with five barges aboard which he had arrayed the very finest of his commanders and troops. Takīn al-Bukhārī engaged him in battle in al-Shadīdiyyah, as Ibn Laythawayh had by then already proceeded to the district of al-Kūfah and Junbulāʾ. Takīn vanquished Sulaymān, seizing his barges with their war machines, weapons, and fighters. In this encounter the most experienced of Sulaymān's commanders were slain. Ibn Laythawayh afterward marched to al-Shadīdiyyah and administered these districts until Abū Aḥmad appointed Muḥammad al-Muwallad governor of Wāsiṭ.[571]

Muḥammad — Jabbāsh said that, when Ibn Laythawayh arrived in al-Shadīdiyyah, Sulaymān marched upon him and for two days they fought against each other. Finally, on the third day Sulaymān fell back and Ibn Laythawayh and his followers rushed to pursue him. Then Sulaymān returned to the attack and threw Ibn Laythawayh into the mouth of the Bardūdā canal; he saved himself after nearly drowning. Sulaymān captured seventeen of his riding animals.

---

568. Juʿlān had been prefect of Wāsiṭ and was replaced by Aḥmad b. Laythawayh.

569. The reading is uncertain.

570. Unless Sulaymān attacked al-Ruṣāfah twice in the same year, this account is out of place in the chronological ordering of events. Ṭabarī has already reported, p. 196, above, Sulaymān's defeat of Maṭar b. Jāmiʿ in al-Ruṣāfah in Dhū al-Qaʿdah, toward the end of the year.

571. That is, replacing Aḥmad Ibn Laythawayh, who had held the post. See Popovic, *Révolte*, 117.

[Muḥammad] continued, saying that Sulaymān communicated with the abominable one requesting reinforcements. The Zanj leader despatched al-Khalīl b. Abān and al-Mudhawwab[572] to him with about fifteen hundred horsemen. Upon the arrival of these reinforcements, Sulaymān straightaway went to engage Muḥammad al-Muwallad in battle. In the course of it Muḥammad fled and the Zanj occupied Wāsiṭ. A large number of persons were killed and the city was pillaged and burned. Kanjūr al-Bukhārī was in Wāsiṭ at the time and he held on, putting up a defense throughout that day until the afternoon, when he was killed. The ones who led the horsemen
[1926] in Sulaymān's army that day were al-Khalīl b. Abān and ʿAbdallāh, who was known as al-Mudhawwab. Al-Jubbāʾī was in charge of the galleys; al-Zanjī b. Mihrān was in charge of the barges. Sulaymān b. Jāmiʿ led his black commanders and their infantry; Sulaymān b. Mūsā al-Shaʿrānī and his two brothers led his horses and foot soldiers along with Sulaymān b. Jāmiʿ. The entire force performed to perfection.[573]

Sulaymān b. Jāmiʿ later left Wāsiṭ and with his entire army headed for Junbulāʾ, causing de poliation and destruction. Discord broke out between him and al-Khalīl b. Abān who wrote to his brother ʿAlī about it. ʿAlī b. Abān begged the Zanj leader to relieve al-Khalīl of his duties with Sulaymān, and permission was given for al-Khalīl to return to the abominable one's city with ʿAlī b. Abān's associates and slaves. Al-Mudhawwab remained behind with Sulaymān in charge of the Arab tribesmen. Sulaymān stayed in his camp for some days and then moved to the Nahr al-Amīr where he reestablished his camp. He despatched al-Jubbāʾī and al-Mudhawwab to Junbulāʾ, where they remained for ninety days while Sulaymān was encamped at the Nahr al-Amīr.

Muḥammad—Jabbāsh said that Sulaymān's camp was in al-Shadīdiyyah.

In this year Sulaymān b. Wahb departed from Baghdad for Sāmarrā. He was accompanied by al-Ḥasan b. Wahb, while Aḥmad b. al-Muwaffaq, Masrūr al-Balkhī, and the army commanders escorted them in public procession. When Sulaymān reached Sāmarrā, al-Muʿtamid grew angry with him and imprisoned him, bound in fet-

572. Ṭabarī enlightens us a few lines below. This man's name was ʿAbdallāh, his nickname al-Mudhawwab, literally "melted (fat)."

573. Literally "as one hand."

ters. His palace and those of his sons Wahb and Ibrāhīm were confiscated.

Al-Ḥasan b. Makhlad was made vizier on the 27th of Dhū al-Qaʿdah (July 31, 878).[574] [1927]

[Abū Aḥmad] al-Muwaffaq left Baghdad with ʿAbdallāh b. Sulaymān.[575] As he approached Sāmarrā, al-Muʿtamid transferred to the west bank [of the Tigris] and assembled his camp there, while Abū Aḥmad and his entourage settled on the island of al-Muʾayyad. Messengers went back and forth[576] between the two. A few days after the beginning of Dhū al-Ḥijjah al-Muʿtamid boarded a fire boat[577] on the Tigris, as his brother Abū Aḥmad headed toward him in a light rivercraft. Then the Caliph bestowed robes of honor upon Abū Aḥmad, Masrūr al-Balkhī, Kayghalagh, and Aḥmad b. Mūsā b. Bughā. On Tuesday, the 8th of Dhū al-Ḥijjah, which was *yawm al-tarwiyah*[578] (August 11, 878), Abū Aḥmad's troops crossed over the river to al-Muʿtamid's camp.

Sulaymān b. Wahb was released from prison, and al-Muʿtamid returned to the Jawsaq palace. Al-Ḥasan b. Makhlad fled with Aḥmad b. Ṣāliḥ b. Shirzād, and instructions were given for the confiscation of their property and that of their supporters.[579] Aḥmad b. Abī al-Aṣbagh was imprisoned. The army commanders stationed in Sāmarrā fled to Takrīt.[580] Abū Mūsā b. al-Mutawakkil went into hiding but reappeared thereafter. Those commanders who had gone to Takrīt went farther on, to Mosul, and began to help themselves to the tax revenues.

This year the pilgrimage was led by Hārūn b. Muḥammad b. Isḥāq b. Mūsā b. ʿĪsā al-Hāshimī al-Kūfī.

---

574. See Sourdel, *Vizirat*, I, 315–26, for details.

575. Manuscript C and Ibn al-Athīr, *Kāmil*, VII, 316, both have ʿUbaydallāh b. Sulaymān b. Wahb.

576. Ibn al-Athīr, *Kāmil*, VII, 316, reproduces this passage from Ṭabarī almost verbatim, though with certain shifts in the order of sentences. He glosses this sentence, stating that al-Muʿtamid was angry with al-Muwaffaq, and then an agreement was reached.

577. *Ḥarrāqah*. See Lane, *Lexicon*, s.v. *ḥ-r-q*.

578. Literally "day of providing oneself with water" the 8th of Dhū al-Ḥijjah, during the annual pilgrimage ceremonies. See *EI*,[2] s.v. "Ḥadjdj."

579. Al-Ḥasan b. Makhlad and Sulaymān b. Wahb were bitter rivals. See Sourdel, *Vizirat*, I, 309–15.

580. See Ibn al-Athīr, *Kāmil*, VII, 316, where he explains that the commanders fled in fear of al-Muwaffaq.

The Events of the Year 265

(September 3, 878–August 22, 879)

Among the events taking place during this year was a battle in the district of Junbulāʾ[581] between Aḥmad b. Laythawayh and Sulaymān b. Jāmiʿ, the Zanj master's commander.

[1928] *An Account of [the] Battle [of Junbulāʾ]*[582]

Sulaymān b. Jāmiʿ had reportedly written to the Zanj leader, informing him of the situation on Nahr al-Zuhayrī. He requested permission for expenses to dig a canal from it into the Sawād al-Kūfah and the plain.[583] Sulaymān informed him the distance was not great and that once the canal was dug it would be easy for the Zanj leader [to arrange] shipments of food supplies from the districts of Junbulāʾ and the Sawād al-Kūfah. The abominable one sent him a man called Muḥammad b. Yazīd al-Baṣrī to help in carrying out the task. He

---

581. A hamlet between Wāsiṭ and al-Kūfah. See Yāqūt, *Muʿjam*, II, 126.

582. See Popovic, *Révolte*, 118; Ibn al-Athīr, *Kāmil*, VII, 322.

583. Reading *al-barāz*, according to Ṭabarī, *Addenda et Emendanda*, DCCXCII, rather than *al-barār*, as in the text.

wrote to Sulaymān to supply all his needs in terms of expenses and lodging with him and his army until the task for which he had been sent was completed. Sulaymān moved his entire force to stay in al-Sharīṭiyyah[584] for almost a month and set the laborers to work on the canal. During this time Sulaymān did not touch [the provisions] at hand belonging to the villagers from nearby Khusrū Sābūr.[585] Rather, supplies reached him from the district of al-Ṣīn[586] and adjacent areas, until the moment when Ibn Laythawayh, Abū Aḥmad's financial administrator over Junbulā', attacked Sulaymān and killed fourteen[587] of his commanders.

Muḥammad b. al-Ḥasan said that forty-seven commanders had been killed and untold numbers of others. Sulaymān's camp was pillaged and his boats, which were moored in this canal that he was engaged in digging, were burned. Sulaymān withdrew in utter defeat to Ṭahītha, where he remained. Al-Jubbā'ī arrived in the wake of the defeat and later went back upstream to stay in Barratimurtā,[588] leaving a boat master called al-Zanjī b. Mihrān in charge of the barges.

The central authorities had sent [Abū Ḥamzah] Nuṣayr to have [1929] Shāmraj[589] sent in bonds to the court and appointed him to Shāmraj's duties. After this, Nuṣayr came upon al-Zanjī b. Mihrān on the Barratimurtā canal and seized nine of his barges, six of which al-Zanjī was able to recover.

Muḥammad b. al-Ḥasan said that Jabbāsh denied that al-Zanjī b. Mihrān had recovered any of the barges, claiming that Nuṣayr got away with them all.

Al-Zanjī headed for Ṭahītha, forwarding a letter to Sulaymān before he arrived. Sulaymān stayed in Ṭahītha until news reached him that al-Muwaffaq was coming his way.

In al-Muḥarram of this year (September 3–October 2, 878) Aḥmad b. Ṭūlūn[590] fought against Sīmā the Tall in Antioch,[591] besieging him until he conquered the city and killed Sīmā.

584. Ibn al-Athīr, *Kāmil*, VII, 322, calls the place al-Sharīṭah.
585. Well-known village near Wāsiṭ. See Yāqūt, *Mu'jam*, II, 96.
586. A location in the region of al-Kūfah. See Yāqūt, *Mu'jam*, III, 440.
587. Ibn al-Athīr, *Kāmil*, VII, 322, has forty.
588. The reading is uncertain.
589. This person remains unidentified.
590. Ṭabarī, III, 1697, notes that in the year 254/868 Bāyakbāk appointed him governor of Egypt. See *EI*,[2] s.v. "Aḥmad b. Ṭūlūn."
591. Le Strange, *Lands*, 152 n. 2, calls attention to the confusion, in the early Ara-

Al-Qāsim b. Mimāh[592] assaulted Dulaf b. ʿAbd al-ʿAzīz b. Abī Dulaf[593] in Iṣfahān and killed him. Later a group of Dulaf's companions killed al-Qāsim in revenge and declared Aḥmad b. ʿAbd al-ʿAzīz their chief.

In al-Muḥarram of this year (September 3 – October 2, 878) Muḥammad al-Muwallad joined Yaʿqūb b. al-Layth. The central authorities ordered the confiscation of his money and lands.

In Jumādā I of this year (December 30, 878 – January 28, 879) Arab tribesmen killed Juʿlān the ruffian (*al-ʿayyār*) in Dimimmā.[594] He had been providing protection for a caravan when he was killed. The central authorities despatched a group of *mawlās* to seek out the
[1930] perpetrators of the crime, but they fled. The searchers got as far as ʿAyn al-Tamr[595] and then returned to Baghdad, a number of them having died of the gripping cold that lasted for some days, with snow even falling in Baghdad.

Abū Aḥmad ordered the imprisonment in his palace of Sulaymān and his son ʿUbaydallāh,[596] along with a number of their relations. The palaces of some of these latter were plundered, but a guard was ordered to protect the palaces of Sulaymān and his son. Their estates and wealth, along with the wealth and estates of their relatives, with the exception of Aḥmad b. Sulaymān, were confiscated. A settlement was later arranged with Sulaymān and his son ʿAbdallāh for the sum of nine hundred thousand dinars, and they were moved to a location where anyone they wished could come to visit.

This same year as well witnessed the assembly of troops of Mūsā b. Utāmish, Isḥāq b. Kundājīq, Yanghajūr b. Urkhūz, and al-Faḍl b. Mūsā b. Bughā at the Shammāsiyyah Gate. They crossed over the [main] Baghdad bridge[597] and ventured to al-Safīnatayn, followed by

---

bic chronicles, between Antioch in Syria and other places of the same name in Asia Minor—e.g., Antioch of Pisidia. Here the locale intended is Antioch in Syria, the ancient Antiocheia; this is confirmed on p. 204, below, and by the report in Ibn al-Athīr, *Kāmil*, VII, 324, that, when Ibn Ṭūlūn left Egypt for Syria in this year he appointed his son ʿAbbās his deputy. See *EI*,² s.v. "Anṭākiya."

592. Ibn al-Athīr, *Kāmil*, VII, 327, calls him al-Qāsim b. Mahāh.

593. In 254/868 his father had sent him to Junday Sābūr and Tustar to collect taxes. See Ṭabarī, III, 1697.

594. A village on the Euphrates just below al-Anbār. See Le Strange, *Lands*, 66; Le Strange, "Ibn Serapion's Description," 69.

595. The district of ʿAyn al-Tamr lay west of the Euphrates; the fortified town itself was situated just south of Hīt. See Le Strange, *Lands*, 65, 81.

596. The text has incorrect ʿAbdallāh; see Sourdel, *Vizirat*, I, 311.

597. See n. 21, above.

Aḥmad b. al-Muwaffaq.[598] They did not return but encamped at Ṣarṣar.[599]

On the 17th of Jumādā II (February 14, 879) Abū Aḥmad appointed Saʿīd b. Makhlad as his secretary. After having bestowed upon him a robe of honor, Saʿīd traveled to the commanders in Ṣarṣar. Abū Aḥmad next sent his son Aḥmad to them. He discussed matters with them, and they returned together, after which robes of honor were bestowed upon them.

According to report, five of the Byzantine commanders, with thirty thousand troops, marched toward Adhanah.[600] Having reached the oratory,[601] they captured Urkhūz, who had been the governor of the frontier districts, then removed from his post, but had [1931] stayed on as part of the frontier guard. Some four hundred men were captured with him, and the Byzantines killed some fourteen hundred men who had rallied to them. The Byzantines withdrew after four days; this was in Jumādā I (January 2, 879) of this year.

In Rajab (February 27–March 28, 879) of this year Mūsā b. Utāmish, Isḥāq b. Kundājīq, and Yanghajūr b. Urkhūz assembled troops on Nahr Dayālā.[602]

In this same year Aḥmad b. ʿAbdallāh al-Khujustānī conquered Naysābūr. Al-Ḥusayn b. Ṭāhir, Muḥammad b. Ṭāhir's prefect, went to Marv and settled there. The brother of Sharkab al-Jammāl was between al-Ḥusayn and al-Khujustānī.

Ṭūs was devastated this year.

Ismāʿīl b. Bulbul was appointed vizier.[603]

Yaʿqūb b. al-Layth died this year[604] in al-Ahwāz and was succeeded by his brother ʿAmr b. al-Layth, who wrote to the central authorities to his obedience and loyalty. Aḥmad b. Abī al-Aṣbagh was

598. Ibn al-Athīr, *Kāmil*, VII, 326, who reproduces this passage with glosses, says that al-Muwaffaq prevented the return of the soldiers.

599. A town on the Ṣarṣar canal, reached by way of the southern road leading to al-Kūfah from Baghdad. See Le Strange, *Lands*, 32.

600. The modern Adana. See Le Strange, *Lands*, 128, 130–31. It was one of the line of fortresses (*al-thughūr*) protecting Syria and was situated near the northern coast of the bay of Alexandretta; *EI*,² s.vv. "Adana," "al-ʿAwāṣim."

601. *Al-muṣallā.*

602. Having moved from their camp in Ṣarṣar (see p. 174, above) to the eastern bank of the Tigris, to the canal that irrigated the gardens of east Baghdad. See Le Strange, *Lands*, 59 (vocalized Diyālā).

603. See Sourdel, *Vizirat*, 315–16.

604. See Ibn al-Athīr, *Kāmil*, VII, 325, for additional details.

despatched to him in Dhū al-Qaʿdah (June 25–July 24, 879) of this year.

A group of tribesmen of the Banū Asad this year killed ʿAlī b. Masrūr al-Balkhī on the Mecca Road before he arrived at al-Mughīthah. Abū Aḥmad had appointed Muḥammad b. Masrūr al-Balkhī governor of the Mecca Road, and it was he who appointed his brother ʿAlī b. Masrūr to the post.

The Byzantine emperor sent ʿAbdallāh b. Rashīd b. Kāwus, the tax collector of the frontier districts who had been captured by him, to Aḥmad b. Ṭulūn, along with many other Muslim prisoners. The emperor also sent him a number of manuscripts as a gift.

[1932] A detachment of Zanj went to Jabbul[605] in thirty galleys, seized four boats containing foodstuffs, and then returned.

Al-ʿAbbās b. Aḥmad b. Ṭulūn and his followers took themselves off to Barqah,[606] in defiance of his father, Aḥmad who, according to report, had left him in charge of his administrative duties in Egypt when he departed for Syria. Upon Aḥmad's return from Syria to Egypt, Al-ʿAbbās took what money there was in the Egyptian treasury, as well as furnishings and other things belonging to his father, and left for Barqah.[607] Aḥmad despatched a force against him, which captured and brought al-ʿAbbās back. Aḥmad imprisoned him in his own quarters. Because of this action of al-ʿAbbās, a group of men who had joined up with him in this venture were killed.[608]

The Zanj this year occupied al-Nuʿmāniyyah,[609] burned its market and most of the inhabitants' dwellings, and took prisoners. They next moved to Jarjarāyā,[610] causing people of the Sawād region to enter Baghdad.[611]

---

605. See Le Strange, *Lands*, 38. It lay on the eastern bank of the Tigris, about 50 km. below Jarjarāyā; Yāqūt, *Muʿjam*, II, 23; Popovic, *Révolte*, 119.

606. For further details, see Ibn al-Athīr, *Kāmil*, VII, 324–25; *EI*,² s.v. "Barḳa." The town and region attached to it were the classical Cyrenaica.

607. Ibn al-Athīr, *Kāmil*, VII, 324, gives the date of his arrival in the month of Rabīʿ I, 265 (January 11–30, 878).

608. Ibn al-Athīr, *Kāmil*, VII, 325, where it is stated that al-ʿAbbās was still in prison in the year 268/881–82.

609. A town on the western bank of the Tigris about halfway between Baghdad and Wāsiṭ. See Le Strange, *Lands*, 37; Ibn al-Athīr, *Kāmil*, VII, 322.

610. A town below Dayr al-ʿĀqūl, which lay on both banks of the Tigris. See Le Strange, *Lands*, 37; Yāqūt, *Muʿjam*, II, 54.

611. This marked the northernmost point of the Zanj expansion, the closest to Baghdad that their campaigns brought them.

During the course of this year Abū Aḥmad made ʿAmr b. al-Layth governor of Khurāsān, Fārs, Iṣfahān, Sijistān, Kirmān, and al-Sind,[612] and had the formal investiture declared in the presence of witnesses. Aḥmad b. Abī al-Aṣbagh was sent to ʿAmr with the document of his investiture, together with a contract and robe of honor.

In Dhū al-Ḥijjah (July 25–August 22, 879) of this year Masrūr al-Balkhī marched on al-Nīl,[613] and ʿAbdallāh b. Laythawayh withdrew from it with his brother's troops. ʿAbdallāh had been in open conflict with the central authorities and had gone with his followers to Aḥmadābādh. He was pursued by Masrūr al-Balkhī, who intended to engage him in battle. Then ʿAbdallāh b. Laythawayh and his followers unexpectedly came to Masrūr on foot and yielded to him in [1933] obedience and loyalty. ʿAbdallāh b. Laythawayh, with his sword and girdle hung about his neck, proferred his apologies to Masrūr and swore an oath that he had been incited to do what he did. His apology was accepted, and robes of honor were ordered bestowed upon him and several of his commanders.

Takīn al-Bukhārī ventured forth to al-Ahwāz as vanguard for Masrūr al-Balkhī.

An Account of Takīn's Arrival in al-Ahwāz[614]

According to Muḥammad b. al-Ḥasan, Masrūr al-Balkhī appointed Takīn al-Bukhārī governor of the districts of al-Ahwāz at the time Abū Aḥmad had appointed Masrūr over them.[615] Takīn set out and arrived at al-Ahwāz. ʿAlī b. Abān had already reached there and was on his way to Tustar, which he surrounded with a large force of his Zanj troops and others. The populace was terrified at the development and was about to surrender the city when, in this situation, Takīn arrived. He had not even had time to change from his travel attire when he went into battle against ʿAlī b. Abān and his troops. Defeat was the lot of the Zanj, as they were slain, routed, and scat-

612. Ibn al-Athīr, *Kāmil,* VII, 326, adds to these posts that of commandant of police in Baghdad.

613. A town on Nahr al-Nīl, which was a continuation, of the Great Ṣarāt canal west of the town; it flowed from the Euphrates to the Tigris below Baghdad. See Le Strange, *Lands,* 73; Le Strange, "Ibn Serapion's Description," 261.

614. Ibn al-Athīr, *Kāmil,* VII, 323.

615. See Popovic, *Révolte,* 119.

tered. ʿAlī was forced to retreat with the remnants of his shattered forces. This was the famous battle of Bāb Kūdak[616] [at Tustar], after which Takīn al-Bukhārī returned and settled in the city. Many freebooters (*ṣaʿālīk*) and others swelled his forces. ʿAlī b. Abān also set out for Tustar with a sizable collection of his troops and encamped on the eastern side of the Masruqān canal. He placed his brother on the western side, together with a troop of horse and Zanj infantry. He sent on ahead a number of the Zanj commanders, among them An-
[1934] kluwayh and Ḥusayn al-Ḥammāmī and others, and ordered them to station themselves at the Fārs bridge (*qanṭarah*). Information about ʿAlī b. Abān's arrangements reached Takīn by means of a slave called Waṣīf al-Rūmī, who was a fugitive from ʿAlī b. Abān's army. He reported on the enemy's position at the Fārs bridge, on their indulgence in wine drinking, and on the dispersal of their troops to gather food. So during the night Takīn made his way toward them with a detachment of troops and attacked, killing from among their commanders Ankalwayh, Ḥusayn al-Ḥammāmī, Abū Ṣāliḥ Mufarraj, and Andarūn. The rest fled and caught up with al-Khalīl b. Abān, telling him what had happened to them. Takīn then ventured along the eastern side of the Masruqān and eventually found ʿAlī b. Abān with a detachment of troops. But ʿAlī did not pause to fight and withdrew, although a slave called Jaʿfarawayh from ʿAlī's cavalry was taken captive. ʿAlī and al-Khalīl returned with their detachments to al-Ahwāz, while Takīn went back to Tustar. ʿAlī wrote to Takīn to request he refrain from killing Jaʿfarawayh, and so he was imprisoned. There then occurred an exchange of messages and courtesies between ʿAlī and Takīn, news of which reached Masrūr, who thoroughly disapproved. Masrūr even heard that Takīn had besmirched his loyalty by going over to ʿAlī b. Abān.

Muḥammad b. al-Ḥasan—Muḥammad b. Dīnār—Muḥammad b. ʿAbdallāh b. al-Ḥasan b. ʿAlī al-Maʾmūnī al-Bādhghīsī, who was one of the associates of Takīn al-Bukhārī, said that when Masrūr
[1935] heard the news of Takīn's audacious behavior against him, he paused until he learned the true state of affairs and then set out toward the districts of al-Ahwāz, making a show of his pleasure with and approval of Takīn. He took the road to Shābarzān[617] and

616. The reading is very uncertain, Manuscript B having *k-d-d*, C *m-r-dh-k*, and Ibn al-Athīr, *Kāmil*, VII, 323, Kūrak.

617. The reading is uncertain.

thence to al-Sūs. Takīn already knew what Masrūr had heard about him, and this distressed him very much, as well as the group of his commanders who had followed in Masrūr's company. Messages went back and forth between Masrūr and Takīn until Takīn felt safe and secure. Masrūr went to Wādī Tustar, where he sent for Takīn, who crossed over to greet Masrūr. Masrūr ordered that his sword be removed and that he be placed in custody. When Takīn's army saw that, they immediately dispersed, a section of them making for the territory of the Zanj leader, another section joining the Kurd Muḥammad b. ʿUbaydallāh. When Masrūr heard of this [reaction], he extended a safe-conduct to all who remained of Takīn's army, and they joined him.

Muḥammad b. ʿAbdallāh b. al-Ḥasan al-Maʾmūnī said, "I was among those who went to Masrūr's camp when he handed Takīn over to Ibrāhīm b. Juʿlān. Takīn remained in his custody until his appointed time arrived and he died." Some of the affair of Masrūr and Takīn that we have mentioned occurred in the year 265 (878–79) and some in the year 266 (879–80).

The pilgrimage this year was led by Hārūn b. Muḥammad b. Isḥāq b. Mūsā b. ʿĪsā al-Hāshimī.

In this year as well, a detachment of Zanj under Abū al-Mughīrah b. ʿĪsā b. Muḥammad al-Makhzūmī attacked Mecca.[618] [1936]

---

618. See Popovic, *Révolte*, 120, who queries whether Ṭabarī intends "attack," rather than "conquer," which is what the Arabic word *mutaghalliban* suggests.

Bibliography of Cited Works

I. Primary Sources

al-Dīnawarī, Abū Ḥanīfah Aḥmad b. Dā'ūd. *Kitāb al-akhbār al-ṭiwāl.* 2 vols. Ed. W. Guirgass and I. Kratchkovsky. Leiden: 1888–1912.

Fragmenta Historicorum Arabicorum. Ed. M. J. de Goeje. 2 vols. Leiden: 1869.

Ibn al-Athīr, ʿIzz al-Dīn Abū al-Ḥasan ʿAlī b. Muḥammad. *al-Kāmil fī al-ta'rīkh.* 13 vols. Beirut: 1385–87/1965–67.

Ibn Ḥawqal, Abū al-Qāsim b. ʿAlī al-Nasībī. *Kitāb al-masālik wa-al-mamālik.* Ed. M. J. de Goeje. Bibliotheca Geographorum Arabicorum II. Leiden: 1873.

———. *Configuration de la terre (Kitāb ṣūrat al-arḍ).* Tr. J. H. Kramers and G. Wiet. 2vols. Paris: 1964.

Ibn al-Jawzī, ʿAbd al-Raḥmān b. ʿAlī. *al-Muntaẓam fī ta'rīkh al-mulūk wa-al-umam.* Ed. F. Krenkow. Hyderabad: 1357–59/1938–40.

Ibn Kathīr, Ismāʿīl b. ʿUmar. *al-Bidāyah wa-al-nihāyah.* 14 vols. Cairo: 1351–58/1932–40.

Ibn Manẓūr, Jamāl al-Dīn Abū al-Faḍl Muḥammad b. Mukarram al-Anṣārī, *Lisān al-ʿArab.* 5 vols. Cairo: 1979.

Ibn Sayyār al-Warrāq. *Kitāb al-ṭabīkh.* Ed. K. Ohrnberg and S. Mroueh. Helsinki: 1987.

Ibn al-Ṭiqṭaqā, Ṣafī al-Dīn Muḥammad b. ʿAlī. *al-Fakhrī.* Tr. C. E. J. Whitting as *Al-Fakhri: On the System of Government and the Moslem Dynasties.* London: 1947.

al-Iṣṭakhrī, Ibrāhīm b. Muḥammad. *Kitāb al-masālik wa-al-mamālik.* Ed. M. J. de Goeje. Bibliotheca Geographorum Arabicorum I. Leiden: 1870.

al-Jāḥiẓ, Abū ʿUthmān ʿAmr al-Fuqaymī al-Baṣrī. *Kitāb al-qiyān.* Ed. and tr. A. F. L. Beeston as *The Epistle on Singing Girls.* Warminster, Eng.: 1980.

al-Masʿūdī, Abū al-Ḥasan ʿAlī b. al-Ḥusayn. *Kitāb al-tanbīh wa-al-ishrāf.* Ed. M. J. de Goeje. Bibliotheca Geographorum Arabicorum VIII. Leiden: 1894.

______. *Murūj al-dhahab wa-maʿādin al-jawhar.* Ed. and tr. C. Barbier de Meynard and Pavet de Courteille as *Les prairies d'or.* 9 vols. Paris: 1861–77.

al-Shābushtī, Abū al-Ḥasan ʿAlī b. Muḥammad. *Kitāb al-diyārāt.* Ed. G. ʿAwwād. Baghdad: 1370/1951.

al-Ṭabarī, Abū Jaʿfar Muḥammad b. Jarīr. *Taʾrīkh al-rusul wa-al-mulūk.* Ed. M. J. de Goeje et al. 13 vols. plus *Introductio. Glossarium. Addenda et Emendanda* and *Index.* Leiden: 1879–1901.

al-Yaʿqūbī, Abū al-ʿAbbās Aḥmad b. Isḥāq, called Ibn Wāḍiḥ. *Kitāb al-buldān.* Ed. M. J. de Goeje. Bibliotheca Geographorum Arabicorum VII. Leiden: 1892.

______. *Taʾrīkh.* Ed. M. T. Houtsma. Leiden: 1883.

Yāqūt, Abū ʿAbdallāh Yaʿqūb b. ʿAbdallāh al-Ḥamawī al-Rūmī. *Muʿjam al-buldān.* Ed. F. Wüstenfeld. 6 vols. Leipzig: 1866–73.

II. Secondary Sources and Reference Works

Artúr, A.-P. U. *Tablas teóricas de equivalencia diaria entre los calendarios islámico y cristiano.* 2 vols. Zaragoza: 1984.

Ayalon, D. "On the Eunuchs in Islam." *Jerusalem Studies in Arabic and Islam,* VI (1979): 67–124.

______. "Preliminary Remarks on the Mamluk Military Institution in Islam." In *War, Technology and Society in the Middle East.* Ed. V. J. Parry and M. E. Yapp. London: 1975. Pp. 44–58.

Biberstein Kazimirski, A. de *Dictionnaire arabe-français.* Paris: 1860.

Bosworth, C. E. "Abū ʿAbdallāh al-Khwārazmī on the Technical Terms of the Secretary's Art: A Contribution to the Administrative History of Medieval Islam." *Journal of the Economic and Social History of the Orient,* XX (1969): 113–64.

______. *The Islamic Dynasties.* Rev. ed. Edinburgh: 1980.

______. "Recruitment, Muster and Review in Medieval Islamic Armies." In *War, Technology and Society in the Middle East.* Ed. V. J. Parry and M. E. Yapp. London: 1975. Pp. 59–77.

______. "The Ṭāhirids and Ṣaffārids." In *The Cambridge History of Iran.* IV. Cambridge: 1975. Pp. 90–135.

Cahen, C. "Mouvements populaires et autonomisme urbain dans l'Asie musulmane du Moyen Age." *Arabica,* V (1958): 225–40; VI (1959): 25–56, 233–65.

Creswell, K. A. C. *A Short Account of Early Muslim Architecture.* London: 1958.

Crone, P. *Slaves on Horses: The Evolution of the Islamic Polity.* Cambridge, 1980.
Dozy, R. *Supplément aux dictionnaires arabes.* 2 vols. Leiden: 1881.
Forstner, M. *Al-Muʿtazz billāh (252/866–255/869): Die Krise des abbasidischen Kalifats in 3./9. Jahrhundert: Ein Beitrag zur politischen Geschichte der sogennanten Periode der Anarchie von Samarra.* Germersheim, W. Ger.: 1976.
Fraenkel, S. *Die aramäischen Fremdwörter im Arabischen.* Leiden: 1886.
Frye, R. N. "The Sāmānids." In *The Cambridge History of Iran.* IV. Cambridge: 1975. Pp. 136–61.
de Goeje, M. J. *Mémoire sur les Carmathes du Bahrain et les Fatimides.* Leiden: 1886.
______. "Ṭabarī." In *Encyclopaedia Britannica,* XXIII. London: 1898. Pp. 2–5.
Halm, H. *Die Traditionen über den Aufstand ʿAlī Ibn Muḥammads, des "Herrn der Zanǧ": Eine quellenkritische Untersuchung.* Bonn: 1967.
Hinz, W. *Islamische Masse und Gewichte.* Leiden: 1955.
Hoenerbach, W. "Zur Heeresverwaltung der Abbasiden: Studie über Abufaraǧ Qudama: Diwān al-ǧais." *Der Islam,* XXIX (1950): 257–90.
Ismail, O. "The Founding of a New Capital: Sāmarrā." *Bulletin of the School of Oriental and African Studies,* XXXI (1968): 315–26.
Kennedy, H. *The Prophet and the Age of the Caliphs.* London: 1986.
Lane, E. W. *An Arabic-English Lexicon.* 2 vols. London: 1863–93. Repr. 8 vols. Beirut: 1984.
Lassner, J. *The Shaping of ʿAbbāsid Rule.* Princeton: 1980.
______. *The Topography of Baghdad in the Early Middle Ages.* Detroit: 1970.
Le Strange, G. *Baghdad during the Abbasid Caliphate.* Oxford: 1900.
______. "Ibn Serapion's Description of Mesopotamia and Baghdad." *Journal of the Royal Asiatic Society* (1895): 1–76, 255–315.
______. *The Lands of the Eastern Caliphate.* London: 1905. Repr. London: 1966.
Levy, R. *A Baghdad Chronicle.* Cambridge: 1929. Repr. Cambridge: 1977.
______. *The Social Structure of Islam.* Cambridge: 1965.
Løkkegaard, F. *Islamic Taxation in the Classic Period with Special Reference to Circumstances in Iraq.* Copenhagen: 1950.
Mez, A. *The Renaissance of Islam.* Tr. S. Khuda Bakhsh. Patna: 1937.
Morony, M. *Iraq after the Muslim Conquest.* Princeton: 1984.
Mottahedeh, R. "The ʿAbbāsid Caliphate in Iran." In *The Cambridge History of Iran,* IV. Cambridge: 1975. Pp. 57–89.
Nöldeke, T. "A Servile War in the East." In *Sketches from Eastern History.* Tr. J. S. Black. London: 1892. Pp. 146–75.

Ocaña Jiménez, M. *Nuevas tablas de conversión de datas islámicas a cristianas y viceversa.* Madrid: 1981.
Ostrogorsky, G. *History of the Byzantine State.* Oxford: 1968.
Pellat, C. *Le milieu baṣrien et la formation de Ǧāḥiẓ.* Paris: 1953.
Popovic, A. "Quelques renseignements inédits concernant le maître de Zanj, ʿAlī b. Muḥammad." *Arabica,* XII/2 (1965): 175–87.
______. *La révolte des esclaves en Iraq au III/IX siècle.* Paris: 1976.
Shaban, M. A. *The ʿAbbāsid Revolution.* Cambridge: 1970.
______. *Islamic History: A New Interpretation,* II. Cambridge: 1976.
Shir, S. A. *A Dictionary of Persian Loan-Words in the Arabic Language.* Beirut: 1980.
Sourdel, D. *Le vizirat ʿabbāside de 749 à 936 (132 à 324 de l'Hégire).* 2 vols. Damascus: 1959.
Thesiger, W. *The Marsh Arabs.* London: 1964.
Tyan, E. "Judicial Organization." In *Law in the Middle East.* Ed. M. Khadduri and H. Liebesny. Washington, D.C.: 1955. Pp. 123–45.
Vasiliev, A. A. *History of the Byzantine Empire.* I. Madison: 1970.
Waines, D. "The Crisis of the Abbasid Third Century." *Journal of the Economic and Social History of the Orient,* XX (1977): 339–48.
Wehr, H. *A Dictionary of Modern Writing Arabic.* Wiesbaden: 1971.
Wiet, G. *Baghdad: metropolis of the ʿAbbāsid Caliphate.* Norman, Okla.: 1971.
Wright, W. *A Grammar of the Arabic Language.* 2 vols. London and Edinburgh: 1874–75.
Young, G. *A Reed Shaken by the Wind.* London: 1983.

Index

The index contains all proper names of persons, places, and tribal and other groups, as well as topographical data and most transliterated technical terms that occur in the Translator's Foreword, the text, and the footnotes, except that only names belonging to the medieval and earlier periods are listed for the footnotes. When a name occurs in both the text and the footnotes on the same page, only the page number is given. The definite article, the abbreviation b. *(for* ibn *"son") and* bt. *(for* bint *"daughter"), and everything in parentheses have been disregarded for the purposes of alphabetization.*

A

ʿAbartā 23
Abbā al-Turkī 175, 178, 195, 196 n
ʿAbbād mosque 33, 53
ʿAbbādān xix, 43, 110, 111, 132, 136, 152, 195
al-ʿAbbās b. Aḥmad b. Ṭulūn 204
al-ʿAbbāsī al-ʿAtīq 41
ʿAbbāsid(s), Hāshimite(s) xvi, 19 n. 72, 27, 28, 40, 41, 48, 65, 75, 90, 93 nn. 292–93, 105, 107, 108, 121, 137 n. 391
ʿAbd al-Qays 30
ʿAbd al-Raḥmān b. Dīnār 102
ʿAbd al-Raḥmān al-Khārijī 157
ʿAbd al-Raḥmān b. Mufliḥ 151–55, 164, 165
ʿAbd al-Raḥmān b. Nāʾil al-Baṣrī 67
ʿAbd al-Ṣamad b. Mūsā 27
ʿAbdallāh b. ʿAlī 133
ʿAbdallāh b. Bughā al-Sharābī 107
ʿAbdallāh b. Ḥumayd al-Ṭūsī 111
ʿAbdallāh Karīkhā 37
ʿAbdallāh b. Manṣūr 71
ʿAbdallāh al-Mudhawwab 198
ʿAbdallāh b. Muḥammad 3
ʿAbdallāh b. Muḥammad al-ʿĀmirī 3
ʿAbdallāh b. Muḥammad b. Sulaymān al-Zaynabī, Abū Manṣūr 35, 52, 53, 57, 61, 108, 109
ʿAbdallāh b. Muḥammad b. Yazdād al-Marwazī, Abū Ṣāliḥ 12, 71, 72, 73, 94, 98, 105
ʿAbdallāh b. Rashīd b. Kāwus 190, 204
ʿAbdallāh al-Sijzī 151, 158, 159, 161
ʿAbdallāh b. Sulaymān 202
ʿAbdallāh b. Sulaymān b. Wahb 199

ʿAbdallāh b. Ṭāhir 172
ʿAbdallāh b. Takīn 97, 101, 102
ʿAbdallāh b. ʿUmar al-Bāzyār 95
ʿAbdallāh b. al-Wāthiq, Abū al-Qāsim 76–80, 82–86, 91, 96, 99, 102, 106, 163
ʿAbdān al-Kasibī 61
al-ʿabīd 15, 35, 38, 42, 106, 111
abominable one. *See* ʿAlī b. Muḥammad
Abrasān 43
Abrūn 138
Abū al-ʿAbbās b. Ayman (Abū al-Kubāsh) 54–56
Abū ʿAbdallāh b. al-Mutawakkil ʿalā-Allāh 2
Abū Aḥmad b. al-Mutawakkil ʿalā-Allāh. *See* al-Muwaffaq
Abū Aḥmad street 86, 87
Abū al-Aḥwaṣ b. Aḥmad b. Saʿīd b. Salm b. Qutaybah al-Bāhilī 67, 88, 110
Abū al-ʿAlāʾ al-Balkhī 54
Abū ʿAwn 180
Abū Bakr 88
Abū Dāʾūd al-Ṣuʿlūk 14 n. 48, 164, 181–83
Abū Dulaf 56, 140, 141
Abū Faqʿas 148
Abū al-Faraj 71
Abū Ghālib 121
Abū Ḥarmalah al-Ḥajjām 88
Abū al-Ḥasan 109
Abū Hilāl 50, 51
Abū Ḥudayd 36
Abū ʿĪsā b. al-Mutawakkil 148
Abū al-Jawn 62
Abū Jaysh ʿAbbād 145
Abū al-Khanjar 36, 61
Abū al-Layth al-Qawārīrī 61
Abū Manārah 43
Abū Manṣūr 52
Abū Muʿādh al-Qurashī 176
Abū al-Mughīrah b. ʿĪsā b. Muḥammad al-Makhzūmī 207
Abū Mūsā b. al-Mutawakkil 199
Abū Muslim 93
Abū al-Nidāʾ 179
Abū al-Ṣahbāʾ 116, 117
Abū Saʿīd al-Anṣārī 119
Abū Ṣāliḥ the Short 38
Abū al-Shawk 63
Abū Tamīm 180 192
Abū al-Wazīr 95
Adhanah 203
Adharbayjān 161
Aghartimish 178, 179, 191
ahl 5, 20 n. 78
ahl al-Baṣrah 64 n. 233
Aḥmad b. ʿAbd al-ʿAzīz 202
Aḥmad b. ʿAbdallāh al-Khujustānī 203
Aḥmad b. Abī al-Aṣbagh 199, 203, 205
Aḥmad b. Ayyūb 129
Aḥmad b. al-Faḍl b. Yaḥyā 3
Aḥmad b. Farīdūn 102
Aḥmad b. ʿĪsā b. Zayd 33, 134
Aḥmad b. Isrāʾīl al-Anbārī, Abū Jaʿfar, 6 n. 24, 9, 10–12
Aḥmad b. Janāb 3
Aḥmad b. Jumayl 94, 95, 98, 105
Aḥmad b. Khāqān al-Wāthiqī 8, 9, 73, 74, 92, 94, 97, 98, 103
Aḥmad b. al-Layth 116
Aḥmad b. Laythawayh 181–86, 197, 200, 201, 205
Aḥmad b. Mahdī al-Jubbāʾī 174–76, 177–80, 191, 192, 193 n. 552, 195, 196, 198, 201
Aḥmad b. al-Mudabbir 111 n. 328
Aḥmad b. Muḥammad al-Qābūs 156
Aḥmad b. Muḥammad b. Thawābah 76, 82, 107
Aḥmad b. Mūsā b. Bughā 199
Aḥmad b. al-Mutawakkil b. Fityān 68, 69, 95, 99, 105, 115; *see also* al-Muʿtamid
Aḥmad b. al-Muwaffaq 185, 198, 203; *see also* al-Muʿtaḍid
Aḥmad b. Rūḥ 153
Aḥmad b. Sahl al-Luṭfī 181

Aḥmad b. Ṣāliḥ b. Shīrzād 19, 199
Aḥmad b. Sharīk 177
Aḥmad b. Sulaymān 202
Aḥmad b. Ṭulūn 201, 204
Aḥmad b. Waṣīf 107
Aḥmadābādh 205
al-aḥrār 35
al-Aḥsā' 31
al-Ahwāz xvi, 24 n. 94, 29, 37 n. 152, 38–39 n. 158, 50 n. 205, 76, 111, 112, 120, 122–24, 137, 142, 152, 153, 154 n. 434, 156, 164–66, 168, 180–83, 187, 203, 205, 206
Akramahr 191
Āl al-Muhallab 128, 131
al-ʿAlā' b. Aḥmad al-Azdī 161
Alburz mountains 155 n. 437
ʿAlī b. Abān al-Muhallabī 32, 34, 39, 42, 44, 45, 48, 49, 52, 54, 55, 59, 61, 62, 65, 123–30, 132, 137, 138, 140, 142, 143, 152, 153, 165, 180, 182–84, 186, 187, 198, 205, 206
ʿAlī b. Abī Ṭālib 30 n. 123, 133 n. 378
ʿAlī b. Aḥmad b. ʿĪsā b. Zayd 133
ʿAlī b. Bāris 97
ʿAlī al-Ḍarrāb 33
ʿAlī b. al-Ḥasan b. Ismāʿīl b. al-ʿAbbās b. Muḥammad b. ʿAlī 67
ʿAlī b. Masrūr al-Balkhī 204
ʿAlī b. Muḥammad (leader of the Zanj) xv, xvi, xvii, 29–67, 108–12, 120–35, 137–49, 152–56, 158–67, 174–81, 186, 187, 190–207
ʿAlī b. Muḥammad b. Abī al-Shawārib 180
ʿAlī b. Muḥammad al-Akbar 33
ʿAlī b. al-Ḥusayn b. Quraysh 28
ʿAlī al-Qāsim b. ʿAlī 182
ʿAlī b. Raḥīb b. Muḥammad b. Ḥakīm 30
ʿAlī b. Zayd b. al-Ḥusayn b. ʿĪsā b. Zayd b. ʿAlī b. al-Ḥusayn b. ʿAlī b. Abī Ṭālib al-ʿAlawī al-Ṭālibī 115, 116, 158
Alṭūn 99
Amājūr 116, 117
al-ʿamāmah 61
al-Amīn 19 n. 72
amīr 35, 40
ʿAmr b. al-Layth 203, 205
ʿAmr b. Masʿadah al-Kātib al-Rāwī 51
al-ʿAmūd 154, 155
Āmul 24 n. 100, 159, 163 n. 462
amwāl nujūm 15 n. 54
al-Anbār 16, 181, 202 n. 594
ʿAnbar al-Barbarī 64
Anburān 185 n. 519
al-Andalus 161 n. 460
Andarūn 206
Ankalāy 120, 195
Ankalwayh 61, 186, 206
ʿAntarah b. Ḥajanā 58
Antioch 201, 201–2 n. 591
Anūshirwān 160 n. 457
ʿAqīl al-Ubullī 39, 41, 46, 47, 49, 50
ʿAqr Māwar 177
Aqshā 47, 49, 50
ʿArafāt 181 n. 509
Arbuk bridge 123, 153
ʿārif 79 n. 269
al-arkhanj 59
Arkhanj al-Muṭahhirī 59
Armenia 116 n. 337, 117, 166
Artakīn b. B.r.n.m. kātakīn 96
arzāq 70, 81, 82, 85
Asātakīn 97, 103
Asfarā'īm 159
Aṣghajūn 139, 142–44, 152
aṣḥāb al-nawbah 70
aṣḥāb al-sulṭān 50 n. 204
ʿĀṣim b. Yūnus al-ʿIjlī 23
ʿAskar Mukram 165, 169, 182, 183, 186
ʿaṭā' 81, 85
ʿAṭā' al-Barbarī 62
ʿAttāb b. ʿAttāb 93, 97, 98, 102
al-ʿAṭṭār 36
al-ʿAwāṣim 137
ʿAyn al-Tamr 202
ʿayyār 88, 104, 202

B

Bāb Ḥulwān 24
Bāb Kūdak 206
Bāb al-Sulṭān 122 n. 350
Bāb Ṭanj 179
Bāb al-Ṭāq 5 n. 21, 139
Bābak 12 n. 39
al-Badandūn 190
Bādhāward xix, 39, 147, 148, 152–54, 174
Bādhghīs 151
Badīl al-Kashshī 159
Badr al-Rūmī al-Shaʿrānī 184
Baghdad xv, xvi, xvii, 3–5, 7, 9 nn. 32 and 34, 13, 14 nn. 47 and 52–53, 15, 16, 18 nn. 70–71, 19 nn. 72 and 76, 20–23, 28 n. 108, 29, 33, 34, 37 n. 152, 40 n. 162, 45 n. 186, 50 n. 72, 90 n. 93, 94, 106 n. 112, 120, 123, 139, 142, 149, 151 n. 162, 161, 163, 166, 168, 169, 171, 172, 174 n. 487, 180, 181, 188, 189, 198, 199, 202, 203 nn. 599 and 602, 204, 205 nn. 612–13
Baghdad street 86
Bahbūdh b. ʿAbd al-Wahhāb 183, 187
Bāhilīs 33
al-Baḥrayn 17 n. 65, 31–33, 120, 126, 164, 165
Bakālabā 73, 79, 82, 96, 101
Baktimur b. Tashtimur 161
Balad 87
Balkh 30 n. 122, 119, 151
Balkh river 165
Banū Asad 127, 204
Banū Asad b. Khuzaymah 30
Banū Dārim 31
Banū Ḍubayʿah 32
Banū Ḥanẓalah 31
Banū Hāshim. *See* ʿAbbāsid(s)
Banū Ḥimmām 128, 130
Banū Ḥiṣn 131
Banū ʿIjl 45
Banū Mūsā b. al-Munajjim 34
Banū Rabīʿah. *See* Rabīʿah
Banū Saʿd 31, 126–30, 132
Banū al-Shammās 31
Banū Shaybān 128, 194
Banū Tamīm 31, 127, 128, 131
Banū Thawābah 95
Banū Yashkur 131
al-Baradān 4, 5
Barāmikah 59
Baranjān 183
Barankhal 34, 35
Bardūdā 191
barīd 129
Barmakids 19 n. 76, 20 n. 77
Barqah 204
Barr Musāwir 176, 195
barrāniyyūn 81, 97 n. 302
Barratimurtā 201
Barsūna 52
Bashīr al-Qaysī 54, 55
Basīl al-Ṣaqlabī (Basil I) 135, 156, 188, 204
al-Baṣrah xvi, xvii, xix, 9 n. 32, 17 n. 65, 29, 30 n. 119, 32–35, 37, 39 nn. 159–61, 45 n. 184, 46 nn. 189–90, 49 n. 198, 51, 52 n. 210, 53, 56 n. 219, 57–59, 61, 62 nn. 228–29, 64, 66, 67, 108, 109, 110, 112, 120, 122, 125–29, 132–34, 136, 137, 140, 147 n. 410, 153, 155, 164, 165, 175 n. 492
al-Baṣrah Gate (Baghdād) 16 n. 61
baṭāʾiḥ (sg. *baṭīḥah*) xvi, 33, 39 n. 161, 96 n. 300, 191 n. 543
Baṭīḥat al-Ṣaḥnāh xix, 143
Baṭn Jūkhā 24
al-Bawāzīj 18 n. 67, 148
Bāyakbāk 22–24, 29, 69, 73–76, 79, 80, 82, 85, 87–90, 92–98, 102–4, 107, 201 n. 590
Bayān xix, 38, 52, 54, 154, 155
Bayān Āzar 155
Bazkuwār 137
al-Bazzāq 194
al-Bilāliyyah 32, 34, 35, 43, 52, 58, 60, 61, 65, 109, 129, 131, 176
Bīnak 197

Birkat Zalzal 123
biṭrīq 190
Bughā al-Kabīr 7 n. 26, 22 n. 87, 85
Bughā the Younger (al-Sharābī) 14 n. 52, 24 n. 98, 88, 90
Bughrāj 120, 122, 126, 127, 130, 168
Bukhtīshū' b. Jibrīl 71
Bulbul 39
Burayh. *See* Ibrāhīm b. Muḥammad b. Ismā'īl
Buraysh al-Quray'ī 33
Bursān 57
Būshanj 151
Byzantium 135, 137 n. 391, 142, 162, 203

C

canal. *See nahr*
Chalcis 137 n. 390
Cilician Gates 190 n. 537
Ctesiphon 23 n. 89

D

al-Dabbāsūn 36
Dabīlā 46, 49, 50
al-Dakar 154
al-Dakkā 86, 104
Damascus 116
al-Damghān 155–56 n. 437
dār al-'āmmah 106 n. 315, 166
Darb al-Salāmah 190 n. 537
Dārim b. Mālik b. Ḥanẓalah 31 n. 129
al-Daskarah 24
Dast Arbuk 123
Dastimārān 152
Dastumīsān 175
Dā'ūd b. al-'Abbās al-Ṭūsī 12
Dā'ūd b. Sulaymān al-Ja'farī, Abū Hāshim 164
Dā'ūdābādh 156
Dawraq 187
al-Daylam 24–26, 159, 160, 163
Daylamites 107, 163
Dayr al-'Āqūl 170, 194, 204 n. 610
Dayr al-Dihdar 49 n. 198
al-Dayrānī, Abū Aḥmad 170, 172, 185
dhū al-yamīnayn 14 n. 50
dihqān 18 n. 67
Dimimmā 202
Dīnār 54, 55
dīnār khafīf 49 n. 200
al-Dīnārī 30
Dīnawar 166, 189
Dirham b. Naṣr 169
dīwān 14, 81
dīwān al-jund wa-al-Shākiriyyah 7 n. 27
Diwdad b. Diwdast, Abū al-Sāj 165, 167, 169, 172
Diyār Muḍar 137, 156 n. 442
Dubbā xix, 57, 58
Dujayl xix, 37, 40, 46–48, 52 n. 212, 123 n. 355, 124 n. 359, 154 nn. 432 and 434, 182
al-dukhalā 77 n. 267
al-Dūlāb 155, 165
Dulaf b. 'Abd al-'Azīz b. Abī Dulaf 29, 190, 202
al-Dūr 19, 20, 76, 78, 81, 84, 86, 87, 91, 95, 96, 99
al-durrā'ah 61

E

Egypt 111 n. 328, 166, 201–2 nn. 590–91, 204
Euphrates 16 n. 64, 33 n. 136, 43, 120, 121, 137 n. 389, 148 n. 414, 156 n. 442, 202 nn. 594–95, 205 n. 613
Euphrates road 124

F

al-Faḍl b. 'Adī al-Dārimī 60, 64, 127, 128, 183
al-Faḍl b. al-'Anbar 187

al-Faḍl b. Isḥāq b. al-Ḥasan b. Ismāʿīl b. al-ʿAbbās b. Muḥammad b. ʿAlī b. ʿAbdallāh b. al-ʿAbbās 135, 149, 167, 184, 188
al-Faḍl b. Maymūn 64
al-Faḍl b. Mūsā b. Bughā 202
Fam al-Ṣilḥ 124 n. 362
al-Fandam 124
Farāghinah 70, 93–95, 97, 102–4, 106, 107, 141, 185
Faraj the younger 96
Fārs 28, 76, 116, 119, 120, 122 n. 351, 123, 135, 137, 164–66, 168, 170, 172, 181, 185, 205
Fārs bridge 182, 183, 206
farsakh 47 n. 192, 108, 157, 169, 178, 186, 191, 192, 196
Fatḥ (slave of Abū al-Ḥadīd) 184
Fatḥ (slave of Abū Shīth) 60, 62, 64, 128, 130
Fatḥ al-Ḥajjām 39, 54
fatwā 13
fayḍ 45 n. 184
Fayrūz the Elder 60
fitnah 5
al-Furāt (al-Baṣrah) xix, 29
al-Furātiyyah 43

G

ghallah 74 n. 262
Ghānim al-Shiṭranjī 31
al-ghawghā' 4, 5 n. 17
ghulām (pl. *ghilmān*) 15, 34, 35, 38 n. 156, 48 n. 193, 70, 86

H

Ḥabīb 7
ḥabl 132, 141
Ḥabshūn b. Bughā 96–99, 101
al-Ḥadīthah 102, 148
Hajar 31
al-Ḥajar 56
ḥājib 28 n. 108
al-Ḥajjājiyyah 193, 196
al-Ḥajjām 45
Hamadhān 27, 29, 189 n. 534
Ḥammād b. Isḥāq 3
Ḥammād b. Muḥammad b. Ḥammād b. Danqash 11, 12
Ḥammād al-Sājī 65
al-ḥannāṭūn 181
Ḥaramayn 120
Ḥārith al-Qaysī 62
al-Ḥārith b. Sīmā al-Sharābī 116, 123, 164
al-Ḥarjaliyyah 196
ḥarrāqah 199 n. 577
Hārūn b. ʿAbd al-Raḥmān b. al-Azhar al-Shīʿī 88, 102, 129
Hārūn b. Muḥammad b. Isḥāq b. Mūsā b. ʿĪsā al-Hāshimī al-Kūfī, 199, 207
Hārūn al-Rashīd 9 n. 34, 20 n. 77
Ḥasak ʿImrān 57
al-Ḥasan b. ʿAlī b. Abī Ṭālib 115 n. 333
al-Ḥasan al-Dirhamī 170
al-Ḥasan b. Harthama al-Shār 152, 153
al-Ḥasan b. Jaʿfar Zāwashār 152, 153
al-Ḥasan b. Makhlad 6 n. 24, 10–13, 72, 73, 76, 107, 188, 199
al-Ḥasan b. al-Ma'mūn 96
al-Ḥasan b. Muḥammad b. Abī al-Shawārib al-Qāḍī 3, 67, 167
al-Ḥasan b. Sulaymān al-Dūshābī 10, 11
al-Ḥasan b. ʿUthmān al-Muhallabī, Mundaliqah 131, 132
al-Ḥasan b. Wahb 198
al-Ḥasan b. Zayd al-Ṭālibī 24–26, 27 n. 104, 106, 116, 148, 155, 156 n. 438, 158–61, 163
Ḥātim b. Zayrak b. Salām 157
Haṭmah 120
al-Ḥawānīt 135, 174–77, 178, 180, 190, 195
hawr (pl. *ahwār*) 39 n. 161, 194 n. 554
al-Ḥayr 68–70, 82, 84, 86, 89, 95, 100, 103, 145
Ḥayyān 124

Hazārdar 109
Ḥāzim 182
Herāt 151, 156, 157
Ḥimṣ 161
al-Ḥimyarī 38, 39, 41, 44–46
Hishām b. ʿAbd al-Mālik 30
Hishām al-Dāff 131
Ḥiṣn b. al-ʿAnbar 187
Ḥiṣn Mahdī, xix, 154
Ḥiṣnayn 190
Ḥulwān 112 n. 331, 166, 189 n. 534, 190
Ḥusayn the eunuch (ʿAraq al-Mawt) 117
Ḥusayn al-Ḥammāmī 65, 206
al-Ḥusayn b. Ismāʿīl b. Ibrāhīm b. Muṣʿab b. Ruzayq 16–19, 21
al-Ḥusayn al-Ṣaydanānī 33, 53, 55
al-Ḥusayn b. Ṭāhir b. ʿAbdallāh b. Ṭāhir 167, 180, 188, 203

I

Ibn ʿAṭāʾ 36
Ibn al-Dayrānī 189, 190
Ibn ʿĪsā 117
Ibn ʿIyāḍ 189
Ibn Ṭulūn 115 n. 333, 201
Ibn Tūmanī al-Saʿdī 64
Ibrāhīm (al-Muhtadī's brother) 29
Ibrāhīm b. Isḥāq b. Ibrāhīm 16, 18
Ibrāhīm b. Jaʿfar al-Hamdānī 42, 43
Ibrāhīm b. Juʿlān 207
Ibrāhīm al-Muʾayyad 28 n. 108
Ibrāhīm b. Muḥammad 3
Ibrāhīm b. Muḥammad b. Ibrāhīm b. Muṣʿab b. Zurayq 88
Ibrāhīm b. Muḥammad b. Ismāʿīl b. Jaʿfar b. Sulaymān b. ʿAlī b. ʿAbdallāh b. ʿAbbās, Burayh 108, 127–29, 134, 157, 161, 162
Ibrāhīm b. Muḥammad b. al-Mudabbir 111, 112, 121
Ibrāhīm b. Saʿdān al-Nahwī 88
Ibrāhīm b. Sīmā al-Turkī 112 n. 330, 123–25, 153–55, 165, 170, 172
Ibrāhīm b. Sulaymān b. Wahb 199
Ibrāhīm al-Ṭālibī 88
Ibrāhīm b. Yaḥyā al-Muhallabī 127, 131, 132
Idṭarbad 170
Ifrīqiyah 161 n. 460, 166
ʿImrān 120
iqṭāʿ 77
Iraq xv, xvi, 9 n. 32, 14, 30
ʿĪsā b. Farrukhānshāh 99–101
ʿĪsā b. Ibrāhīm, Abū Nūḥ 6 n. 24, 9, 11, 12
ʿĪsā al-Karkhī 76, 77, 87, 103
ʿĪsā b. al-Shaykh 116, 117
Iṣfahān 166, 202, 205
Isḥāq b. Ibrāhīm 86
Isḥāq b. Kundāj (Kundājīq) 153, 155, 202, 203
Ishtākhaniyyah 107
Iskāf Banī Junayd 23
Ismāʿīl 36
Ismāʿīl b. ʿAbdallāh al-Marwazī, Abū Naṣr 117
Ismāʿīl b. Bulbul 203
Ismāʿīl b. Isḥāq al-Qāḍī 119, 164, 168, 180
Iṭākh Gate 98

J

al-Jabal (al-Jibāl) 27, 97, 112, 151 n. 427, 160, 180, 189 n. 534
Jabal Zaynī 91
Jabbāsh 175, 180, 195–98, 201
Jabbul 204
Jaʿfar b. ʿAbd al-Wāḥid 99, 105
Jaʿfar b. Aḥmad 195
Jaʿfar b. Ibrāhīm al-Sajjān 141
Jaʿfar b. Maʿlūf 133
Jaʿfar b. Muḥammad al-Ṣūḥānī 34
Jaʿfar b. al-Muʿtamid al-Mufawwaḍ ilā-Allāh 148, 157, 166, 167, 169, 188
Jaʿfar b. Sulaymān b. ʿAlī al-Hāshimī 41, 66
Jaʿfar b. Yaḥyā b. Khālid b. Barmak 19

Ja'farawayh 206
Ja'fariyyah xix, 41, 42, 44, 45, 59–61
al-Jālah 135
al-Jāmidah 135
Jannāba 122 n. 351
jarībiyyāt 46, 66
Jarjarāyā 204
al-Jawharī 59
al-Jawsaq al-Muḥdath (Baghdād) 6 n. 25
Jawsaq palace (Sāmarrā) 6, 28 n. 108, 68, 69, 72, 73, 74 n. 261, 82, 84, 87, 91, 93–99, 101, 103, 105, 107, 157, 199
Jaxartes 70 n. 248, 93 n. 296
Jaysh b. Ḥamartakīn 194
al-Jazīrah 18 n. 67, 136 n. 388, 137 n. 389, 156 n. 442, 160, 166, 176, 195
jisr (pl. *jusūr*) 5 n. 21
jisrayn 19
Jūbak 52
Jubbā xix, 40, 56, 111, 112, 124, 125, 137, 140, 174
Jūkhāniyyūn 175
Ju'lān *al-'ayyār* 202
Ju'lān al-Turkī 66, 67, 108–10, 148, 174, 190, 193, 195–97
Junbulā 116 n. 336, 197, 198, 200, 201
al-jund 4, 5 n. 17, 7, 15 n. 56
Junday Sābūr 182, 187, 202 n. 593
Jurayḥ 67
Jurbān, Abū Ya'qūb 34, 41, 44
Jurjān 160, 163, 166, 168
al-Juwayth 15

K

Ka'bah 167
Kābul 119
Kaftimur 'Alī b. al-Ḥusayn b. Dā'ūd 181
Kāfūr 72
al-Kāmilī 97
Kanjūr al-Bukhārī 28, 29, 72, 102, 116, 150, 151, 156 n. 440, 198
al-Karaj 166
al-kārawān 52
al-Karkh *(baṭā'iḥ)* xix, 40, 46
al-Karkh (Sāmarrā) 69, 76–78, 82, 84–87, 91, 93, 95, 96, 99, 104, 107
Karkh Fīrūz 69 n. 246
Karkh Juddān 164
Karkhah river 181 n. 511
Karnabā 138
Kaskar 166
Kathīr b. 'Abdallāh al-Salmī 62 n. 228
Kawkab 190
Kāyakbāk 94
Kayghalagh 96, 97, 99, 101, 156, 180, 188, 199
kaylajah 9
kayyāl 31
al-khabīth. See 'Alī b. Muḥammad
khādim 72, 175
khā'in. See 'Alī b. Muḥammad
Khalaf b. Ja'far 138
khalīfah 79
al-Khalīl b. Abān 32, 182, 186, 198, 206
khamr 46 n. 188
Khamūsh 71
Khāniqīn 112, 115, 116 n. 335
kharāj 26, 137, 181
Khārijites 161
Kharshanah 190
Khashabat Bābak 12, 94, 104
al-khāṣṣah 5 n. 18
Khaṭārimush 103
al-khawal 38, 55, 56, 59
Khaybar 46
al-Khayzurāniyyah 124, 125, 137, 138
khil'ah 72 n. 257, 157 n. 447
Khuld 5 n. 21
Khurāsān 3 n. 7, 5 n. 20, 14, 15, 19, 22, 28 n. 110, 74, 133 n. 378, 151 nn. 423–24 and 426, 157, 159 n. 453, 160, 163, 166–68, 171, 205
Khurāsān Road 23, 24, 92, 95, 103, 164–66
Khuraskhāris 142
al-Khuraybah 127, 129, 130
Khurramah 166
Khurshād b. Jīlaw 160
Khushanaj 103
Khushaysh 178–80, 190, 192
Khusrū Sābūr 201

Khuṭārish 97
khuṭbah 38, 183
Khūzistān 24 n. 94, 169 n. 476, 181 n. 511, 187 n. 527
Khwārazm Shāh 188
Kirmān 119, 166, 205
al-Kūfah 9 n. 32, 19, 30, 32, 33 n. 136, 115, 116, 149 n. 417, 150, 158, 165, 166, 194 n. 557, 197, 200, 203 n. 599
al-Kūfah Gate (Baghdād) 16
al-Kuḥayl 91
Kurds 136
kurr 161
Kurramites 12 n. 39
Kūtakīn 103

L

Laḥsā 31 n. 128
al-laʿīn. *See* ʿAlī b. Muḥammad
liwāʾ 36
Lubbādah 170
Lujayn mosque 86
Luʾluʾah 162, 188, 190

M

al-Madāʾin 23, 170 nn. 480–81, 172, 174
al-Madhār xix, 42, 43, 174
Madīnat al-Salām. *See* Baghdād
al-Mādiyān road 175
Maftaḥ xix, 46
Maghāribah 55, 81, 93–95, 97, 98, 104, 106
Maghrib 161 n. 460
al-Mahdī 9 n. 34
Main Bridge (Baghdād) 5, 139 n. 400, 202
makkūk 9
māl al-bayʿah 17 n. 66
Malaṭyah 156
mamālīk 111
al-Maʾmūn 3 n. 7, 190 n. 538
Māndawayh 46
Manīnā 191
Manjūr 161, 193
al-Manṣūr 16 nn. 61–62, 58 n. 223, 93, 109 n. 324, 117 n. 341
Manṣūr camp 120
Manṣūr b. Jaʿfar b. Dīnār al-Khayyāṭ 120, 122, 123, 125, 137, 138
Marv 16, 18, 151, 188, 203
al-Maṣāff Gate 98
Mashraʿah al-Qayyār 66
al-Maskanīn 190
Maskin 16
Masrūr al-Balkhī, Abū Hāshim 97, 99, 136, 148, 155, 158, 164–67, 169, 170, 172, 174, 176–78, 181, 198, 199, 205–7
Masrūr market 98
Maṭar b. Jāmiʿ 196, 197
al-Maṭbaq (Baghdād) 16
al-Maṭbaq (Sāmarrā) 87
mawlā (pl. *mawālī*) 2, 7, 9, 18, 24, 26–29, 31, 33, 40–42, 48, 52, 69–71, 73, 75–86, 88, 90, 95–97, 100–3, 107, 108, 154, 193, 202
Mayān Rūdhān 43
maẓālim 24, 68
Māzrawān 193, 195, 197
Mecca 8, 117, 120 n. 343, 149 n. 417, 157 n. 448, 160, 161, 181, 207
Mecca Road 119–20, 165 n. 467, 166, 181, 204
Medina 120, 161, 166
Melitene 156 n. 443
Michael b. Tawfīl (Michael III) 135
Mihrajānqadhaq 166
mīl 47 n. 192
minbar 183
al-Mirbad 128, 130
Mirbad Road 130, 131
Mirdās 166
mithqāl 96
Mosul 87 n. 280, 102 n. 309, 166, 181, 199
Mosul road 185
al-Muʿallā b. Ayyūb 57, 63
al-Muʾayyad 4, 71

al-Mu'ayyad (island) 199
Mubārak al-Baḥrānī 62
al-Mubaraqa' al-Maghribī 170
Mufarraj al-Nūbī the Younger, Abū Ṣāliḥ 39, 40, 41, 206
Mufliḥ 24–26, 69, 71, 73, 79, 82, 86, 87, 89, 90–92, 97, 99, 102, 103, 107, 116, 136, 137, 139–42, 181
muftī 13 n. 45
al-Mughīthah 204
muhakkim 18 n. 67
al-Muhallabī 49
al-Muhallabiyyah 50
Muḥammad (the Prophet) 27 n. 103, 30 n. 123, 77, 78, 80
Muḥammad b. Abān 32, 183
Muḥammad b. 'Abdallāh b. Ḥasan b. 'Alī al-Ma'mūnī al-Bādhghīsī 206, 207
Muḥammad b. 'Abdallāh al-Iṣbahānī, Abū al-Layth 61, 65, 121, 132, 134, 137, 138, 143
Muḥammad b. 'Abdallāh b. Ṭāhir 14 n. 52, 16 n. 60, 17 n. 65, 18 n. 71, 19 nn. 72–73, 21 n. 82
Muḥammad b. Abī 'Awn 17, 33, 39, 42, 44, 45, 49, 53, 56
Muḥammad b. Aḥmad b. 'Īsā b. Abī Ja'far al-Manṣūr 117
Muḥammad b. 'Alī b. Fayd al-Ṭā'ī 172
Muḥammad b. 'Alī b. Ḥabīb al-Yashkūrī 193, 194
Muḥammad b. 'Alī b. Ṭāhir 22
Muḥammad b. 'Attāb b. 'Attāb 181
Muḥammad b. Aws al-Balkhī 13, 15, 16, 18–24, 165, 170, 185
Muḥammad al-Azraq al-Qawārīrī 61
Muḥammad b. Bughā, Abū Naṣr 75, 80, 82, 85, 87, 91, 96, 97, 99, 100, 101, 106–8
Muḥammad b. Dīnār 206
Muḥammad b. al-Faḍl b. Sinān al-Qazwīnī 156
Muḥammad b. Ḥakīm 30
Muḥammad b. Hārūn b. al-Mu'ammar 158
Muḥammad b. al-Ḥasan al-Baghdādī 45
Muḥammad b. al-Ḥasan al-Iyādī 33
Muḥammad b. al-Ḥasan b. Sahl 55, 60, 61, 64, 65, 109, 121, 125–27, 129, 133, 134, 139, 142, 146, 152, 175, 176, 180, 183, 195–98, 201, 205, 206
Muḥammad b. al-Ḥusayn b. al-Fayyāḍ 137
Muḥammad b. 'Īsā b. 'Abd al-Raḥmān al-Kātib al-Khurāsānī 15, 22
Muḥammad b. 'Īsā al-Qurashī 106
Muḥammad b. Ja'far al-Muraydī 57, 58
Muḥammad b. Kathīr 169, 170
Muḥammad b. Masrūr al-Balkhī 204
Muḥammad b. Mubāshir al-Karkhī 76, 77, 84, 93–95, 100
Muḥammad al-Muwallad 134, 135, 150, 167, 169, 190, 197, 198, 202
Muḥammad b. al-Muẓaffar b. Saysal 23
Muḥammad b. Naṣr b. Ḥamzah b. Mālik al-Khuzā'ī 21
Muḥammad b. Naṣr b. Manṣūr b. Bassām 23
Muḥammad b. al-Qāsim 34
Muḥammad b. Rajā' al-Ḥiḍārī 32–34
Muḥammad b. Ṣāliḥ, Abū Sahl 183, 186
Muḥammad b. Salm al-Qaṣṣāb al-Ḥajarī 33, 34, 39, 41–43, 46, 48, 52, 54, 58, 60–62, 64
Muḥammad b. Sim'ān al-Kātib 64, 129, 130, 131, 142, 144, 146
Muḥammad b. Ṭāhir b. 'Abdallāh, Abū 'Abdallāh 151, 156, 157, 159, 163, 168, 171, 172, 188, 203
Muḥammad b. Tarkashah 169
Muḥammad b. Thaqīf al-Aswad 77
Muḥammad Ṭughtā al-Turkī 170
Muḥammad b. Turksh 71
Muḥammad b. 'Ubaydallāh b. Azārmard al-Kurdī 181–83, 207
Muḥammad b. 'Ubaydallāh al-Kurayzī 117
Muḥammad b. 'Uthmān al-'Abbādānī 175, 176, 180
Muḥammad b. Wāṣil b. Ibrāhīm al-Tamīmī 116, 135, 137, 164, 166, 172, 181, 185

Muḥammad b. al-Wāthiq 3, 4, 90, 112, 115
Muḥammad b. Yaḥyā 3
Muḥammad b. Yaḥyā al-Kirmānī 183
Muḥammad b. Yaḥyā al-Wāthiqī 102
Muḥammad b. Yazīd al-Baṣrī 200
Muḥammad b. Yazīd al-Dārimī 126
Muḥammad b. Zaydawayh 167, 169, 180
al-Muḥammadiyyah 39, 47, 96, 100, 101
al-Muhtadī (bi-Allāh), Abū ʿAbdallāh Muḥammad b. al-Wāthiq xv, 1, 5, 7, 10–12, 16, 24, 25, 27–29, 68–70, 72–80, 82–87, 89, 91–99, 100, 101, 104–8
al-Muhtadī, mother of. *See* Qurb
mujāwirah 21 n. 83
mujawniḥāt 46
al-Mukhtārah xvi, xix, 109 n. 324, 186 n. 522, 196 n. 566
Mundhirān 57
al-Muntaṣir 31, 94 n. 298, 99
Mūsā 24
Mūsā b. Bughā, Abū ʿImrān 7, 24–29, 68–73, 74 n. 261, 76, 79–88, 90–92, 95–99, 102, 103, 105–7, 112, 115, 116, 119 n. 342, 148, 153, 155, 156, 164–67, 170, 172, 174, 181, 188, 189
Mūsā Dālijuwayh 185
Mūsā b. Jaʿfar 152
Mūsā b. Mihrān al-Kurdī 166
Mūsā b. Utāmish 151, 174, 202, 203
al-muṣallā 203 n. 601
al-musannah 51
Musāwir b. ʿAbd al-Ḥamīd 4 n. 13, 18, 24, 87, 90–92, 95, 96, 112, 116, 136, 148, 158, 164, 187
Mushriq (Ḥamzah), Abū Aḥmad 34, 41, 44, 49, 62
Muṣliḥ 63, 65, 138
al-Mustaʿīn 1 n. 3, 9, 12 n. 43, 32 n. 132, 74, 79, 80
al-Muʿtaḍid 106 n. 315
al-Muʿtamid xv, 28 n. 107, 68 n. 244, 115, 116, 119, 123, 137, 139, 145, 153, 164 n. 466, 166, 169, 170, 172, 174, 183, 189, 198, 199
al-Muʿtaṣim xv, 6 n. 25, 69 n. 246, 70
al-Mutawakkil xv, 7, 9, 26, 34 n. 140, 70, 71 n. 255, 74, 86, 99
al-Muʿtazz 1–4, 6 nn. 22–23, 8, 12 n. 43, 14 nn. 47 and 52, 15, 17, n. 65, 25, 26, 28, 70, 75, 189
al-Muṭṭawwiʿah 175
al-Muwaffaq, Abū Aḥmad (b. al-Mutawakkil) xv, xvi, xvii, 4, 73, 117, 119, 120, 137, 139, 140–48, 150, 152, 157, 164–74, 176, 185, 187, 189, 197, 199–205
al-Muẓaffar b. Saysal 19, 21

N

nabīdh 46 n. 188, 48, 74
Nādir, Abū Naʿjah 64
al-naffāṭīn 20 n. 80
nahr 37 n. 153
Nahr Abān 176, 195, 197
Nahr al-ʿAbbās 139, 142–44
Nahr Abī al-ʿAbbās 124
Nahr Abī al-Asad 45, 142, 143, 144, 146
Nahr Abī al-Khaṣīb xix, 109, 141, 147, 175 n. 492
Nahr Abī Qurrah 67
Nahr ʿAdī 126
Nahr Amīr al-Muʾminīn xix, 58, 59, 198
Nahr ʿAmūd ibn al-Munajjim 34
Nahr al-ʿAtīq 175–77
Nahr al-Atrāk 109 n. 324
Nahr Awwā 134
Nahr Bāmdād 42
Nahr Bāqthā 46
Nahr Bard al-Khiyār 47–49
Nahr Bardūdā 197
Nahr Barratimurtā 201
Nahr al-Barūr 177
Nahr Bayān xix, 52, 53, 55, 56
Nahr Bithq Shīrīn xix
Nahr Būr 38
Nahr al-Dāwardānī 58

Nahr Dayālā 203
Nahr al-Dayr xix, 49
Nahr Dīnārī xix, 59, 60
Nahr Dubayrān 54
Nahr Farīd 45
Nahr al-Fayyāḍ 58, 59
Nahr al-Ghūthā 134
Nahr al-Ḥājir 67
Nahr Ḥarb 60, 61, 63
Nahr al-Ḥasan b. Muḥammad al-Qāḍī 45
Nahr al-Ḥasanī 57, 58
Nahr Ibn ʿUmar xix
Nahr Jārūrah Banī Marwān 179
Nahr Jaṭṭā xix
Nahr Jubbā 124, 138
Nahr Kathīr 62, 64
Nahr al-Mādiyān 50 n. 202
Nahr Mankā 147
Nahr Maʿqil xix, 110, 111, 120, 121, 123, 135, 139
Nahr al-Mara' xix, 174
Nahr Masruqān 169 n. 476, 182, 184, 186, 206
Nahr Maymūn xix, 37, 40, 46, 47
Nahr Muḥaddath xix
Nahr al-Muḥdath 59
Nahr al-Mukāthir 36
Nahr Murghāb 120
Nahr Mūsā 124
Nahr Nāfidh xix, 61, 109
Nahr al-Nīl 205 n. 613
Nahr al-Qandal xix, 43, 56, 57
Nahr al-Rayyān xix, 50 n. 205
Nahr Riyāḥī xix, 59
Nahr al-Sabābijah 62
Nahr al-Ṣāliḥī 57, 58
Nahr al-Ṣarāt 205 n. 613
Nahr al-Shādhānī 62
Nahr Sharīkān 55
Nahr Shayṭān 62, 63, 65
Nahr al-Sīb 41, 42, 44, 45, 47
Nahr al-Sidrah xix, 154, 155, 187
Nahr Sindād 176
Nahr Ṭahīthā 178
Nahr Ṭīn 39
Nahr al-Ubullah xix, 110, 175 n. 492
Nahr Umm Ḥabīb 65, 66
Nahr al-Yahūdī xix, 175
Nahr Yaḥyā 154
Nahr Yaʿqūb b. al-Naḍr 176
Nahr al-Zuhayrī 200
al-Nahrawān 22, 23, 24 n. 93
al-nā'ibah 21
Najāḥ b. Salamah 71 n. 255
al-nās 5, 131 n. 372
Naṣībīn 87 n. 280
Nāṣiḥ al-Ramlī 47, 64
Naṣr b. Aḥmad b. Asad al-Sāmānī 165
Naṣr b. Aḥmad al-Zubayrī 98
Naṣr al-Iqrīṭashī 156
Naṣr al-Rūmī 184
Naṣr b. Shabath 102
Nasūkhā 154
Nawfaliyyūn 134
Naysābūr 3 n. 7, 151, 156, 157, 159, 188, 203
Nayzak 152
al-Nazālah Gate 99
al-Nīl 205
Nūbah 43
al-Nūbandajān 185
al-Nuʿmāniyyah 23, 169, 204
al-Numayrī 45
Nuṣayr, Abū Ḥamzah 111, 175, 201
al-Nūshurī 23, 24, 71, 90

O

Oxus river 30 n. 122, 165–66 n. 469

P

Public Audience Hall 105, 166
Public Gate (Sāmarrā) 11, 90, 98, 136, 148, 151

Q

qabālah 79
Qabīḥah 6–8, 24, 25, 73–75, 189

Qadhaydhīyah 190
al-Qādisiyyah 40, 48, 137 n. 392, 175
qā'id 79, 190 n. 539
al-Qā'im (Sāmarrā) 169, 189
al-qalansuwah 61
al-qanāt 96
al-Qandal 126
qanṭarah 49 n. 197, 62, 123, 144, 182, 206
Qāquwayh 48, 49
al-Qarʿā' 149
Qarmaṭiyyūn 43
Qaryat Ḥassān 194
Qaryat Marwān 177, 194 n. 556
al-Qāshānī 26
al-Qāsim b. al-Ḥasan al-Nawfalī 134
al-Qāsim b. Jaʿfar b. Sulaymān al-Hāshimī 130
al-Qāsim b. Mimāh 202
Qaṣr al-Aḥmar 68, 100
Qaṣr Anas 127
Qaṣr ʿĪsā b. Jaʿfar 127
Qaṣr Ma'mūn xix
qaṭā'iʿ 69 n. 246
Qaṭrabbul 16
al-Qaṭṭān 181
al-Qāṭūl 29, 71, 108
Qaṭūṭā 20
Qayyārān 49
Qazwīn 166, 171
qiblah 89
Qinnasrīn 137
al-Qufṣ 45
Quhistān 151
Qūmis 155
Qumm 160, 166
Qūraj al-ʿAbbās bridge 144
al-Qurashī 34–36
Qurayshites 65
Qurb 1, 9
Qurrah 30, 190

R

Rabʿ al-Qubbah 88
(Banū) Rabīʿah 158
al-Radm 32
Rāfiʿ b. Bisṭām 143
al-Rafīf 102, 103, 106
Rafīq (Jaʿfar), Abū al-Faḍl 34, 35, 41, 63, 129
Rajā' al-Rabābī 7
Rāmhurmuz 29, 164, 168
raqīq 112
al-Raqqah 181
Raqqat al-Baradān 22
Rāshid al-Maghribī 36
Rāshid al-Qarmaṭī 36
Rashīq 188
Rayḥān b. Ṣāliḥ 35, 39, 41, 50–52, 54, 55, 57, 60, 62–64
al-Rayy 14, 22 n. 84, 24–27, 30, 106, 116, 156, 161, 163, 166, 168, 171, 180
Rāziqiyyah xix, 39
Riyāḥ al-Qandalī 176
al-Riyāḥī 61
Rumays 41–45, 47–50, 175, 176
al-Ruṣāfah 9, 172, 195–97
rustāq 45
Rūzbah 88

S

Sabkhat al-Qandal 38, 39 n. 159
ṣadaqah 2
al-Saʿdiyyah 32, 34, 35, 52, 60, 65, 109, 128–31
safātij 8 n. 28
al-Safīnatayn 202
ṣaḥārā 26
ṣāḥib al-barīd 27
ṣāḥib al-ḥarb 152 n. 428
Sahl al-Ṭaḥḥān 36
Saʿīd b. Aḥmad b. Saʿīd b. Salm al-Bāhilī 135, 136
Saʿīd b. Makhlad 203
Saʿīd b. Ṣāliḥ al-Ḥājib 109, 112, 120–22, 125
Saʿīd b. al-Sayyid al-ʿAdawī 196
Saʿīd b. Yaksīn 112, 124
Saʿīd the Younger 31

al-Ṣalābī 156, 161, 180
salaf 148
Salām al-Shāmī 62
Salamah b. Khāqān 90
ṣalāt al-fiṭr 37
ṣalghah 175
Salhab, Abū Naṣr 184
Ṣāliḥ b. ʿAlī b. Yaʿqūb b. Abī Jaʿfar al-Manṣūr 93, 94, 107, 180
Ṣāliḥ al-ʿAṭṭār 73
Ṣāliḥ b. Waṣīf 6–13, 22, 23 n. 92, 24 n. 98, 26, 27, 29, 68–73, 75, 81–83, 85–88, 89, 90, 104, 106
Salīm 61
Sālim al-Zaghāwī 44
salkh 3 n. 8
al-Salūlī 90
Salūqīyah 190
samād 37
Samarqand 93 n. 296
Sāmarrā xv, xvi, 4 n. 13, 6 n. 25, 7, 12 n. 39, 15 n. 59, 22, 24–29, 31, 67, 68, 69 n. 246, 73, 78, 79, 81, 84–86, 90 n. 287, 91, 92, 96, 97, 99, 100 n. 307, 102, 105, 106, 115–17, 119, 122, 133, 134, 137, 139, 142, 145, 148, 150, 151, 153, 156, 158, 165, 167, 168, 169, 188, 198, 199
al-Sanāʾī 36
Sandādān Bayān 52, 54
Saqlabtūyā 64
al-Ṣaqr b. al-Ḥusayn al-ʿAbbādānī 195, 196
Sarakhs 19
al-Sarakhsī 12, 88
Sāriyah 159, 160
Ṣarṣar 203 n. 599
Sāsānians 23 n. 89
Sātikīn 69, 87, 89, 151, 172
Sawād 14 n. 47, 15, 24, 72, 120, 166
Sawād al-Kūfah 200
ṣawālijah 88 n. 281
sawīq 35, 93
Ṣayghūn 189
Sayḥān 132
al-Ṣaymarah 148, 189
Sayrān b. ʿAfwiallāh 51, 52
Seleucia 190 n. 540
Shābarzān 206
shadhah 56 n. 218
al-Shadīdiyyah 197, 198
al-Shāh b. Mīkāl 18, 19, 21, 115
Shāhīn b. Bisṭām 112, 123, 124, 125
Shākiriyyah 7, 13, 15–17, 21, 69, 98, 102
Shālūs 163
al-Shām 160
al-Shammāsiyyah 4, 20, 22
Shammāsiyyah Gate (Baghdad) 19 n. 76, 20, 202
Shāmraj 201
al-Sharīṭiyyah 201
Shāriyah 88
Sharkab al-Jammāl 151, 188, 203
Shāṭiʾ ʿUthmān 53, 110, 111
Shīʿah 16, 22 n. 84, 24 n. 100, 27 n. 104
Shibl b. Sālim 36, 42, 60, 61, 64, 65, 67, 126, 132, 134, 138, 192
al-Shīfiyā 48
Shihāb b. al-ʿAlāʾ al-ʿAnbarī 59, 129
shihrī 11, 19
Shīrāz 28 n. 109, 166 n. 470
al-Shirriz 159, 160
Shūrajiyyūn 35–37, 39, 40, 43–45, 48, 51 n. 207, 59
al-Sīb 177, 181
Sīb Banī Kūmā 170
sibākh 30, 34, 35 n. 143
Sijistān 119, 151, 158, 166, 205
Sīmā al-Sharābī 72
Sīmā the Tall 97, 201
al-Ṣīn 201
Sind 30, 119, 166, 205
al-Sinn 91, 102, 103, 148 n. 415
Sīstān xvi, 28 n. 110
Ṣubayḥ al-Aʿsar 36
al-sudān 37, 38 n. 156, 48 n. 195, 51 n. 206
Sughd 93 n. 296
Suḥayl 62
Sulaymān b. ʿAbdallāh b. Ṭāhir 3–5, 13–22, 32, 72, 156 n. 438
Sulaymān b. Jāmiʿ 33, 34, 41, 42, 64, 121, 144, 152, 174–80, 190–201, 202

Sulaymān b. Muḥammad b. Sulaymān 58, 61
Sulaymān b. Mūsā al-Shaʿrānī 126, 152, 155, 175, 198
Sulaymān b. Wahb 28, 71–73, 79, 80, 82, 188, 198, 199
Sulaymān b. Wahb al-Qaṭṭān 107
Sulaymānān xix, 43, 53
Sulbān 52, 56
ṣuʿlūk (pl. *ṣaʿālīk*) 14 n. 48, 20 n. 81, 182, 206
sumayriyyah 41 n. 171
Sumaysāṭ 156
Sūq al-Ahwāz 152
Sūq al-Rayyān 50
ṣurnay 49
al-Sūs 24, 181, 182, 207
Sūsa 181 n. 511
Syria 117, 137 nn. 390–91, 166, 204; *see also* al-Shām
Syrian Gate (Baghdād) 16–18

T

Ṭabāghū al-Turkī 170
al-Ṭabarī, Abū Jaʿfar Muḥammad b. Jarīr xv–xvii
Ṭabaristān 3 n. 7, 13 n. 46, 20, 24–26, 158, 159, 160, 161, 163, 166, 168
Ṭabariyyah 5, 107
al-Ṭabasayn 151
Ṭabāyaghū b. Ṣūl Artakīn 91, 96, 97
Ṭafāwah 132
al-Ṭaff 194
Ṭaghūtyā 94, 97
Ṭāhir b. al-Ḥusayn 14 n. 51
Ṭāhir b. Muḥammad b. ʿAbdallāh 18 n. 70
Ṭāhirids xvi, 14, 22 n. 84, 28 n. 110
Ṭahīthā 177, 179, 193, 195, 196, 201
Takīn al-Bukhārī 151, 156, 191–93, 195–97, 205–6
Takrīt 136, 199
talājī 81
al-Ṭalāqānī 182
al-Ṭāliqān 30
Tall Rumānā 195
Tallfakhkhār 194
Ṭalmajūr 12, 70, 71
Ṭamīs 160
tannūr ḥadīd 60
Ṭāriq 36
Tarsus 162
tasbīb 15 n. 57
Ṭāshtimur al-Turkī 104, 144, 154, 155
ṭassūj 16
Taurus mountains 190
tawqīʿ 71 n. 255
Thaʿlab b. Ḥafṣ al-Baḥrānī 174, 191, 196
Thītal 101
thughūr 190
Thumāl 58
al-Ṭīb 180
Tigris xix, 15, 22, 23 nn. 89–90, 30, 33 n. 36, 37 n. 152, 38, 39, 42, 44, 49, 52 n. 212, 56, 102 n. 309, 109, 110, 120, 121, 123, 124 n. 362, 137 n. 392, 142, 143, 148 nn. 414–15, 151 n. 422, 165, 169, 170, 174, 175, 191 n. 543, 199, 203 n. 602, 204 nn. 605 and 609–10, 205 n. 613
Tigris Street (Baghdad) 5
al-Ṭufūf 177
Ṭughtā b. al-Ṣayghūn 71, 119
Ṭukhāristān 30 n. 122, 119
Ṭulūnids 111 n. 328
Turks 6, 8, 25, 69, 74, 75, 83, 84, 86, 92, 93, 95, 97, 103, 104, 105, 106, 107
Ṭurnāj 197
Tursā 52
Ṭūs 203
Tustar 182, 183, 186, 202 n. 593, 205, 206

U

ʿUbaydah al-ʿUmrūsī 90, 91
ʿUbaydallāh b. ʿAbdallah b. Ṭāhir 14–17, 72, 163
ʿUbaydallāh b. Sulaymān 188, 202
ʿUbaydallāh b. Yaḥyā b. Khāqān 34 n. 140, 115, 157, 170, 188

al-Ubullah xix, 39, 46, 47, 53, 67, 110–12, 134, 142–44
Ūkashiyyah 93
ʿUkbarā' 45 n. 186, 151
ʿUmar b. ʿAlī b. Murr, Abū al-Rudaynī 161
ʿUmar b. al-Khaṭṭāb 76
ʿUmar b. Mihrān 138
ʿUmar b. Sīmā 169
ʿUmayr b. ʿAmmār al-Bāhilī 33, 174, 177, 194
Umayyads 62 nn. 228–29, 93 n. 293
Umm al-Faḍl 90
ʿUmrān 56
ʿuqābān 123
Urkhūz 203
Ushnās palace 77
Ushrūsaniyyah 93, 107
ʿUthmān Gate 131
ʿUzayz b. al-Sarī 157, 185

W

Wādī Tustar 207
Wah 142
Waḥash 7
Wahb b. Sulaymān b. Wahb 199
Wahsūdhān b. Justān al-Daylamī 156
Wājin 86
Warzanīn 30
Waṣīf 168
Waṣīf (clan) 86, 88, 107
Waṣīf (al-Turkī) 29, 85, 180
Waṣīf al-Kūfī 61
Waṣīf al-Raḥḥāl 177
Waṣīf al-Rūmī 205
Wāsiṭ xvi, 4 n. 11, 9 n. 32, 23 n. 90, 24 nn. 94–95, 28 n. 107, 33, 39, 44, 58 n. 223, 120, 135 n. 384, 142, 146, 147 n. 410, 148, 150, 165, 169, 170, 174, 176, 177, 185, 190, 194, 196–98, 200, 204 n. 609
al-Wāthiq 8 n. 30, 34, 70
Wāthiq street 98
al-Wazīriyyah 95

Y

al-Yahūd 42
Yaḥyā b. ʿAbd al-Raḥmān b. Khāqān 34, 35, 41, 129
Yaḥyā b. Abī Thaʿlab 31, 33
Yaḥyā b. Ḥafṣ 164
Yaḥyā b. Isḥāq b. Mūsā b. ʿĪsā b. ʿAlī b. ʿAbdallāh b. ʿAbbās, Abū ʿĪsā 27
Yaḥyā b. Khalaf al-Nahrabaṭṭī 152
Yaḥyā b. Muḥammad al-Azraq (al-Baḥrānī) 31, 33, 34, 41, 48, 49, 52, 54, 56, 64, 112, 121, 123, 126–28, 130–35, 139, 142–46, 152
Yaḥyā b. Muḥammad b. Dā'ūd 102
Yaḥyā b. ʿUmar, Abū al-Ḥusayn 32
Yaḥyā b. Yaḥyā al-Zubayrī 41
Yaḥyā b. Zakariyā' b. Abī Yaʿqūb al-Iṣbahānī 3
Yaḥyā b. Zayd b. ʿAlī 133, 134
Yājūr 68–73, 79, 82, 86, 89
al-Yamāmah 17 n. 65, 28 n. 108, 120, 164, 165
Yanghajūr b. Urkhūz 202, 203
Yaʿqūb b. al-Layth al-Ṣaffār xvi, 28, 119, 151, 156–61, 163, 164 n. 466, 166–70, 171, 173, 174, 176, 177, 181–83, 185–87, 189, 202, 203
Yaʿqūbiyyah 136
Yārjūkh 4, 5, 87, 95, 97, 99, 103–5, 120, 138, 148
yawm al-Shaʿānīn 172
yawm al-Shadhā 66
yawm al-Tarwiyah 181, 199
Yemen 120, 166
Yusr the Eunuch 31

Z

Zāb(s) 23, 102 n. 309, 148 n. 415
al-Zaʿfarāniyyah 169, 170
Zahrān 130, 131
al-Ẓahrān 31 n. 128
Zamm 166
Zandaward Bridge 19 n. 72

Zanj xvi, xvii, 29, 30 n. 119, 34 n. 139, 35, 36 n. 149, 37 n. 154, 38, 39, 43–46, 49–51, 53, 54, 108 n. 322, 110–12, 119 n. 342, 122, 124, 126, 130, 131, 132, 134, 138, 140, 141, 143–45, 147, 148, 153, 154, 165, 179, 181, 186, 192, 198, 204–7
Zanj, leader of. *See* ʿAlī b. Muḥammad
Zanjān 166, 171
al-Zanjī b. Mihrān 198, 201
zarnūq (pl. *zarānīq*) 44
al-Zawāriqah 63
Zayd b. ʿAlī b. al-Ḥusayn, Abū al-Ḥasan 30, 133 n. 378
Zayd b. Ṣūḥān 34
al-Zaydān road 144
al-Zaynabī. *See* ʿAbdallāh b. Muḥammad b. Sulaymān
Ziyād b. Abīhi 62 n. 229
Ziyādiyyūn 41
Zuhayr 56
Zurayq 36, 61, 64, 65

www.ingramcontent.com/pod-product-compliance
Lightning Source LLC
Chambersburg PA
CBHW020648230426
43665CB00008B/353
* 9 7 8 0 7 9 1 4 0 7 6 4 6 *